THE FASCIST
REVOLUTION

THE FASCIST REVOLUTION

TOWARD A GENERAL THEORY OF FASCISM

GEORGE L. MOSSE

HOWARD FERTIG

NEW YORK

Library of Congress Cataloging in Publication Data
Mosse, George L. (George Lachmann), 1918–1999
    The fascist revolution : toward a general theory of fascism /
    George L. Mosse.
        p.   cm.
    Includes bibliographical references (p.   ) and index.
    ISBN 0-86527-432-0 (cloth)
    ISBN 0-86527-435-5 (pbk)
    1. Fascism.   2. National socialism.   3. Racism.
4. Europe—Intellectual life—20th century.   I. Title.
JC481.M63   1999
320.53'3—dc21   98-16770
                                                                              CIP

Design by Albert Burkhardt

Manufactured in the United States of America

The following page constitutes an extension
of the copyright notice.

For permission to reprint copyright material, the author is indebted to the following:

1. *Toward a General Theory of Fascism*, reprinted in greatly revised form from *International Fascism, New Thoughts and New Approaches*, ed. George L. Mosse, Sage Publications, London and Beverly Hills, 1979, pp. 1–45.

2. *Fascist Aesthetics and Society*, reprinted from *The Journal of Contemporary History*, Vol. 31, No. 2, April 1996, pp. 245–252.

3. *Racism and Nationalism*, reprinted from *Nations and Nationalism*, Vol. 1, No. 2, 1995, pp. 163–73, by permission.

4. *Fascism and the French Revolution*, reprinted by permission of *The Journal of Contemporary History*, Vol. 224, January 1989, Sage Publications Ltd., London, pp. 5–26.

5. *Fascism and the Intellectuals*, reprinted from *The Nature of Fascism*, Stuart Woolf, ed., Chapter 6 (London: Weidenfeld and Nicolson, 1968), The Graduate School of Contemporary European Studies, University of Reading, pp. 205–25.

6. *The Occult Origins of National Socialism*, reprinted from *The Journal of the History of Ideas*, Vol. XXII, No. 1, January–March 1961, pp. 81–96.

7. *Fascism and the Avant Garde*, first published as "Faschismus und Avant-Garde" in *Faschismus und Avant-Garde*, ed. Reinhold Grimm and Jost Hermand, Athenäeum Verlag, Frankfurt-am-Main, 1980.

8. *Nazi Polemical Theater: The Kampfbühne*, first published as "Die NS Kampf-bühne, in *Geschichte im Gegenwartsdrama*, ed. Reinhold Grimm and Jost Hermand, Verlag W. Kohlhammer, Stuttgart, 1976, pp. 24–39.

9. *On Homosexuality and French Fascism*, first published in *Sociétés*, No. 17, March 1988, pp. 14–16, reprinted in revised form.

10. *Nazi Aesthetics: Beauty without Sensuality*, originally published in *"Degenerate Art": The Fate of the Avant-Garde in Nazi Germany*, Museum Associates, Los Angeles County Museum of Art, 1991, pp. 25–32, reprinted by permission.

Contents

Introduction

MODERN HISTORICAL SCHOLARSHIP has made great advances in our understanding of fascism as it existed in its epoch, overturning most older interpretations and reevaluating its consequences.

Historians in the past were prone to look for a single key to unlock the secrets of fascism's existence and success. The development of the social structures or of the economy was most often singled out as the explanation for fascism's rise and triumphs. Social and economic factors were congenial tools of historical analysis, while at the same time fascism was said to lack any coherent political thought or ideology. The structure of valid political thought, regardless of content, was supposed to follow established classical models like that of the ancients, or in modern times that put forward by Karl Marx or Adam Smith. This book hopes to challenge such traditional attitudes towards politics.

Here, as in many analyses of fascism, Germany was simply considered an occupied country, brutally taken over by the Nazis. The optimism about the good and rational nature of "the people" was a heritage of the enlightenment which had long ago informed so-called progressive political thought, and which was not abandoned but rather reenforced by many analyses of fascism. This held for Germany which was not able to create a true anti-fascist movement in order to redeem the people, but also for Italy which did have an anti-fascist movement tied to the political left which was strong enough to attempt a civil war during the last years of the fascist regime.

However, while in the past historians did make crucial contributions to our understanding of fascism, they could not grapple successfully with a key question which must be answered about the fascist movement: why it could attract so much popular support and govern by consensus for some time after it took power. Economic and social factors certainly played a role, even if fascism can no longer be thought of simply as a movement of the bourgeoisie. We now know about its largely cross-class appeal, and that while it came to power only in two highly developed countries, it also played an important role in undeveloped nations like Romania or Hungary. Class analysis, a favorite of many historians, cannot really capture the essence of fascism. In addition, the accumulation of historical knowledge has meant that different approaches have naturally come into play. This book attempts to point in one such direction which is finding increasing favor with contemporary historians.[1]

Fascism considered as a cultural movement means seeing fascism as it saw itself and as its followers saw it, to attempt to understand the movement on its own terms. Only then, when we have grasped fascism from the inside out, can we truly judge its appeal and its power. For fascism created a political environment which attempted to encompass the entire man or woman, to address, above all, the senses and emotions, and at the same time to make the abstract concrete as something uplifting and familiar which can be seen and touched. That is why, for example, considerations of beauty usually not thought of as an element of politics played such an important role in defining the political liturgy as well as the human stereotypes used as symbols of the movement. Moreover, the *mis-en-scène* was crucial to fascist self-representation, while the visual expression of fascism in architecture, art and city planning played a leading role as expressions of the movement's political thought. The cultural interpretation of fascism opens up a means to penetrate fascist self-understanding, and such empathy is crucial in order to grasp how people saw the movement, something which cannot be ignored or evaluated merely in retrospect.

Culture in our case must not be narrowly defined as a history of ideas, or as confined to popular culture, but instead understood as dealing with life seen as a whole—a totality, as indeed the fascist movement sought to define itself. Cultural history centers above all upon the perceptions of men and women, and how these are shaped and enlisted in politics at a particular place and time. Quite consciously fascism addressed people's perceptions of their situation in life and their hopes for the future, and therefore it is essential to understand how fascist self-representation was so successful in taking up and satisfying these perceptions if we want to gauge the depth of the movement's appeal. To be sure, writing about self-representation has become popular among some scholars of late, but when they address "representation," they are almost always concerned with loose psychological or textual associations, rather than with the specific historical context in which visual self-representation takes place.

This approach to the various fascist movements encompasses other surprisingly neglected and yet crucial aspects of fascism, above all that of fascism seen as an integral element of European nationalism, as well as fascism viewed as a revolutionary movement.

Nationalism is a belief-system which provided the foundation for all fascist movements, it was the bed rock upon which they were built. Racism, of prime importance in Germany, enhanced nationalism and gave it its cutting edge. Finally, fascism must be understood as a nationalist revolution with its own ideology and its own goals. A cultural interpretation takes account of fascism as a system of belief based upon heightened nationalism, as well as of fascism understood as a right-wing revolution. The model of socialist, communist or anarchist revolutions taken as representing the only valid use of the term must be abandoned, as Karl Dietrich Bracher suggested some years ago.[2] A revolution from the political Right is as possible as one from the political Left, once revolution is defined as the forceful reordering of society in the light of a projected utopia.[3]

Nationalism has been a stepchild of historians, and a renewed interest in nationalism as collective self-understanding through a belief system has surfaced only recently, nearly half a century since the end of the Second World War, in the midst of clear signs that nationalism in Europe was alive and well—not merely a patriotism which tolerated ethnic and national differences, but the integral nationalism which had found its climax in fascism.

Modern nationalism found its fulfillment as a belief-system seeking legitimacy through the construction of a largely mythical past and through easily understood symbols which could serve as rallying points. The national flag, national monuments or national anthems, for example, reenforced by national ceremonies and parades provided such symbols which date back to the beginnings of modern national consciousness. But now, in fascism, the liturgy of nationalism moved to the forefront as people were transformed from spectators to participants.

This liturgy borrowed liberally from that of the Christian churches with its martyrs as well as its hymns, responses, and the confession of faith in which all could join. Adolf Hitler's constant use of a Christian vocabulary in which to sheath his movement is well documented.[4] Christianity was used in order to give fascism a familiar cast, to make it correspond to something people knew well. The structure of one belief-system reenforced another. These borrowings from Christianity were, of course, stripped of their content, and nationalism was substituted instead.

Traditional Christianity was the most important inspiration for the rites and liturgy of fascism, but in German National Socialism the tradition of bourgeois, artisan and workers' festivals must have played its role as well. Bourgeois festivals, for example, during the nineteenth century were not so much exceptional occasions as an integral part of daily life.[5] These were regional and civic festivals which by the end of the nineteenth century had often been subordinated to national concerns. The connection between this culture of festivals and the political liturgy which is our concern still needs to be investigated.

Nationalism with its symbols, rites and confession of faith became a civic religion in the hands of German National Socialists or Italian fascists and their imitators—they completed a sacralization of politics which had always been latent in modern nationalism. Fascism's expansionist drives were to a large extent fueled by long-standing nationalist ambitions, whether it was to transform the Mediterranean into a *Mare Nostrum*, or the search for living space in eastern Europe.

The three vital elements necessary for the constitution of a nation are said to be collective memory essential to any national consciousness, the belief in the nation's mission and its regenerative power.[6] The heightened nationalism of the fascists added little to this definition but used it as a springboard in order to cement the bonds between the movement and its people, and to give meaning to the activism which it both encouraged and disciplined through giving it a goal and direction. The traditional nationalist myths and slogans, the use of the nationalist liturgy, the constant and unremitting appeals to national solidarity and greatness informed all of fascism, and should have made nationalism's importance obvious—perhaps too obvious to many historians of the movement who have not bothered to analyze nationalism itself as a belief-system. This is certainly a crucial reason why in the past many failed to discuss fascism as a civic religion, and that, for example, it was only in the 1990s that Emilio Gentile gave us the first and masterful analysis of Italian fascism's sacralization of politics. National Socialism had already been analyzed in that context somewhat earlier.[7] The principal difficulty any historian of fascism has to overcome is indeed daunting: how to analyze the irrational rationally is no easy task.

Like nationalism, racism has been on the whole a stepchild of modern historiography. To be sure, not all fascist movements were racist. Jews, for example, were well represented in the Italian fascist party during the first sixteen years of its rule, and even held some important positions. The Rexist movement in Belgium, a fascist party in a multi-ethnic state, repudiated racism while, to cite another example, the Spanish Falange, the Spanish fascist movement, was not racist. Racism was an integral part of fascism in eastern and central Europe, while in western Europe it became an ingredient in some but not all of fascism. How strong or weak the anti-Semitic tradition within any one nation proved to be determined the alliance of racism and nationalism, and therefore with the fascist party. But even in Italy, which outside the Catholic Church (and perhaps just because of its claim to power) had no very strong anti-Semitic tradition, recent research has shown that a wing of the party which was attracted to racism existed long before fascism in power unleashed its own racism, first against blacks during the Ethiopian war, and then against the Jews through the 1938 racial laws.[8]

Racism became part of that nationalism upon which some of fascism based its principle appeal, it brought out in sharp relief the aggressiveness inherent in much of nationalism, it drove the exclusivity of nationalism to new heights and locked it securely in place. This alliance between nationalism and racism must not obscure the fact that racism itself was a fully-fledged world view which stood on its own two feet, similar in this respect to other world views like liberalism, conservatism, and Marxism, which the nineteenth bequeathed to the twentieth century. Here also, historians have tended to see it as a by-product of other more tangible forces: the ruling class, capitalism or the bourgeoisie. But such a downgrading of racism disguises what it could bring to its alliance with nationalism and how it could, in Germany, for example, become the determining factor in the fascist state.

Racism, originating in the eighteenth century, used new sciences like anthropology, eugenics and a freshly fashioned aesthetic consciousness in order to construct its ideology. All of these played a part in racism's search for roots in order to fulfill a longing for immutability and certainty in a world of rapid change, to help get one's bearing and to prove one's superiority. The appeal to science was important especially at a time when theories of heredity and evolution were becoming popularized. The racial myths concerning the far-away origins, the triumphs and the hardships of the race, formed a belief-system to which its scientific garb gave added authority.

But racism was more than just a theoretical construction, it sought to provide concrete examples of the superior and inferior races, constructing stereotypes in order to make the inherent explicit.[9] Man must be judged by the shape of his body, his appearance and comportment. The transformation of humans into stereotypes was a prerequisite of racism.

Enemy and friend were clearly distinguished one from another using criteria of judgement which were familiar: a person's beauty or ugliness, his strength or weakness, his control or his lack of control over his passions. The body of a man of the superior race must be harmonious and yet project strength and self-confidence. Surely it is easy to see how racism could give additional substance to nationalism, define the national character clearly and—unlike the traditional symbols of nationalism such as the flag or national anthems—furnish symbols which were concrete and familiar, which could be seen and touched, whether it was the beautiful body of the superior or the distorted body of the inferior race.

The expansionist drive of fascism, fueled by nationalism, which we have already mentioned, was further sharpened: wars now became race wars, whether against external or internal enemies. Racism here joined the apocalyptic strand in fascism and especially in National Socialism whose occult origins will be discussed in a later chapter. Ideas of regeneration, of sacrifice, and a vision of utopia were the staple of all of fascism, as was the need to triumph over ever-present enemies. If a heightened nationalism became a civic religion, then racism for all its scientific pretensions was a belief-system as well.

The race war was always a crusade, a total war which seemed to require a final solution. What other choice was there if the enmity between races was hereditary, locked into place, and the differences between races absolute and total? However, as in the case of nationalism, racism was not always extreme, mostly it led to exclusion, discrimination and ghettoization. National Socialism, however, largely with the collaboration of its allies in eastern Europe and in the Baltic pushed the race war to its logical conclusion, the complete eradication of the Jews, supposedly the principal enemy of the race. Here, unlike Italy even after its racist laws, racism actually defined the fascist world view and gave a deadly edge to German nationalism.

Fascism was born in the aftermath of the First World War, and everywhere it claimed to continue the war experience into peacetime, with its male camaraderie and its emphasis upon struggle and triumph. Mussolini talked about that violence which cannot be expelled from history.[10] Emphasizing wartime camaraderie meant that fascism everywhere saw itself as a coterie of men, while women were stereotyped not as inferior but as largely passive in their role as wives and mothers. The virile man was considered the driving force of history and one of the principle symbols representing the nation's strength and harmony.[11] The official invitation to the Nazi Party congress of 1934, for example, shows the Nazi Party emblem carried on the hands of half-naked men. The military analogy was never far away from the supposedly disciplined fascist party formations with their hierarchical command structures. Fascism considered itself in a state of permanent war which, in the service of a higher cause, would unleash all the hidden energy of men, foot soldiers of a civic religion.

Fascism needed a supreme leader in order to provide a sharp enough focus, a living symbol of nation and party. As we shall see in the first chapter, fascism nevertheless considered itself a democratic movement even while rejecting representative government. The people were supposed to govern themselves directly through taking part in the liturgy and rites of the new nation as well as in party formations—joining in an activism encouraged and directed by the regime and the party. The leader, the charismatic Führer or Duce, was the living symbol of the people, the embodiment of all its ideals. He could do no wrong, and it is well documented that whenever any German saw what he considered an injustice committed in the name of the Third Reich, the reaction was often "if only the Führer had known!" And indeed, for many, especially in times of crisis, such a direct democracy seemed more meaningful than the far-away Parliaments, the "talking heads" from which they seemed excluded.

Here, the appearance—the perception of meaningful action—was substituted for reality and the same substitution held when fascists talked about individualism but in reality believed that the individual could only be free as an integral part of a disciplined mass. Fascism always appropriated already existing, familiar, and popular ideas while manipulating them and integrating them into its own world view. Fascism was a new political movement but not a movement which invented anything new; it annexed the long familiar and made it a part of its racism and nationalism. That was some of its real strength: it offered regeneration with security and revolution based on the already familiar.

These themes which grow out of the attempt which cultural history provides to comprehend fascist self-understanding and self-representation will be pursued in the chapters which follow. Fascist movements had their differences but they shared a common approach to politics. The first three chapters further extend this approach, dealing concretely and specifically with fascist movements as they existed in their epoch during the inter-war years. The next chapters investigate aspects of the origins of the movement which have a direct bearing upon its course, while the rest of the book probes various facets of fascism. Here is a kaleidoscope which addresses often-neglected themes, all of which contribute to a general theory of fascism.

Though these essays were written on different occasions and at different times they do present a coherent picture based on the approach to fascism which I have attempted to describe. Redundancies have been eliminated and some chapters—especially the seminal chapter on the General Theory of Fascism—have been extensively revised. The chapter on Homosexuality and Fascism has not been available in English up to now, but it has also seen extensive change from the original version. Though there exists no single key which will unlock the secrets of fascism, as we stated at the beginning of this introduction, it is hoped that the essays in this volume come close to fascist reality through the various experiences they analyze within the general framework set by the first chapters.

ONE

Toward a General Theory
of Fascism

I N OUR CENTURY two revolutionary movements have made
their mark upon Europe: that originally springing from Marxism, and the fascist revolution. The various forms of Marxism
have occupied historians and political scientists for many decades,
while the study of fascism was late catching up. Even so, because
of the war and the fascist record in power, fascism has remained
synonymous with oppression and domination; it is alleged that it
was without ideas of its own, but merely a reaction against other
more progressive movements such as liberalism or socialism. Earlier
scholarship concerning fascism has more often than not been used as
an occasion to fight contemporary polemical battles.

In a justified reaction against stereotyping, recent scholarship has
been suspicious of general theories of fascism. As many local and
regional studies show, while on one level fascism may have presented
a kaleidoscope of contradictory attitudes, nevertheless these attitudes
were based upon some common assumptions. We shall attempt to
bring together some of the principal building blocks for such common
assumptions—there seem to be enough of them to construct at least
a provisional dwelling. Germany and Italy will dominate the discussion, as the experience of European fascism was largely dominated by

1

Italian fascism and German National Socialism. The word "fascism" will be used without qualification when both these movements are meant. From time to time I shall also refer to various other fascisms in Europe, but only specifically or as subsidiary examples.

We can best develop a general theory of fascism through a critique of past attempts to accomplish this task. Some historians have seen an integral connection between bolshevism and fascism. Both were totalitarian régimes and, as such, dictatorships based upon the exclusive claim to leadership by one political party.[1] Although such an equation was often politically motivated, it was not, as its opponents claimed, merely a child of the cold war.

Both movements were based on the ideal, however distorted, of popular sovereignty. This meant the rejection of parliamentary government and representative institutions on behalf of a democracy of the masses in which the people would in theory directly govern themselves. The leader symbolized the people; he expressed the "general will"—but such a democracy meant that, instead of representative assemblies, a new secular religion mediated between people and leaders, providing, at the same time, an instrument of social control over the masses. It was expressed on the public level through official ceremonies, festivals, and not least, the use of political imagery, and on a private level through control over all aspects of life by the dictates of the single political party. This system was common in various degrees to fascist and bolshevist movements.

The danger inherent in subsuming both systems under the concept of totalitarianism is that it may serve to disguise real differences, not only between bolshevism and fascism but also between the different forms of fascism themselves. Moreover, the contention that these theories really compare fascism not with the early, more experimental years of bolshevism, but with Stalinism instead seems justified. Indeed, totalitarianism as a static concept often veils the development of both fascism and bolshevism. In Soviet Russia, for example, the kind of public ceremonies and festivals that mark the fascist political style were tried early in the régime but then dropped, and not resumed until after the Second World War, when they came to fulfill the same functions as they had for fascism earlier. In 1966, *Pravda* wrote that rallies, ceremonial processions, speeches, and music gave emotional strength to the political commitment of the people.[2] Fascism, too, did not remain static, although even some critics of totalitarian theory apparently see it as unchanging. There is, for example, a difference between fascism as a political movement and as a government in power.

Theories of totalitarianism have also placed undue emphasis upon the supposedly monolithic leadership cult. Here again, this was introduced into the Soviet Union by Stalin rather than at first by Lenin. Even within fascism, the cult of the leader varied: Piero Melograni has written on how the cult of "Il Duce" and fascism were not identical, and that it was "Mussolinianism" which won the people's allegiance.[3] In Germany there is no discernible difference between Hitlerism and National Socialism.

More serious is the contention, common to most theories of totalitarianism, that the leader manipulates the masses through propaganda and terror: that free volition is incompatible with totalitarian practice.[4] The term "propaganda," always used in this context, leads to a serious misunderstanding of the fascist conception of politics and its essentially organic and religious nature. In times of crisis such politics provided many millions of people with a more meaningful involvement than representative parliamentary government—largely because it was not itself a new phenomenon, but instead based upon an older and still lively tradition of direct democracy, which had always opposed European parliaments.

Even the widespread notion that fascism ruled through terror must be modified; rather, it was built at first upon a popular consensus. Tangible successes, the ability to compromise and to go slow, combined with the responsive chord struck by fascist culture, integrated Italians and Germans into this consensus which undoubtedly was more solid in Germany than Italy. Hitler, after all, shared a volkish faith with many of his fellow Germans, especially in times of crisis, and his tangible successes in domestic and foreign policy up to the Second World War were much more spectacular than Mussolini's achievements.

Terror increased with the continued survival of the régimes, for disillusionment with fascism in power could easily lead to unrest. By the time many earlier fellow travelers woke up to fascist reality, it was too late to resist, except by martyrdom. Mass popular consensus during the first years of fascism in power allowed it to develop a secret police—outside and above regular channels and procedures[5]-as well as the special courts needed to reinforce its actions. This was easier in the Soviet Union since the revolution had destroyed the old legal framework; while in Germany and Italy traditional safeguards paradoxically continued to exist and even to be used side by side with arbitrary action. In Germany, judges freed some concentration camp inmates as late as 1936.

Terror must not then be treated as a static concept, but as something that develops in intensity. Moreover, there was a great deal of disharmony and disunity on the local level in its application. Manpower in Germany, for example, was scarce and the secret police depended in large part on plentiful private denunciations.[6] Not only must historical development be taken into account, but also the existence and extent of a popular consensus, which, although differing in scope in the so-called totalitarian nations, did exist at some time in each of them.

Despite all these caveats, both bolshevists and fascists reached back into the anti-parliamentary and anti-pluralistic traditions of the nineteenth century in order to face the collapse of social, economic, and political structures in their nations during and after the First World War. So-called totalitarianism was new only as a form of legitimate government: it derived from a long tradition; otherwise it would not have received such immediate mass support. Beginning its modern history with the French Revolution, that tradition continued to inform both the nationalism and the quest for social justice of the nineteenth century. Even if Jacob Talmon's concept of "totalitarian democracy" rests, as some have claimed, upon a misreading of the Enlightenment,[7] men like Robespierre and Saint-Just shared in such misconceptions. Rousseau's "general will," his exaltation of "the people," was bent by the Jacobins into a dictatorship in which the people worshipped themselves through public festivals and symbols (such as the Goddess of Reason), where traditional religious enthusiasm was first transferred to civic rites.[8]

The distinction between private and public life was eradicated, just as totalitarian régimes would later attempt to abolish such differences. Public allegiance through active participation in the national cults or party organizations, was the road to survival, and as, for example, the Jacobins used dress as an outward sign of true inner allegiance (the revolutionary cap and trousers instead of breeches), so fascists and bolshevists integrated various dress codes into their systems. Nationalist movements during the nineteenth century carried on these traditions, even if at times they attempted to compromise with liberal values. The workers' movement, though most of it was in fact wedded to parliamentary democracy, also stressed outward symbols of unity as in the serried ranks and Sunday dress of May Day parades, massed flags, and the clenched fist salute. Italy was less influenced by this legacy, but it also played a part in the fight for national unity. At the turn of the century, the radical Left and the radical Right were apt to demand control of the whole man, not just a political piece of him.

Bolshevism and fascism attempted to mobilize the masses, to substitute modern mass politics for pluralistic and parliamentary government. Indeed, parliamentary government found it difficult to cope with the crises of the postwar world, and abdicated without a struggle, not only in Germany and Italy but also in Portugal and, where it had existed immediately after the war, in the nations of eastern Europe. The fascists helped the demise of parliamentary government, but that it succumbed so readily points to deep inherent structural and ideological problems—and, indeed, few representative governments have withstood the pressures of modern economic, political, and social crises, especially when these coincided with unsatisfied national aspirations and defeat in war.[9] Wherever during the interwar years one-party governments came to power, they merely toppled régimes ripe for the picking; this holds good for Russia as well as for Germany and Italy. But unlike bolshevism, fascism never had to fight a proper civil war on its road to power: Mussolini marched on Rome in the comfort of a railway carriage, and Hitler simply presented himself to the German president. Certainly, representative government and liberal politics allowed individual freedom to breathe and prosper, but the new post First World War political movements cannot be condemned without taking the collapse of existing parliaments and social structures into account. We must not look at a historical movement mainly from the viewpoint of our political predilections, lest we falsify historical necessity.

If some historians have used the model of totalitarianism in order to analyze fascism, others, and they are in the majority, have used the model of the "good revolution."[10] The French, American, and especially the Russian revolutions, so it is said, led to the progress of mankind, while fascism was an attempt to stop the clock, to maintain old privilege against the demands of the new classes as represented by the proletariat. In reality, fascism was itself a revolution, seizing power by using twentieth-century methods of mass mobilization and control, and replacing an old with a new élite. (In this sense, National Socialism brought about a more fundamental change than Italian fascism, where new and traditional élites co-existed to a greater extent.) Economic policy was subordinated to the political goals of fascism, but in Germany, at least, this did not preclude nationalization (as for example, the huge Hermann Goering Steel Works). By and large, however, fascism worked hand in hand with the larger industrial enterprises. Fascism, as Stanley Payne, writing the most authoritative history of fascism sees it, was a radical force seeking to create a new social order.[11]

Yet a one-sided emphasis either upon economic factors or upon the proletariat obscures our view of the revolutionary side of fascism. Fascism condemned the French Revolution but was also, at least in its beginnings, a direct descendant of the Jacobin political style.[12] Above all, the fascist revolution saw itself as a "Third Force," rejecting both "materialistic Marxism" and "finance capitalism" in the capitalist and materialist present. This was the revolutionary tradition within which fascism worked. But it was not alone in such an aim; in the postwar world, many left-wing intellectuals rejected both Marxist orthodoxy and capitalism. Unlike the fascists, however, they sought to transcend both by emphasis on the triumphant goodness of man once capitalism was abolished.

Fascism retreated instead into the nationalist mystique. But here, once more, it followed a precedent. French socialists of the mid-nineteenth century, and men like Édouard Drumont toward the end of the century, had combined opposition to finance capitalism and the advocacy of greater social equality with an impassioned nationalism. They were National Socialists long before the small German Workers' Party took this name. Such National Socialism was in the air as a "Third Force" in the last decades of the nineteenth century, when Marxism was to be reckoned with and capitalist development seemed accompanied by a soulless positivism in a world where only material values counted. There were early national socialist movements in France (in which former leaders of the Paris Commune, with their Jacobin traditions, joined, but also some anarchists and bourgeois *bien-pensants*), in Bohemia, and even in Germany, advocated at the turn of the century by the Hessian Peasants' League led by Otto Boeckel.[13]

In Italy, argument for the "Third Force" resulted from the First World War—the struggle to get Italy to intervene in this war, and the subsequent war experience seemed to transcend vested interests and political parties.[14] There was indeed a similar reaction among a good many veterans in Germany (but not in France, which had won the war and successfully weathered postwar upheaval). Yet in Italy, unlike Germany, the "war experience" carried revolutionary implications. Mussolini was joined in this hope by students and by revolutionary syndicalists who wanted to abolish the existing social and economic order so that the nation could be regenerated through the searing experience of war. After the war as "revolutionary veterans" they appealed both to the revolutionary spirit and to a sense of Italy's historic national mission. It is typical that when the local Fascist Party was founded in 1920 in Ferrara, it was a youth group called the "Third Italy" which took the initiative.[15] In Germany and Italy—nations plunged into crisis by the war—and also among many political groups of other nations, the "Third Force" became an alternative revolution to Marxism, a retreat into the organic community of the nation when the world seemed to be dominated on the one hand by the mysterious power of money and on the other by the Marxist conspiracy.[16]

Yet this "Third Force" became ever less revolutionary and more nationalistic as fascists and Nazis strove for power. Mussolini broke with the revolutionary syndicalists early on and tamed his youth organization but stayed with the Futurists, whose revolutionary ardor took the fast sports car as its model rather than the nationalization of production. Hitler got rid of social revolutionaries like Otto Strasser who wanted to challenge property relationships, however slightly. Yet we must not limit our gaze to property relationships or the naked play of power and interest; such issues alone do not motivate men. It was the strength of fascism everywhere that it appeared to transcend these concerns, gave people a meaningful sense of political participation (though, of course, in reality they did not participate at all), and sheltered them within the national community against the menace of rapid change and the all too swift passage of time. At the same time it gave them hope through projecting a utopia, taking advantage of apocalyptic longings.

National Socialism was able to contain the revolutionary impetus better than Italian fascism because in Germany the very term "Third Force" was fraught with mystical and millenarian meaning. The mythos of the "Third Force" became a part of the mythos of the "Third Reich," carrying on a Germanic messianic tradition that had no real equivalent in Catholic Italy. The prophecy by Joachim of Flora about the future "Third Age," which would be a kingdom of the spirit—the biblical millennium—had become an essential ingredient of German Protestantism, as had the three mystical kingdoms of Paracelsus: that of God, the planets, and the Earth. The German mystics such as Jakob Böhme believed that man, by overcoming his baser self and seeking harmony within nature, could rise from Earth to the kingdom of God—an important emphasis on "becoming" or joining the eternal spirit of the race rather than "being"; on the quest for the "genuine" as exemplified first by nature and, later, by the "Volk" itself.[17]

Moeller van den Bruck, whose book *The Third Reich* (1923) was originally entitled *The Third Way*, brought this tradition up to date for a defeated nation: the Germanic mission would transcend all the contradictions inherent in modern life, including Germany's defeat in war; Germans must struggle continually toward utopia, which he equated with the German Reich of the future. To be sure, Moeller was pragmatic in his demand for political action, his advocacy of the corporate state, and his desire to institute a planned economy (hence his praise of Lenin's new economic policy).[18] Yet he also retained the traditional elements that were so much a part of this kind of revolution, calling for the maintenance of state authority, preferably that of a monarchy, as well as of the family structure.

However, for Moeller the pragmatic was always subsumed under the messianic. The arrival of the "Third Reich" would automatically solve all outstanding problems. Such a belief was part of the "Third Force" in Germany: the purified national community of the future would end all present difficulties and anxieties, social inequalities and economic crises. Man would then "overcome" the dialectic of earthly life. Small wonder that the Nazis enthusiastically annexed the fairy tale and folk legend to their cause. However, this vision of the future was rooted in the past—it was the traditional fairy tale which the Nazis used in creating their emphasis upon the modern Volk. Precedent was always an integral part of the Nazi ideology, and of Italian fascism too—as when in the fourth year of Mussolini's government the ancient monuments of Rome were restored. For Mussolini, however, history was never more than a platform from which to jump into an ill-defined future.

Hitler and Goebbels's obsession with history reached a climax at the moment of defeat: in 1945, they clung to memories of Frederick the Great, who had been saved from certain defeat by the opportune death of the Czarina Elizabeth, as well as remembering the victory of Rome over Carthage.[19] Utopia and traditionalism were linked, a point to which we shall return when discussing the new fascist man.

Ernst Bloch called this urge to "overcome"—the mystical and millenarian dynamic—the "hidden revolution" essential to the realization of the true socialist revolution.[20] Men must hope before they can act. National Socialism claimed to represent this "inner dynamic," though it was always careful to state that the "Third Reich" stood at the threshold of fulfillment and that a period of struggle and suffering must precede eventual salvation. And indeed, in the end, this revolutionary tradition did transfer a religious enthusiasm to secular government.

While few would deny that in order to understand communism or bolshevism we have to comprehend their revolutionary tradition, fascism has often been discussed as if it had no such tradition. The revolutionary appeal of fascism is easy to underestimate in our own time; the object has been to de-mystify, and a new positivism has captured the historical imagination.

The fascist revolution built upon a deep bedrock of popular piety and, especially in Germany, upon a millenarianism that was apt to come to the fore in times of crisis. More about this tradition will be said in the chapter below on the occult origins of National Socialism. The myths and symbols of nationalism were superimposed upon those of Christianity—not only in the rhythms of public rites and ceremonies (even the Duce's famed dialogues with the masses from his balcony are related to Christian "responses")—but also in the appeal to apocalyptic and millenarian thought. Such appeals can be found in the very vocabulary of Nazi leaders. Their language grew out of Christianity as we mentioned in the introduction; it was, after all, a language of faith. In 1935, for example, at Munich's *Feldherrnhalle*, where his *putsch* of 1923 had resulted in a bloody fiasco, Hitler called those who had fallen earlier "my apostles," and proclaimed that "with the Third Reich you have risen from the dead." Many other examples spring to mind, as when the leader of the Labor Front, Robert Ley, asserted that "we have found the road to eternity." The whole vocabulary of blood and soil was filled with Christian liturgical and religious meaning—the "blood" itself, the "martyrdom," the "incarnation."[21]

Moreover, historians have recently found that in the past, millenarianism was not simply a protest by the poor against the rich, but a belief shared by most classes;[22] not inherently psychotic, but a normal strain of popular piety running through the nineteenth century and into twentieth-century Europe, and common to all nations. This background was vital for the cross-class appeal of National Socialism, and perhaps, despite a different emphasis, for Italian fascism as well: the "new man," for whom all fascism yearned, was certainly easily integrated into such popular piety as it became transformed into political thought.

The "Third Force" in Italy did not directly build upon a mystical tradition, though it existed there as well as in Germany. Rather than referring to Savonarola, for example, Giovanni Gentile the important fascist philosopher saw in the fascist state a Hegelian synthesis, which resolved all contradictions. In consequence, German idealism was more important in Italian fascism, derived from Gentile, than in National Socialism, though some Nazi philosophers used Hegel to prove that Hitler had ended the dialectic of history. After the Concordat of 1929, Italian fascism, seeking to rival the Church, became increasingly the religion of the state. The will to believe was emphasized, and the Italian anti-rational tradition was searched for precedents.[23] Yet when all was said and done, such efforts were sporadic, and some leading fascists retained their skepticism about "*romanità*" or civil religions.

While the "Third Force" is vital for understanding fascism, its importance should not be exaggerated. For fascism, it was always "the experience" that counted, and not appeals to the intellect. In a play by Hans Johst, written in 1934, the young Leo Schlageter, about to fight against the French occupation of the Ruhr Valley after the First World War, facing his socialist father speaks these lines:

> *Son:* The young people don't pay much attention to these old slogans anymore . . . the class struggle is dying out.
> *Father:* So . . . and what do you live on then?
> *Son:* The Volk Community . . .
> *Father:* And that's a slogan . . . ?
> *Son:* No, it's an experience![24]

It was an organic view of the world, which was supposed to take in the whole man and thus end his alienation. A fundamental redefinition is involved in such a view of man and his place in the world. "Politics," wrote the Italian fascist Giuseppe Bottai, "is an attitude toward life itself,"[25] and this phrase is repeated word for word in National Socialist literature. Horia Sima, one of Codreanu's successors in the leadership of the Romanian Iron Guard, summed it up: "We must cease to separate the spiritual from the political man. All history is a commentary upon the life of the spirit."[26] When fascists spoke of culture, they meant a proper attitude toward life: encompassing the ability to accept a faith, the work ethic, and discipline, but also receptivity to art and the appreciation of the native landscape.[27] The true community was symbolized by factors opposed to materialism, by art and literature, the symbols of the past and the stereotypes of the present. The National Socialist emphasis upon myth, symbol, literature and art is indeed common to all fascism.

If, then, fascism saw itself as a cultural movement, any comparative study must be based upon an analysis of cultural similarities and differences. Social and economic programs varied widely, not only between different fascisms but within each fascist movement. Some historians and political scientists have stumbled over this fact; for them, culture defined as "attitudes toward life" is no substitute for neatly coherent systems of political thought. They believe, as mentioned in our introduction, that fascism was devoid of intellectual substance, a mere reflection of movements which depend upon well-constructed ideologies. This has led many of them to underestimate fascism, to see it as a temporary response to crises, vanishing when normality is restored (though Italian fascism, with its twenty years in power, is surely more than a "temporary response"). In reality, fascism was based upon a strong and unique revolutionary tradition, fired by the emphasis on youth and the war experience; it was able to create a mass consensus that was finally broken only by a lost war.

Fascism was a movement of youth, not only in the sense that it covered a definite span of time but also in its membership. The *fin de siècle* had seen a rebellion of the young against society, parents, and school; they longed for a new sense of community. These youths were of bourgeois background, and their dominant concern for several generations had been with national unity rather than with social and economic change—for which they felt little need. Thus they were quite prepared to have their urge to revolt directed into national channels, on behalf of a community which seemed to them one of the "soul" and not an artificial creation. Such were the young who streamed not only into the earlier German Youth Movement but also into the *fasci* and the S.A., and who made up the cadres of other fascist movements. Returned from the war, they wanted to prolong the camaraderie of the trenches or if they were too young to have fought, repeat an experience which had been idealized in retrospect. Fascism offered them this chance. It is well to note in this connection that the early fascists were a new grouping, not yet bureaucratized, and that their supposed open-endedness made them appear more dynamic than rival political parties. The leaders, too, were young by the standards of that age—Mussolini became prime minister at thirty-nine; Hitler attained the chancellorship at forty-four.

Youth symbolized vigor and action; ideology was joined to fact. Fascist heroes and martyrs died at an early age in order to enter the pantheon, and symbolic representations of youth expressed the ideal type in artistic form. This was the classical ideal of beauty, which had become the manly stereotype. There must have been many who, like Albert Speer's mother, voted for the Nazis because they were young and clean-cut. The hero of the Italian novel *Generazione* (*Generations*, 1930), by Adolfo Baiocchi, finds his way from communism to fascism. His final conversion comes when he sees his former comrades, now unattractive, dirty, and disheveled, taken away by the police after an unsuccessful attempt at revolution: "These are the men of the future?" Similarly in the Nazi film *Hitler-Junge Quex* (1933), the communists were slovenly and disheveled while the Hitler Youth were clean-cut, true and respectable men. Monuments to the soldiers who fell in the First World War often represented young Siegfrieds or Greek youths. Indeed, this stereotype was reinforced by the war when the cult of youth joined the cult of the nation.

The war became a symbol of youth in its activism, its optimism, and its heroic sacrifice. For Germans, the Battle of Langemarck (November, 1914), where members of the German Youth Movement were mowed down in thousands, came to stand for the sacrifice of heroic youth. The flower of the nation, so the myth tells us, went singing to their death. One writer, Rudolf Binding, asserted that through this sacrifice only German youth had the right to symbolize national renewal among the youth of the world.[28]

Benito Mussolini also declared himself the spokesman of a youth that had shown its mettle in war. While Hitler promised to erase the "shame of Versailles," Mussolini wanted to complete Italy's "mutilated" victory in the Great War. Both took up the slogan of the young and old nations which gained currency after the war, as a reassertion of the defeated against the victors.

Fascism thus built upon the war experience, which, in different ways, had shaped the outlook of Mussolini and Hitler themselves toward the world: the former moving from a Nietzschean rather than a Marxist socialism to ideals of nationalism and struggle; the latter deepening his ever present racist world view. Above all, for millions of their contemporaries the war was the most profound experience of their lives. While a very few became pacifists, many more attempted to confront the mass death they had witnessed by elevating it into myth. Both in Germany and Italy the myth of the war experience— the glory of the struggle, the legacy of the martyrs, the camaraderie of the trenches—defeated any resolve never to have war again. France, the victorious and satisfied nation, saw the rise of powerful veterans' movements which proclaimed an end to all war;[29] but in Germany and Italy such movements proclaimed the coming resurrection of the fatherland.

The Left in Germany and Italy, as in all other nations, had difficulty in coming to grips with this war experience, shared though it was by their own members. Social Democrats and communists sometimes paraded in their old uniforms (but without decorations), and founded self-defense and paramilitary organizations, like the *Reichsbanner* in Germany (which was supposed to defend the Republic). But in the last resort the Left was halfhearted about all this, and its didactic and cosmopolitan heritage, as well as its pacifist traditions, proved stronger. The communists while they were ready to discard this past, found it impossible to redirect loyalty away from the fatherland and toward the Red Army.[30] To this day, few historians have investigated the Left's confrontation with the war experience, perhaps in itself a comment on the continued underestimation of this myth as a political force. Here was a political void readily occupied by the fascists.

The war experience aided fascism in another, more indirect manner. The front-line soldiers had become immune to the horrors of war, mass death, wounded and mutilated comrades. They had faced such unparalleled experiences either with stoicism or with a sense of sacrifice—war had given meaning to their dull and routine lives. Indeed, the war experience, despite all its horrors, catered to the longing for the exceptional, the escape from the treadmill of everyday life and its responsibilities. The political liturgy of fascism with its countless festivals catered to the same dream of excitement, of taking part in meaningful action. Typical was the expression, often repeated during the war, that death in battle had made life worthwhile.

Whatever the actual attitudes of the front-line soldiers during the war, their war experience later took on the appearance of myth, concretized through countless war cemeteries and memorials. The cult of the fallen soldier was central to the myth of the war experience in defeated Germany and Italy, and the dead were used to spur on the living to ever greater efforts of revenge. Mussolini put it succinctly: "A people which deifies its fallen can never be beaten." It was said that Hitler offered up his conquests on the altar of the war dead.[31] The horrors of war became part of an as yet incomplete struggle for national and personal fulfillment.

The acceptance of war was aided by new techniques of communication, which tended to trivialize mass death by making it a familiar part of an organized and channelled experience shared by thousands. For example, the battlefields of France and Flanders were among the tourist attractions organized by Thomas Cook and Sons. The massed and impersonal military cemeteries were faced by an equally impersonal mass of tourists, who could buy souvenir shells, helmets, and decorations. Still more important, the First World War was also the first war in the era of photography. During the war, postcards, films, and newsreels showed happy and healthy soldiers, and emphasized their work of destroying farms, towns, and churches rather than the dead and wounded. After the war, tourists could photograph the trenches, but what had once been experienced in these trenches was now for the most part tidied up and surrounded by flowers and shrubs.

Most people, however, were familiar with the face of war through the countless picture books that appeared after 1918. The illustrations and photographs of the peaceful dead or wounded were presented as a part of a glorious struggle, a desirable sacrifice that would reap its deserved reward. One such book, typical of the genre, called the war both horrible and yet a purveyor of aesthetic values. Arms were depicted as symbols of the highest human accomplishment, armed conflict as the overcoming of self in the service of collective ideals and values.[32] Horror pictures were transcended, suffused with ideals of sacredness and sacrifice; the dead and mangled corpses of soldiers were by association equated with the body of Christ in the service not of individual, but of national salvation.

Through this dual process of trivialization and transcendence, the war experience served the purposes alike of the dynamic of fascism and of the movement's brutality. Death and suffering lost their sting; the martyrs continued to live as a spiritual part of the nation while exhorting it to regenerate itself and to destroy its enemies.

Joseph Goebbels's definition of the nature of a revolutionary, written in 1945 when Germany faced defeat, is typical of the process of brutalization begun by the First World War. The Nazis, in common with all fascists, had always condemned half-measures as typically bourgeois and anti-revolutionary. Goebbels now defined as "revolutionary" those who would accept no compromise in executing a scorched earth policy, or in shooting shirkers and deserters. Refusal to carry out such actions marked the worn-out old bourgeois.[33] During the desperate years of the Republic of Salò, Mussolini also resorted to brutal measures, even at times threatening to execute pupils who refused to attend school.[34] There is little doubt that the myth of the war experience made fascist brutality more acceptable and fascism itself more attractive. Here was none of the ambivalence, shared by socialists and liberals, toward what millions must have regarded—if they survived—as a great experience, and perhaps, as we have mentioned, even the high point of their otherwise uneventful lives.

The crucial role which the war experience played in National Socialism is well enough known. The war was "a lovely dream" and a "miracle of achievement," as one Nazi children's book put it. Any death in war was a hero's death and thus the true fulfillment of life.[35] There was no doubt here about the "greatness and necessity of war."[36] In Mussolini's hands, this myth had even greater force because of the absence of a truly coherent volkish ideology in Italy. The fascist struggle was a continuation of the war experience. But here, as in Germany, the glorification of struggle was linked to wartime camaraderie and put forward as a method to end class divisions within the nation. "Not class war but class solidarity" reigned in the face of death, wrote an Italian fascist who had been a syndicalist up to the last months of the war; it was not a conflict between potentates or capitalists but a necessity for the defense of the people. Historical materialism was dead.[37]

The *èlan* of the battlefield was transformed into activism at home. The *fasci* and the German storm troopers regarded their postwar world as an enemy, which as patriotic shock troops they must destroy. Indeed, the leaders of these formations were in large part former front-line officers: Roehm, the head of the S.A.; Codreanu, founder of the Iron Guard; De Bono in Italy and Szalasi in Hungary—to give only a few examples. But this activism was tamed by the "magic" of the leadership of which Gustave Le Bon had written toward the end of the nineteenth century. Among the returned veterans it was even more easily controllable, for they desperately sought comradeship and leadership, not only because of the war experience but also to counteract their sense of isolation within a nation that had not lived up to their expectations.

The revolutionary tradition of the "Third Force" contained ingredients essential to this taming process: stress upon the national past and the mystical community of the nation; emphasis upon that middle-class respectability which proved essential for political success. The cult element to which we referred earlier gave it direction by channeling attention toward the eternal verities, which must never be forgotten. Activism there must be, enthusiasm was essential; the leader, aided by fascist methods of self-representation would direct it into the proper channels.

Here the liturgical element must be mentioned again, for the "eternal verities" were purveyed and reinforced through the endless repetition of slogans, choruses, symbols, and participation in group and mass ceremonies. These were the techniques that went into the taming of the revolution and that made fascism a new religion annexing rites long familiar through centuries of religious observance. Fascist mass meetings seemed something new, and so they were in the technology used and the *mis-en-scène*, but they also contained predominantly traditional elements in the technique of mass participation as well as in ideology.

To be sure, this process did not always work. The youthful enthusiasm that reigned at the outset of the movement was apt to be disappointed with its course. Italy, where fascism lasted longest, provides the best example, for the danger point came with the second fascist generation. There, the young men of the "class of '35" wanted to return to the beginnings of the movement, to its activism and its war on alienation—in short, to construct the fascist utopia. By 1936, they had formed a resistance movement within Italian fascism, which stressed that "open-endedness" the revolution had at first seemed to promise: to go to "the limits of fascism where all possibilities are open."[38] Similar signs can be discerned as Nazism developed, but here the SS managed to capture the activist spirit. Had it not been for the Second World War, Hitler might well have had difficulty with the SS, which thought of itself as an activist and spartan èlite. But then fascism never had a chance to grow old except in Italy; given the ingredients that went into the revolution, old age might have presented the movement with a severe crisis.

But in the last resort taming was always combined with activism, traditionalism inevitably went hand in hand with a nostalgic revolution. Both Hitler and Mussolini disliked drawing up party programs, for this smacked of "dogmatism." Fascism stressed "movement"— Hitler called his party a *"Bewegung,"* and Mussolini for some time favored Marinetti's Futurism as an artistic and literary form that stressed both movement and struggle. All European fascisms gave the impression that the movement was open-ended, a continuous Nietzschean ecstasy. But in reality definite limits were provided to this activism by the emphasis upon nationalism, sometimes upon racism, and by the longing for a restoration of traditional morality. The only variety of fascism of which this is not wholly true is to be found among the intellectuals in France. There a man like Drieu La Rochelle continued to exalt the "provisional"—the idea that all existing reality can be destroyed in one moment.[39] Elsewhere that reality was "eternal," and activism was directed into destroying the existing order so that the eternal verity of Volk or nation could triumph, and with it the restoration of traditional morality.

The traditionalism of the fascist movement coincided with existing society's most basic moral values. This was to be a respectable revolution. When Hans Naumann spoke at the Nazi book-burning in 1933, he exalted activism; the more books burned the better. But he ended his speech by stressing the traditional bonds of family and Volk. Giuseppe Bottai, too, had called for a "spiritual renewal," and, in Belgium, the leading Rexist Jean Denis held that without a moral revolution there could be no revolution at all.[40] Some fascisms defined the moral revolution within the context of a traditional Christianity: this is true of the Belgian Rexist movement, for example, as well as of the Romanian Iron Guard. The Nazis substituted racism for religion, but once more, the morality was that shared with the rest of respectable society.

Almost all analyses of fascism have been preoccupied with the crucial support it received from the bourgeoisie. However, the Marxist model, based upon the function of each class in the process of production, is much too narrow to account for the general support of fascism. A common ethos united businessmen, government officials, and the intellectual professions that made up the bourgeoisie.[41] They were concerned about their status, access to education, and opportunity for advancement. At the same time they saw their world as resting upon the pillars of respectability: hard work, self-discipline, and good manners—always exemplified in a stereotyped ideal of male beauty which the Nazis annexed as one of their prime symbols.[42] The so-called middle-class morality, which had come to dominate Europe since the end of the eighteenth century, gave them security in a competitive world. Moreover, toward the end of the nineteenth century, the very structure of this world was challenged through the youthful revolt against accepted manners and morals by some schoolboys, bohemians, radicals, and the cultural avant garde.

Nationalism annexed this world of respectability, as did racism in central and eastern Europe, promising to protect it and to restore its purity against all challengers. This explains the puritanism of National Socialism, its emphasis upon chastity, the family, good manners, and the banishment of women from public life. However, there is no evidence that the workers did not also share such longings: the workers' culture did not oppose the virtues of the bourgeois consensus, it had co-opted the standards of respectability long ago. There was no repeating the brief relaxation of normative manners and morals that occurred in the years following the October Revolution in Russia.

Thomas Childers has supplied much evidence concerning the amorphous nature of the Nazi electorate. The Nazis, in the end, capitalized on the resentment felt by all classes, including the working class.[43] Italian fascism, Renzo De Felice has told us, was in large part an expression of the emerging, mobile, middle classes, the bourgeois who were already an important social force and were now attempting to acquire political power.[44] This is exactly the opposite of the Bonapartist analysis, once so popular among the Left, which adapts to fascism Karl Marx's discussion of the dictatorship of Napoleon III. The middle class gave up political power, so the argument runs, in order to keep their social and economic power.

As a matter of fact, in Italy, and also in other European fascist movements, some important leaders came from the Left: for the most part they were syndicalists inspired by the war and the activism promised by the movement. Jacques Doriot, the only really significant leader of French fascism, traveled from the militant Left to fascism—a road, as Gilbert Allardyce has shown, not so different from that of Mussolini earlier. Doriot wanted a greater dynamic within French communism, and was impatient with party bureaucracy and discipline. As a fascist, he advocated "a revolution in France with French materials."[45] Nationalism became the refuge for such frustrated revolutionaries. National Socialism did not, by and large, attract former leaders of the Left. German Social Democrats and communists were too disciplined to desert so easily; moreover, they formed an almost self-contained subculture, whose comfort was not readily rejected. Revolutionary traditions, lively in Italy and France, easily became fossilized dogma in Germany.

Fascism thus attracted a motley crowd of followers from different backgrounds and of all classes, even though the bourgeoisie provided the backbone of the movement and most of the leaders. Rather than renewed attempts to show that fascism could not attract the working class, at best a partial truth, the very diversity of such support needs analysis. Most large-scale business and industrial enterprise, as we now know, did not support the Nazis before their seizure of power, and indeed looked upon them as potential radicals.[46] The Hitler government of 1933, which they did support, was at first a coalition in which conservatives predominated. When, six months later, the conservatives left the cabinet, industrialists compromised with Hitler, just as the Industrial Alliance in Italy came to support Mussolini. But even so, the primacy of fascist politics over economics remains a fact: the myth pushed economic interests into a subservient position. Until the very end, Adolf Hitler believed that a political confession of faith was the prerequisite for all action. From his experience in the First World War, he drew the lesson that man's world view was primary in determining his fate.[47] It was the fascist myth which had cross-class appeal, and which, together with the very tangible successes of the régimes, made possible the consensus upon which they were at first based.

Fascist movements seems to have been most successful in mobilizing the lower classes in underdeveloped European countries where the middle class was small and isolated. Spain provides one example in the West, and it is true of the Iron Guard as well as of the Hungarian fascist movement in eastern Europe. To be sure, in those countries the bourgeoisie was not as strong as elsewhere; but another factor is of greater importance in explaining the fascist appeal to the laboring and peasant classes. Here, for the first time, was a movement which tried to bring these segments of society into political participation, for in such nations Marxist movements were strictly prohibited. The stress upon an end to alienation, the ideal of the organic community, brought dividends—for the exclusion of workers and peasants from society had been so total that purely economic considerations did not provide the sole or perhaps even the principal reason for joining.

The fascist myth was based upon the national mystique, its own revolutionary and dynamic traditions, which we have discussed, and the continuation of the war experience in peacetime. It also encompassed remnants of previous ideologies and political attitudes, many of them paradoxically hostile to fascist traditions. It was a scavenger which attempted to co-opt all that had appealed to people in the nineteenth- and twentieth-century past: romanticism, liberalism, and socialism, as well as Darwinism and modern technology. Too little attention has been paid to this co-optation; it has been subsumed under the so-called eclecticism of fascism. But in reality all these fragments of the past were integrated into a coherent attitude toward life through the basic fascist nationalist myth.

The romantic tradition infused the national mystique, but it was also present in the literature and art supported by the fascists, especially by the Nazis. It had supplied the framework for a popular culture that had changed little during the preceding century. Adventure, danger, and romantic love were the constant themes, but always combined with the virtues we have mentioned: hard work, sexual purity, in short the respectability at the core of normative morality. Here the novels of Karl May in Germany, with a circulation of half a million by 1913 and 18 million by 1938, are typical. They were set in faraway places—the American plains or the Orient—and combined a romantic setting with the defense of good against evil, bodily purity, law and order, against those who would destroy them. Interestingly enough, many Nazis wanted to ban May's stories because he exalted the American Indian race and pleaded for tolerance and understanding between peoples. Hitler, however, had his novels distributed to the armed forces during the Second World War. He once said that

Karl May had opened his eyes to the world, and this was true of many millions of German youth. The virtues which American Indian heroes defended against evil European trappers were precisely those the Nazis also promised to defend. They called themselves tolerant—but the tolerance and compassion that fill May's novels would come about only after Hitler had won his battles, and eliminated the "intolerant" Jewish world conspiracy.[48]

Unfortunately, we have seen no detailed analysis of similar novels popular in the Italy of the 1920s and 1930s.[49] But both National Socialism and Italian fascism used the phrase "romantic realism" to describe realistic character portrayal within a romantic setting.[50] In Italy, such realism was expressed through the strictness of classical form. Thus Francesco Sapori could summarize these aspirations: "Live romantically, as well as according to the classical idea. Long live Italy!"[51] Sapori was a member of the "Novocento" (Twentieth Century) group of writers and artists who wanted to create a native Italian style that was both natural and neo-classical. Though inspired by Mussolini's friend (and mistress) Margherita Sarfatti, it was but one of several competing cultural groups in fascist Italy. "Magic realism" was their formula, created by the writer Massimo Bontempelli. Such romantic realism had already informed popular literature in the past, and provided a mystical and sentimental dimension even while proclaiming a clarity of purpose everyone could understand. Painters like Casorati in fascist Italy or Adolf Ziegler in Germany (Hitler's own favorite) provided corresponding examples in the visual arts.

Admittedly, here as elsewhere "magic realism" exemplified only one trend in Italy, while in Germany it was officially approved and furthered. But even in Germany non-approved literature could be obtained, at least until the war broke out. Parallels can also be drawn between Italian and German architecture under fascism, though in Italy even a party building could still reflect avant-garde style. (In Germany, among non-representational buildings and even in military barracks, the otherwise condemned Bauhaus style often surfaced.) The athletic stadium, "Forum Mussolini," was praised for the same "simplicity of style," the hard lines, displayed by the Nazi Nuremberg Stadium. The plea that architectural material must be genuine and subordinated to that "divine harmony" which reflected the Italian spirit was duplicated in Germany.[52]

Romanticism was integrated into fascism all the more easily because it had always provided the major inspiration for nationalist thought. "Magic realism" stood side by side with the romanticized view of the past: whether it was the ancient Germans who had defeated the Roman Legions, or those Roman ruins that were now bathed nightly in a romantic light, the kind of illumination so attractive to Italian fascism. Differences between the two political styles existed. The liturgy was not quite as all-embracing in Italy as in Germany; and the regime was less concerned with the total control over culture. There was some truth to the contention that the Italian fascist dictatorship was an innovative force in the arts which could persist into the 1930s,[53] but in Germany no such assertion was ever possible except in the first years of the regime when some leaders like Goebbels patronized the Expressionists until Hitler himself put a stop to it. However, for such nationalist movements, these differences are matters of degree, not absolutes. Some of the differences may relate to the fact that Mussolini was a journalist, never really comfortable with the visual expressions of fascism, while Hitler thought of himself as an architect and was not truly interested in the written word.

Liberal ideas were interwoven with romanticism. Middle-class manners and morals would lead to success (the Cinderellas of popular literature were models of respectability). But as there was no real Horatio Alger tradition in Europe, it was the "pure heart" that counted and made possible Cinderella's progress from kitchen to ballroom. Moreover, fascists everywhere believed in the threat posed by degeneration which the liberal Max Nordau had popularized during the last decade of the nineteenth century.

Nordau saw the moderns in art and literature as literally sick people, maintaining that their lack of clarity, inability to uphold moral standards, and absence of self-discipline all sprang from the degeneration of their physical organism. The Nazis, of course, illustrated their opposition to artistic modernism by the exhibition of "degenerate art," and Hitler and Mussolini prided themselves on the supposed clarity of their rhetoric. Fascism deprived the concept of degeneration of its original foundations: clinical observation linked to a universe ruled by scientific laws. But this was typical of such annexations—the popular and traditional superstructure was absorbed but now set upon racial or nationalist foundation.

The concept of degeneration had provided the foil to the liberal's concept of clarity, decency, and natural laws. Fascism also took over the ideals of tolerance and freedom, changing both to fit its model. Tolerance, as mentioned earlier, was claimed by fascists in antithesis to their supposedly intolerant enemies, while freedom was placed within the community. To be tolerant meant not tolerating those who opposed fascism: individual liberty was possible only within the collectivity. Here once more, concepts that had become part and parcel of established patterns of thought were not rejected (as so many historians have claimed) but instead co-opted—fascism would bring about ideals with which people were comfortable, but only on its own terms.

Socialism was also emasculated. The hatred of capitalism was directed against finance capitalism only. At first glance, the opposition to the bourgeoisie seemed shared equally between Nazis and socialists, as both thundered against the moribund bourgeois era. However, fascism cut away the class basis of socialist opposition to the bourgeoisie and substituted the war between generations. "Bourgeois" no longer meant a class of exploiters, but the old and worn out, those who lacked a vibrant dynamic. The setting of the young against the old was a theme which, as we saw earlier, fascism co-opted from the *fin de siècle* and then transferred from people to nations. Thus young nations with their dynamic fascist youth confronted the old nations with their ancient pot-bellied parliamentarians. This was the fascist "class struggle," and here the socialist vocabulary was employed. In this, the Italian fascists went beyond the National

Socialists. Fascist students exalted the Latin, Roman, fascist revolution at the expense of the fat and pacifist bourgeois. Indeed, in Italy the lower middle class (never clearly defined) was constantly berated as being incapable of grasping the myths of nationalism and war, and as lacking any power of social interaction. It is perhaps ironic that certain Italian fascists saw their adversary as precisely that lower middle class which, according to some modern historians, constituted the most important social basis of fascism. This anti-bourgeois rhetoric was undoubtedly also part of the resentment that fascist leaders, usually from modest backgrounds, felt against so-called established society.

Fascists not only borrowed socialist rhetoric, they also made use of some rituals provided by working-class meetings: the massed flags, and the color red, for example. Moreover, some of the socialist workers' cultural and sports organizations were adapted to fascist ends. The liturgy was for the most part based on nationalist precedent from the previous century, but, with typical eclecticism, useful socialist examples were also appropriated.[54]

Fascism absorbed important parts of well-established ideologies like romanticism, liberalism, or socialism; but it was also not afraid to annex modern technology if this could be embedded within fascist myths. Indeed, the dictators were singularly perceptive in their appreciation of technological advance.

Both Hitler and Mussolini had a passion for speed—aircraft and powerful cars provided one outlet for their activism. Hitler was the first German politician to use an airplane in order to make campaign appearances throughout Germany on the same day. Use of the latest technology was immediately linked to Nazi ideology: Hitler literally dropping from the sky, Hitler by his personal courage helping to pilot his plane throughout an awesome storm (this story with its obvious biblical analogy was required reading in Third Reich schools). But Mussolini shared this passion, and in both régimes air aces like Hermann Goering or Italo Balbo had a special status and were surrounded by an aura of adventure and daring.

Anson Rabinbach has shown how technology was used to improve modes of production in Germany, how the program known as the "Beauty of Labor" turned fear of the machine into a glorification of technology through emphasis on efficiency and volkish aesthetics.[55] The newest technology was annexed to an ideology that looked to the past in order to determine the future.

Little is as yet known of how Italian fascism absorbed and used traditional modes of thought as well as the newest technology. In fact, the Italian Nationalist Association (founded in 1910), which was to be Mussolini's partner in fascist rule, combined emphasis upon industrial growth and modern technology with the nationalist mystique.[56] Nationalism, and even volkish thought, were not necessarily opposed to modernization, provided it was made to serve the ideology of the régime, which in turn justified it. That is why, for example, the Nazis supported modern technology and industrial planning, but opposed modern physics as a "Jewish science"—pragmatism was accepted, but any science resting on an abstract theoretical base had to be examined for racial purity.

Italian fascism had no such anti-scientific bias. There, for example, the physicist and Nobel Laureate Enrico Fermi flourished during the 1930s until the proclamation of the racial laws. In Germany, Volkish thought transformed the scientist into a provincial. Films in the Third Reich, for example, praised the faithful family physician, and favorably contrasted this avuncular type to a many-sided scientist like Rudolf Virchow. For all that, Germany as well as Italy integrated technology into fascism, using it to praise and further modernization as well as to enhance the political liturgy (as in Albert Speer's dome of light in mass festivals, borrowed from the anti-aircraft batteries of the defense establishment).[57]

Within its basic presuppositions of revolution, nationalism, and the war experience, fascism contained two rhythms: the amoeba-like absorption of ideas from the mainstream of popular thought and culture, countered by the urge toward activism and its taming. Both were set within the nationalist myth, and all together provided the proper attitude toward life. Fascism attempted to cater to everything people held dear, to give new meaning to daily routine and to offer salvation without risk. The fact that Adolf Hitler shared in popular tastes and longings, that in this sense he was a man of the people, was one vital ingredient of his success. Mussolini entertained intellectual pretensions that Hitler never claimed, nor did he share the tastes of the people, perhaps because in Italy popular culture was diversified in a nation with stronger regional traditions and ties than Germany.

The frequent contention that fascist culture diverged from the mainstream of European culture cannot be upheld; on the contrary, it absorbed most of what had the greatest mass appeal in the past. In fact, it positioned itself much more in this mainstream than socialism, which tried to educate and elevate the tastes of the worker. Fascism made no such attempt: it accepted the common man's preferences and went on to direct them to its own ends. Moreover, the lack of original ideas was not a disadvantage, as many historians have implied, for originality does not necessarily lead to success in an age of democratic mass politics. The synthesis which fascism attempted between activism and order, revolution and the absorption of past traditions, proved singularly successful. To be sure, Marxism, conservatism, and liberalism made original contributions to European thought, but they underwent a long period of gestation, and by the time they became politically important movements, they had founded their own traditions. Fascism, appearing as a political force only after the First World War, had no time to create a tradition for itself: like Hitler, it was in a hurry, confronted with an old order that seemed about to fall. Those who did not strike at once were sure to be overtaken by other radicals of the Left or Right.

Yet fascism would never have worked without the tangible successes achieved by fascist régimes; social and economic factors are not to be ignored and we shall return to them later. But the preeminence of the cultural factors already discussed is certainly the other half of the dialectic. Without them, the ways in which the men and women of those times were motivated cannot be properly understood.

What, then, of the fascist utopia? It was certainly a part of the fascist myth. The fairy tale would come true once the enemies had been defeated. The happy ending was assured. But first men must "overcome"—the mystical ingredient of National Socialism was strong here; and in Italy, the ideal of continuing the wartime sacrifice was stressed. The happy end would bring about the "new Rome" or the Third German Empire, infused with middle-class virtues, a combination of the ancient past and the nineteenth-century bourgeois ideal. The new fascist man would usher in this utopia—and he already existed, exemplified by the Führer and the Duce. Eventually, it was implied, all Germans or Italians would approach their example.

The new fascist man provided the ideal stereotype for all fascist movements. He was, naturally, masculine: fascism represented itself as a society of males, re-enforced by the struggle for national unity that had created fellowships such as "Young Italy," or the German fraternities and gymnastic societies. Moreover, the cult of masculinity of the *fin de siècle*, which Nietzsche himself so well exemplified, contributed its influence. More immediately, a male society continued into the peace the wartime camaraderie of the trenches, that myth of the war experience so important in all of fascism. The masculine ideal did not remain abstract, but was personified in ideals of male strength and beauty.

Such an ideal may be vague, as in a children's book where the Duce is described as being as beautiful as the sun, as good as the light, and as strong as the hurricane.[58] It is less vague in sculptures of the Duce as a Renaissance prince or, more often, as the emperor Augustus. In addition, the innumerable pictures of the Duce harvesting, running, boxing—often bare-chested—projected a strong and invulnerable masculinity. Yet such stereotypes were not all-pervasive in Italy; they were all but absent even at such events as the exhibition honoring the tenth anniversary of the March on Rome (1933).[59] The inner characteristics of this new man were expressed through the strength and harmony of his body: athletic, persevering, in control of his passions, filled with self-denial and the spirit of sacrifice. At the same time, the new fascist man must be energetic, courageous, and spartan.[60] The ideal fascist was the very opposite of muddleheaded, talkative, intellectualizing liberals and socialists—the exhausted, tired old men of the old order. Indeed, Italian fascism's dream of an age-old masculine ideal has not vanished from our own time.

Germany shared such ideals of the male society and the new fascist man, but much more consistently. This gave the Nazi utopia quite a different direction from that of Italy. Volkish thought had always advocated the ideal of the "Bund" of males; the German Youth Movement reinforced the link between the fellowship of men and the national mystique, while the war completed the task. Mussolini might talk about the war and the continuing struggle, but right-wing Germans believed that a new race of men had already emerged from the war—energy come alive, as Ernst Jünger put it; lithe, muscular bodies, angular faces, and eyes hardened by the horrors they had seen.[61] Here the inner nature of the new race was immediately connected with its outward features. Whenever Adolf Hitler talked about the "new German," he wasted little time on the inner self of the Aryan but instead defined him immediately through an ideal of beauty—"*Rank und Schlank*" (slim and tall) was his phrase.[62] There was never any doubt about how the ideal German looked, and it is impossible to imagine a Nazi exposition without the presence of this stereotype.

Racism made the difference. It gave to volkish thought a dimension which Italian fascism lacked. To be sure, as we shall see later, an effort was made to introduce this dimension into Italy with the Racial Laws of 1938, but these were by and large less successful as far as the stereotype was concerned. The Aryan myth had from its beginning in the eighteenth century linked the inward to the outward man, and combined scientific pretensions with an aesthetic theory that saw in Greek sculpture the ideal of male beauty.[63] Indeed, while the nude male was commonplace in German volkish art (see Chapter Ten), the female was usually veiled: the modest and chaste bearer of the children of the race had to be hidden from public view.

Was the fascist man then tied to the past or was he the creator of new values? Renzo De Felice has seen here one of the chief differences between Italian fascism and German National Socialism. For the Germans, the man of the future had always existed, even in the past, for the race was eternal, like the trunk of a tree, while the ideal man of Italian fascism created new values.[64] If we look at the famous definition of fascism given by Mussolini and Giovanni Gentile in the *Encyclopedia Italiana* (1932), the new "fascist man" is, on the one hand, set within the Italian patriotic tradition, and, on the other, supposed to live a superior life unconstrained by space and time. He must sacrifice his personal interests and realize that it is his spirituality which gives him human values. But his spirituality must be informed by history, meaning Italian traditions and national memories. Such an apparent paradox of standing within and yet soaring above tradition accompanied most discussions of the new fascist man in Italy. Man must proceed to ever higher forms of consciousness, culture must not crystallize, and yet the great Italian authors of the past must be studied ("These are germs which can fructify our spirit and give us spontaneity").[65] The Universal Roman Exhibition of 1942 illustrated such principles concretely. Indeed, the new Rome built for this exhibition (*Rome Eure*) was supposed to transmit its heritage to its own day, as shown by the effort to imitate all the Italian architectural styles of the past: Roman, Renaissance, and Baroque. But the exhibition was also supposed to be a signpost for the future. These diverse intentions were symbolized by the completion of the archaeological excavations of Ostia Antiqua (Roman Ostia), creating access to it by means of an Autostrada, and as the catalogue tells us, thus making the new Rome encompass the old,[66] except that by 1942 what was supposed to be unique had been tamed into an historical eclecticism.

In fact, the new fascist man in Italy ignored history no more than his Nazi counterpart.[67] The cult of the Roman past was pervasive; it determined the fascist stereotype wherever we do find it. But this past remained, at least until the final years of the régime, a jumping-off point for the ideal fascist man of the future. Tradition informed his consciousness, but he himself had to rise beyond it without losing sight of his starting point. Such a flexible attitude toward the ideal reflected the greater openness of Italian fascism to the new in both art and literature. This utopia was willing to leave the door to the future halfway open, while in Germany it was shut tight. The difference reflects the groping of Italian fascism for an ideology, its greater emphasis upon struggle and energy, its syndicalist and Futurist elements.

The new German incorporated the eternal values of the race, summarized in a frequently used admonition: "You yourself represent a thousand years of the future and a thousand years of the past."[68] The SS, the most dynamic of all party organizations, fits into this picture. True, an official SS publication tells us that the SS man should never be a conformist, and every SS generation should improve upon its predecessors. Yet the maxim that "history is human fate" meant emphasis upon racial ancestry, that the accomplishments of the past dominated the present and determined the future.[69]

Was this ideal man then to be stripped of his individuality? Was individuality not a part of the fascist utopia? For liberal democracy and for social democracy, the final goal of all social organization was the good of the individual. Did fascism really change this goal? To do so, it would have to eradicate one of the deepest utopian traditions. But it was the pattern of fascism to annex and bend to its purpose, rather than change concepts deeply rooted in the national consciousness, and individualism was not exempted from this pattern, being at the same time retained and redefined. In contrast to unlimited economic and social competition, setting man against man, the ideal of an organic community had taken root in the previous century. The German Youth Movement had thought of itself as such a community, voluntarily joined but based upon shared origins. The ideal of the *"équipe"* played a similar role among French fascist intellectuals, a team spirit grounded in a common world view, exalted by the young male writers grouped around the fascist newspaper *Je Suis Partout* (see Chapter Nine). It was the camaraderie of trench life, which, as we have mentioned repeatedly, many men had actually experienced, and which for others had become a myth that seemed to provide the model for the ideal society. To be sure, they had been conscripted, but this awkward fact was ignored as veterans thought back to comradeship under fire, when each man had had to subjugate his will to that of the others in his unit in order to survive.

Fascism could all the more easily co-opt this idea of community since nationalism had always advocated it: individualism is only possible when men voluntarily join together on the basis of a common origin, attitude, and purpose. Fascism dropped the voluntary aspect, of course, but only as a temporary measure. Education was directed to help the young understand that "*Credere, Obedire e Combattere*" on behalf of the national community was the true fulfillment of individualism.[70] The prospectus of the élite Nazi school at Feldafing sums up this redefinition of individualism: "He who can do what he wants is not free, but he is free who does what he should. He who feels himself without chains is not free, but enslaved to his passions."[71]

Individualism under fascism then meant self-fulfillment while sheltering within the collectivity, having the best of both worlds. It is therefore mistaken to characterize fascism simply as anti-individualist, for this ignores the longing for a true community in which the like-minded joined together, each through his own power of will. The French fascist intellectuals, merely a coterie out of power, could as we have seen praise the provisional, yet for all this Nietzschean exaltation, one of their number, Robert Brasillach, not only found refuge in an "inner fatherland" but also saw in his beloved Paris a collection of small villages in which he could be at home.[72] Between the wars the young men in the Latin Quarter wanted to be original and spontaneous, while longing for an end to intellectual anarchy.[73] Fascism gave them the means to do all that and still remain sheltered by the national community.

These French fascists expressed an *élan* typical of fascism as a movement out of power, though even here the dynamic had to be tamed. Fascism in power, as we saw earlier, was often a disappointment to the young fascist activists. Although it kept much of the earlier rhetoric, once in power it inevitably became the Establishment. Indeed, Stanley Payne's suggestion that at that point the differences between fascism and the reaction become less marked seems close to the facts, if not to the professed ideology.[74] The reactionaries, men like Francisco Franco, based themselves on the traditional hierarchies, on the status quo and, as often as not, took as their ideology the Christianity of the Catholic Church. The fascist revolutionary base, the dynamic nationalist attitudes, and the prominent rhythms were lacking. However, before the relationship between fascism and the reaction can be redefined, more detailed comparison is needed between, for example, the various stages of Mussolini's government and the evolution of Franco's rule in Spain. Here, once again, the particular national histories of those countries are of great importance.

Although national differences culminated in the distinctions between the "new fascist man" of Italy and of Germany, all fascism essentially went back to the anti-parliamentary tradition of the nineteenth century in order to redefine popular participation in politics. Both such participation and individual liberty were supposedly part of a collective experience. It must not be forgotten that, in the last resort, all fascisms were nationalisms, sharing the cult of national symbols and myths as well as the preoccupation with mythical national origins. Himmler sent an expedition to Tibet in order to discover Aryan origins, while other young Germans searched for the original Aryans in Scandinavia, closer to home. The Italian fascist Foreign Ministry sponsored archaeological expeditions to revive the idea of the Roman Empire,[75] while Mussolini restored Rome's ancient ruins, saying that the city was Italian fascism's eternal symbol. The Museum of Classical Antiquity, named after the Duce, was situated in the Campodoglio, in the heart of ancient Rome. Nationalism meant emphasis upon origins and continuity, however much the Italian fascist man was supposed to be a man of the future.

Racism and anti-Semitism were not a necessary component of fascism, and certainly not of those parts of the movement that looked

for their model to Italy, where until 1936, racism was not part of official doctrine. Léon Degrelle, the leader of the Belgian Rexists, at one
time explicitly repudiated that racism which he was later to embrace
wholeheartedly (to become Hitler's favorite foreign National Socialist). What, he asked, is the "true race"—the Belgian, the Flemand, or
the Walloon? From the Flemish side, the fascist newspaper *De Daad*
inveighed against race hatred and called upon "upright Jews" to repu-
diate the Marxists in their midst.[76]

Even Dutch National Socialism under Anton Andriaan Mussert did
not at first appeal to racism and kept silent about the Jews, an attitude
the German Nazis were later to find incomprehensible. The French
fascist group around the newspaper *Je Suis Partout* did go in for anti-
Semitism, but even here the Germans were accused of exaggerating
the racial issue, for good relations were possible with a foreign people
like the Jews.[77] This state of affairs did not last. By 1936 Mussolini
had embraced racism and though, as we mentioned, racism was not
really successful in Italy, Mussolini himself first used it in 1936 against
blacks during the Ethiopian war, and then through the racial laws
of 1938 against the Jews. We shall never know whether Mussolini
himself became a convinced racist, but he did increase the severity in
the draft of the racial laws which had been submitted to him.[78] The
proclamation of these laws was not solely due to German influence,
though much of their content and their method had to be imported
from the north. Rather, Mussolini may have embraced racism out of
opportunism (in the Ethiopian war it lay readily at hand), or to give
fascism a clearly defined enemy like the Jews in order to reinvigorate
his ageing movement, to give a new cause to a young generation
becoming disillusioned with his revolution.

It was only in central and eastern Europe that racism was from the
beginning an integral part of fascist ideology. In eastern Europe, the
masses of Jewry were to be found still living under quasi-ghetto conditions. They were a distinctive part of the population and vulnerable
to attack. Jews prayed differently, dressed differently, and spoke a
different language (Yiddish). Even if some were assimilated, enough

non-assimilated Jews remained to demonstrate the clash of cultures that underlay much of the anti-Semitism in the region. Moreover, in underdeveloped countries like Romania or Hungary the Jews had become *the* middle class, forming a vulnerable entity within the nation as that class which seemed to exploit the rest of the population through its commercial activities. No wonder the Romanian Iron Guard, in appealing to the nationalism of the peasants, became violently anti-Semitic and even racist despite their Christian orientation—for they had begun as the "Legion of the Archangel Michael."

From the 1880s on, a great part of East European Jewry began to emigrate into the neighboring countries, predominantly Germany and Austria. The account in *Mein Kampf* of how sharply Hitler reacted to the sight of such strangers in prewar Vienna may well have been typical. However that may be, the facts of the situation in that part of Europe gave fascism an enemy who could be singled out as symbolizing the forces that must be overcome. Hitler built upon the so-called "Jewish question," and until the late 1930s this led to a further differentiation between National Socialism and western or southern fascism. For Hitler, unlike Mussolini, the enemy was not just a vague liberalism or Marxism; he was physically embodied by the Jews who supposedly had created liberalism and Marxism, and who were the sworn enemies of all nations. Building on the central European tradition of a racist-oriented nationalism, he could give to the enemy of his world view a concrete and human shape.

We have discussed Italian fascism and National Socialism as placing their emphasis upon culture. Both Mussolini and Hitler attempted to epitomize their movements, to provide in their own persons living symbols and an integrative force. Discussing the movements without the leaders is rather like describing the body without the soul. Astute politicians that they were, neither could have succeeded without an instinct for the tastes, wishes, and longings of their people; both ended states of near civil war which they themselves had largely created, managing to provide economic stability and success in foreign policy. Hitler's success was the more spectacular.

Between 1933 and 1936, he led Germany from the depths of a depression to full employment. Rearmament played only a limited role in this economic revival, traditional investments and public works were more important. Hitler was instrumental in the building of a powerful army, and his successes in foreign policy need no further comment. It is true, as Sebastian Haffner wrote in one of the most insightful biographies of Hitler, that by 1938 he had converted even those who had earlier voted against him by the sheer weight of his political and economic success.[79] But here again such consensus, in the last resort, rested upon shared myths and aspirations which, because of this achievement, seemed nearer realization.

Mussolini could at first claim equal success. The population had reason to be satisfied. If in Italy the Duce had not restored work to 6 million unemployed or torn up the Treaty of Versailles, he had brought order and a certain dynamic to a government that had been inert and corrupt. Moreover, Italy avoided most of the European depression. Even conservatives, who did not want a fascist revolution, could be content with the quality of life. However, by 1938, under the pressure of the unpopular German alliance and then an unpopular Ethiopian war, Mussolini maintained a consensus only with difficulty.

Like many other historians, Sebastian Haffner fails to recognize Hitler's success as a politician in the age of the masses using the new style of politics based upon traditional emotions and myths. He therefore easily distinguishes between Hitler and a German people who, in his view, merely responded to the Führer's tangible gains. In fact, to the contrary, just because the desires of the people coincided so largely with those of the régime, the new political style won their acclaim. Gustave Le Bon, in his book *The Crowd* (1895), had stressed that successful leadership must genuinely share the myths of the people—and both Hitler and Mussolini were his disciples.[80]

We know that real wages fell in Germany and that the Italian workers and peasants did not materially benefit from the fascist régime. But it would seem that, to many of them, this mattered less than the gain in status. Those who have tried to prove otherwise apparently believe that material interests alone determine men's actions. Hitler and Mussolini knew that what mattered was how people would perceive their position: myth is always more important as a persuader than the sober analysis of reality.

Moreover, people, and not just material forces, do make history—not just the leader himself but also the likes and dislikes, wishes and, above all, the perceptions of the followers. Whenever he took an action which might upset many Germans, Hitler tried—successfully—to appear to be the pushed rather than the pusher. The staging of the local riots that preceded all new steps in his Jewish policy are a good example. His tactic of making an aggressive move in foreign policy and then proclaiming it as his very last, confused friend and foe alike. Mussolini's policies until the mid-1930s were more modest, but he too combined gestures with patience, moving slowly in order to accomplish his ends. Yet Mussolini came to power much earlier than Hitler, and his achievement, as we have seen, was in minimizing the economic depression Hitler had to overcome. Speaking of the fascist consensus in Italy, Renzo De Felice puts it graphically: "The country was thinking more about the evils that fascism had avoided than whether it brought true benefits."[81] There was a difference between the consensus in Italy and in Germany, even though the two dictators' approaches to politics and their successful emphasis upon the myths that determine human perceptions were similar.

The desired end was different also. Mussolini's long-range objectives were traditional: to create an empire built upon the example of ancient Rome. Hitler's long-range goals of racial domination were not traditional. A wide gulf divided Adolf Hitler, the provincial whose exposure to the far-out racist sects of Vienna provided his intellectual awakening, and Mussolini, who emerged from the conflicts within international socialism. Mussolini confessed himself to be influenced by some of the masters of European thought—such men as Gustave Le Bon, Georges Sorel, William James, and Vilfredo Pareto—while Hitler, also a pupil of Le Bon, was mainly taken with the thoughts of obscure racist sectarians like Lanz von Liebenfels, Alfred Schuler, or

Dietrich Eckart, who but for their disciple's success would have remained deservedly unknown. From one perspective Mussolini may be called a man of the world, and Adolf Hitler a true believer, a member of an obscure racist-theosophical sect. But then this man who believed in secret sciences, Aryan mythologies, and battles between the powers of light and darkness, through his political genius turned such ideas into the policies of a powerful nation. Hitler's goal was both the acquisition of a traditional empire—"*Lebensraum*"—and the enslavement of the Slavs to the superior race as well as the extermination of the mentally and physically handicapped, the gypsies and above all the Jews. His devotion to genocide summarized the difference between Germany where the Volkish tradition of nationalism triumphed, and Italy with its more humanitarian nationalism of the *Risorgimento*.

Because of his ideological commitment, Hitler showed a tenacity that was absent in Mussolini. This is exemplified on one level by comparing Mussolini, the bon vivant and womanizer, with Hitler, the lonely, spartan figure. But on a more important level, it may have meant, as Sebastian Haffner states, that Hitler, knowing the war was lost, would nevertheless continue the conflict so that he could kill as many Jews as possible before the inevitable end. Hundreds of thousands of Germans died so that Hitler could, at the last moment, kill hundreds of thousands of Jews.[82]

Mussolini was cynical about the potentialities of his own people, and even came to despise them toward the end of his rule. But while Hitler felt himself in the end betrayed by the German people, for the most part he thought in apocalyptic terms. Every action had to contribute to a "final end": indeed, Hitler himself believed in finite time—it was during the short span of his own life, he was fond of remarking, that the Aryan must triumph over Jew and find his *Lebensraum*. The German occult tradition asserted itself, as we saw when discussing the "Third Way," not mediated by Jakob Böhme but by an obscure and bizarre racism.[83]

Haffner's speculation as to why Hitler kept on fighting fits better into our picture of the Führer than the usual interpretation (adopted by all other biographers as the sole explanation), that in the end he became a captive of his own myth of invincibility. It is quite possible that Hitler lost contact with reality at some point shortly before the end of the war; however, the Hitler who emerges from Joseph Goebbels' Diaries does not seem to have lost control, though perhaps he realized earlier than anyone else that the war was lost.[84] To be sure, Hitler and Mussolini became isolated during the course of the war, but the consistency of Hitler's whole life makes the tenacity of his end believable as well. Mussolini changed, whereas Hitler from the end of the First World War onward remained locked in his unchanging world view.

Any comparison of Hitler and Mussolini becomes difficult because of the absence of works on Hitler that in historical detail and powerful analysis correspond to Renzo De Felice's monumental biography of Benito Mussolini. Admittedly, Mussolini had no Auschwitz and, unlike Germany, Italy had an important anti-fascist movement. The Duce also showed more human dimensions than the Führer. Yet the materials for a large scale biography of Hitler exist, and are certainly as extensive as the resources that made De Felice's biography possible. But in spite of the availability of such documentation, up to now each recent biography of Hitler has merely added minor facts, without any new interpretations of note. To be sure, psychohistorians have begun to analyze the record of Hitler's life in an attempt to find new insights. Yet it is difficult to accept their contention that his mother's death by cancer determined the structure of his entire life, or that the hallucinations of Hitler, the temporarily blinded soldier, led to his hatred of the Jews. Scholarship has not really advanced much beyond Alan Bullock's pioneering work of 1952 *Hitler, A Study in Tyranny.* German historians, even of the younger generation, have for the most part avoided the figure of the Führer and concentrated instead upon the more impersonal causes of National Socialism. The biographies of Hitler which do exist have for the most part been written by those outside the historical profession. Yet to write about National Socialism while omitting to confront Adolf Hitler, who was at the heart of it, means shirking a true confrontation with the past.

The building blocks for a general theory of fascism now seem to lie before us. Fascism was everywhere an "attitude toward life," based upon a national mystique which might vary from nation to nation. It was also a revolution, attempting to find a "Third Way" between Marxism and capitalism, but still emphasizing ideology over economic change, the "revolution of the spirit" of which Mussolini spoke, or Hitler's "German revolution." However, fascism encouraged activism, the fight against the existing order of things. Both in Germany and Italy, fascism's chance at power came during conditions of near civil war. But this activism had to be tamed, fascism had to become respectable for activism was in conflict with the general desire for law and order, with those middle-class virtues that fascism promised to protect against the dissolving spirit of modernity. Fascism in power was also sometimes constrained by a head of state who continued to represent the old order and who could not be ignored. While Hitler was freed from this constraint by President von Hindenburg's death in 1934, Mussolini always had to report to King Victor Emmanuel. The main dilemma, however, which faced fascism was that activism had to exist side by side with the effort to tame it and to keep it under control. This was one of the chief problems faced by Hitler and Mussolini before their rise to power and in the early years of their rule.

Fascism could create a consensus because it annexed and focused those hopes and longings that informed diverse political and intellectual movements of the previous century. Like a scavenger, fascism scooped up scraps of romanticism, liberalism, the new technology, and even socialism, to say nothing of a wide variety of other movements lingering from the nineteenth into the twentieth century. But it threw over all these the mantle of a community conceived as sharing a national past, present, and future—a community that was not enforced but presumably "natural," or "genuine," with its own organic strength and life, analogous to nature. The tree became the favorite symbol; but the native landscape or the ruins of the past were also singled out as exemplifying on one level the national community, a human collectivity represented by the Fascist Party.

Fascism with its glorification of war and struggle needed enemies and some of these we have mentioned already. Foreign nations considered hostile were not close or tangible enough, thus internal enemies were essential. Racism as we saw focused upon tangible enemies like the Jews or Gypsies, but fascism in general also provided a category of "asocials," men and women who were said to be without any sense of community. The so-called asocials were homeless people like the beggars or vagabonds, the mentally impaired and so-called sexual deviants. They were not usually of an inferior race, but as aryans or good Italians were thought to undermine the nation or race, to lead it into degeneration. These enemies could, at times, be reformed, but in Germany if they resisted they too were doomed. Indeed, German homosexuals, for example, were classified as either merely shamming when they could perhaps be saved, or hereditary and must be exterminated.

These were, of course, precisely those members of the population whom normative society had always deplored and pushed to the margins of existence. Here again fascism trod on familiar ground with, in the case of Germany, one all important difference: in the quest for utopia the asocials were to be killed, exterminated, a procedure which settled, respectable society rejected. Indeed, the Nazis felt that the extermination process had to be kept a dark secret. The belief in racism made the difference here between prison, being an outcast and death. Whether it focused upon its enemies or attempted to inculcate its attitude towards life, basically fascism invented nothing new, but pushed already present hopes, fears and prejudices to their logical conclusions.

Support for fascism was not built merely upon appeal to vested interests. Social and economic factors, to be sure, proved crucial in the collapse after the First World War, and in the Great Depression, while the social and economic successes of fascism gave body to fascist theories. But—and this seems equally crucial—political choices are determined by people's actual perception of their situation, their hopes and longings, the utopia toward which they strive. The fascist "attitude toward life" was suffused by cultural factors through which, as we have attempted to show, the movement presented itself; it was the only mass movement between the wars that could claim to have a largely cross-class following.

In the end, it is not likely that Europe will repeat the fascist or the National Socialist experience. However, the fragments of our Western cultural and ideological past which fascism used for its own purposes still lie ready to be formed into a new synthesis, even if in a different way. Most ominously, nationalism, the basic force that made fascism possible in the first place, not only remains but is growing in strength—still the principal integrative force among peoples and nations. Those ideals of mass politics upon which fascism built its political style are very much alive, for ours is still a visual age to which the "new politics" of fascism were so well attuned. The method used to appeal to the masses (or public opinion as it is called today), if not the form or content, is in our time, for example, reflected in the public relations industry[85] and refined through the use of television as an instrument of politics. Symbols and myth are still used today though no longer in order to project a single and official attitude, but instead a wide variety of attitudes towards life. The danger of successful appeals to authoritarianism is always present, however changed from earlier forms or from its present worldwide manifestations.

Speculations about the future depend upon an accurate analysis of the past. This chapter is meant to provide a general framework for a discussion of fascism, in the hope of leading us closer to that historical reality without which we cannot understand the past or the present.

TWO

Fascist Aesthetics and Society:
Some Considerations

ASCIST SCHOLARSHIP has become increasingly aware of the role which aesthetics played in the movement's appeal and that exploring the link between aesthetics, politics and society could open up new dimensions in our understanding of fascism. This aspect of the fascist movement is no longer brushed aside as mere propaganda, an attempt to manipulate the people against their will. Instead of emphasizing propaganda and terror, fascist scholarship has been increasingly concerned with aesthetics, and the building of a temporary consensus.

The study of Italian fascism has been neglected outside Italy and perhaps England, and while Nazi aesthetics have quite often received attention, it was Italy which successfully pioneered the use of aesthetic sensibilities for political purposes. All of fascism shared an aesthetic, but knowing more about the Italian case will enable us better to judge the similarities and possible differences which existed within a common fascist aesthetic between nations like Italy and Germany.

The aesthetic of fascism should be put into the framework of fascism seen as a civic religion, a non-traditional faith which used liturgy and symbols to make its belief come alive. Civic religion is distinguished from traditional religion by its primary concern with life on earth and the nature of the state and nation, making use of the "beauty of holiness" for the purposes of a revolution in government. Fascists were urged to immerse themselves in symbols, a Baroque world, while consecrated rooms and sacred venues inviting pious contemplation were sometimes part of factories, official exhibitions and museums. The new Italy represented itself through public buildings and city planning as well as through practical accomplishments such as the draining of the southern marshes. Fascism, it should be unnecessary to add, was no ideology in the traditional meaning of that term, but a faith which could not be explained in rational terms.

Without a broader framework, fascism is relatively easy to trivialize, especially for those who have never been attracted by any religion. I myself remember how, in the 1930s, even in the midst of our anti-fascist engagement, we could only laugh at Mussolini's posturing, and his gestures—the rigmarole of fascist ritual—without attempting to understand its true import or considering whether a fascist aesthetic could have played a crucial role in its appeal. As historians we were not accustomed to give aesthetics much weight as over against economic or social forces. We failed to see that the fascist aesthetic itself reflected the needs and hopes of contemporary society, that what we brushed aside as the so-called superstructure was in reality the means through which most people grasped the fascist message, transforming politics into a civic religion.

The aesthetic which stood at the center of this civic religion was the climax of a long development. The ideal of beauty was central to this aesthetic, whether that of the human body or of the political liturgy. The longing for a set standard of beauty was deeply ingrained in the European middle classes, and the definition of beauty as the "good, the true, and the holy" was an important background to the fascist cult. Appreciation of the arts played an central role in the self-definition of the middle classes and anyone who wanted to be a respected member of society had to value them properly. The most unmusical person, for example, had to profess his love of music; and how many young boys and girls had to undergo the torture of learning to play the piano? This was no mere German cultural phenomenon, but held true for Europe in general—and what seemed at first glance to have no possible connection to politics became politically charged through the connection between art, beauty and truth which lay readily at hand to be used by modern political movements. Gabriele D'Annunzio, the poet, was, so it seems, the first to practice such a "politics of beauty" which was then taken up by fascism itself. Politics must not be defined in too limited a fashion, what was important in daily life like the cult of beauty was bound sooner or later to have its political consequences. The aesthetics of fascism with some of its most important roots not only in traditional religion but also in middle-class culture can remind us of that.

Here a certain public standard of beauty reigned all over Europe, one which fascism was to annex as its own. The rediscovery of classical antiquity in the eighteenth century set a standard of beauty which never lost its attraction for the educated, who in Germany and Italy—but elsewhere as well—saw it as their own particular heritage. They valued classical beauty of form whether of the human body or, to a lesser extent, of official architecture, as close to the sublime. Many examples which document this standard could be given, whether through a comparison of the pseudo-classical sculptures of Arno Breker in Nazi Germany with those surrounding the Forum Mussolini in Rome, or through a comparison of official German and many Italian fascist architectural styles—and this in spite of the fact that Italian fascism had no officially approved artistic style, and even annexed modernist architecture, while National Socialism enforced a rigid artistic standard. However great or small the variations in the fascist artistic style, when it came to the fascist liturgy itself they were minor.

Indeed, it was the strength of fascism in general that it realized, as other political movements and parties did not, that with the nineteenth century Europe had entered a visual age, the age of political symbols, such as the national flag or the national anthem—which, as instruments of mass politics in the end proved more effective than any didactic speeches. Under fascism, for example, the speech of the leader itself took the form of symbolic action. The populism of fascism helped the movement to arrive at this insight; the need of integrating the masses into a so-called spiritual revolution which represented itself through a largely traditional aesthetic.

Fascist aesthetics was not confined to the public sphere. Just as it took up a concept of beauty which informed middle-class tastes long before the movement itself came into being, so this aesthetic formed a bridge between the public and the private sphere. Here the role which stereotypes played in all of fascism is of prime importance, it informed fascism's view of the ideal type, of the "new fascist man" or the German Aryan. The creation of modern stereotypes as standard-ized mental pictures which encompassed the whole human character, body and soul, was something new at the beginning of the nineteenth century. The idea that the structure of the human body indicates the structure of the mind was to become commonplace. Aesthetics played a determining role in stereotyping: every man must aspire to a classi-cal standard of beauty, and as he builds and sculpts his body (and we must remember the part played by physical exercise in the aesthetics of fascism), his mind will come to encompass all the manly virtues which the fascists prized so highly.

The beautiful male body was an important symbol in all European fascist movements. However, significantly, such a body was not merely a fascist symbol, but one which had already been adopted by society at large. Here we are at the intersection between traditional, normative, society, and fascist aesthetics; here the social and the aesthetic were not strictly separate one from another. The beautiful male body as the eighteenth-century Greek paradigm had it, projects both self-control in its posture and virility in the play of its muscles; it symbolized both the dynamic and the discipline which society wanted and needed. Here order and progress, often in conflict, were reconciled through the symbolism of the male body modelled on the harmonious form of Greek sculpture. This reconciliation was also symbolized by the aesthetic of fascist and Nazi mass meetings: the disciplined marches, the (often violent) appeal to action, the dialogue between leaders and followers.

Through stereotypes fascism worked not only with abstract symbols but with living human symbols as well. The true fascist man must through his looks, body, and comportment, project the ideal of male beauty. Men of flesh and blood were given a symbolic dimension, a fact which added to the fascist appeal. Here was an aesthetic which was not confined to the public realm, but one which penetrated daily life. Perhaps the strength of this particular symbol, and the deep need it fulfilled, can be seen through the fact that while most of the symbols and rituals of the civic religion of fascism have vanished after the Second World War, its stereotypes are still with us. Here fascism had simply co-opted ideal types which had existed ever since modern stereotypes were created, and there is little difference in looks, manly behavior and posture, between Mussolini's new man, the German Aryan, the clean-cut Englishman, or the all-American boy. Fascism and National Socialism built upon a tradition of human beauty and ugliness which like fascist aesthetics in general drew its strength from an already present consensus. Fascist aesthetic invented nothing new or even experimental, and that was its great strength, while fascist politics in contrast did present something new, a so-called political party based upon a civic religion which encompassed all aspects of life.

However, one aspect of the aesthetics of fascism needs additional emphasis. Fascist aesthetic depended upon clear and unambiguous statements. This meant that the ideal human type must be clearly distinguished and set off against what the Nazis called the "counter-type," the exact opposite of the normative ideal. A Nazi book actually called *The Counter-Type* (*Der Gegentyp*, 1938) stated clearly what was involved in the sharp distinction between the ideal and its foil: "through the counter-image we obtain the greatest clarity of what our own ideals should be." This statement, for example, explains the way Jews were pictured in the Nazi press, or blacks before and after the Abyssinian War, in the Italian papers. Only now are scholars paying some attention to the actual construction of stereotypes and their counter-types, though in every case the so-called beautiful or the supposedly deformed body set the standard for judging a person's character and mind. The clear distinction between friend and foe was an integral part of the fascist aesthetic and an important part of its appeal as well.

Here, once more, fascist aesthetic reflected a social reality, just as it symbolized modern society's need for both movement and order. Modern society itself needed and apparently still needs an enemy against which it could define itself; the "outsiders," designated as such, often denigrated and vilified—those who did not seem to fit the established norm—accompanied our society throughout the last two centuries. Fascist aesthetic sharpened and refined the image of the "outsider," while continuing to give him the traditional bodily features—for example, the Jew's nose or his pathological gait—which had marked him for life for at least a century and a half. Settled and respectable society was not adverse to bolstering its self-worth and feeling of superiority in this manner.

Fascist aesthetic supported existing society in another way as well, which has often been addressed, though not always in this context. The sexual division of labor was perceived as important as the economic division of labor for the smooth functioning of society. The ideal which fascism projected so strongly and which symbolized progress and order (or as fascists put it, virility and discipline), was an aggressive masculinity. Indeed, Mussolini pinned his hopes for the future on the new, disciplined and beautiful man which fascism would create. The body beautiful would symbolize a disciplined and committed mind. However, in reality this new fascist man was merely the normative type writ large. The tension between this ideal of manliness and family life was common to all of fascism: the bonding of males which was said to determine the fate of the state, and the virtues of a bourgeois family life which fascism was sworn to uphold. But these were bound to come into conflict when the demands of male camaraderie clashed with the duties of family life.

Enough has been written lately about the place of women in fascism as part of the sexual division of labor, and the only point to be made here is that women's athletics were encouraged (as by the female statues of athletes on the Forum Mussolini), and that the body beautiful played its role in this context as well—not, of course, as enhancing discipline and virility, but in order to highlight its graceful movements. Women's aesthetic differed from that of men. Women in Germany, for example, were usually shown as exercising in the midst of nature, emphasizing an analogy with natural beauty and innocence. Yet in Italy Mussolini did not hinder his oldest daughter, Edda, when she became one of the first Italian women to drive a car, to bicycle in public or even to wear trousers, while in 1944, the Fascist Social Republic even created a woman's auxiliary to the armed forces. Yet in spite of these departures from accepted norms there was no attempt to re-invent woman or to create a new woman in concert with the new fascist man. Here the familiar conventions remained intact.

The interaction between fascist aesthetics and traditional society we have mentioned does throw some light upon the much discussed problem whether or not a fascist revolution took place. Perhaps it would be best to speak about a fascist dynamic, a certain open-endedness, at least in Italy, which exchanged elites but co-opted a traditional social reality. It was surely one of the main attractions of fascism that it promised on the one hand a change of attitudes, a spiritual revolution, a new élan, and on the other addressed those needs which seemed essential to the preservation of established modern society.

While fascism itself worked for the most part with an already existing aesthetic, it did strike out in new directions through the manner in which it presented itself. Fascist liturgy institutionalized the close link between aesthetics and politics which had existed earlier only in isolated examples such as D'Annunzio's regime in the city of Fiume (1919–1921). Now the aesthetics of the human body and of color and form were used in order to nationalize the masses, to shape and control the mass meetings which were an essential part of fascist politics. The aesthetic of the human body has already been mentioned, and the youth who marched and saluted were supposed to be ideal types who represented the movement and the nation. The *mis-en-scène* of these meetings, the setting constructed or chosen for their venue, represented a spectacle suffused with grandeur and beauty, and through their dynamic and virile movements the assembled and disciplined masses once more symbolized both order and progress and served to reconcile both.

Aesthetics shaped the fascist view of man, of his surroundings and of politics. It was a cement which held fascism together. As it was both traditional in its forms and dynamic in its movement, fascist aesthetic reflected fascism itself which, as we have mentioned, meant, at one and the same time, to uphold tradition and symbolize a revolutionary dynamic which was supposed to lead to a better future.

The importance we have given to fascist aesthetic is not supposed to diminish the significance of the social and economic aspects of fascism, but rather this aesthetic must find its important place within the totality of the movement. That the aesthetic and the social cannot easily be separated has been demonstrated in this essay, however briefly. Fascism, in the last resort, was based upon nationalism as a civic religion, and its aesthetic articulated this faith just as it did for the older established religions. The almost complete dominance of social history over recent American, German and French historiography as the single explanatory tool of modern politics and society has tended to ignore nationalism as well as aesthetics. Moreover, the denigration of the leader of the movement in postwar historiography has only recently been rectified—not yet in Germany but in Italy, as was mentioned in the previous chapter. And yet, in the aesthetics of fascism the personal tastes of Hitler and Mussolini did matter, or, rather, the absence of a strong aesthetic taste by Mussolini who was, as we know, eclectic in his own artistic preference, and Hitler's decisive aesthetic judgement. Both, however, influenced the shape of their respective civic religions, and only those who ignore the civic religion of fascism can deny the centrality of the leader to the movement or to the regime.

These remarks have attempted to articulate some important factors which seemed to inform the aesthetics of fascism, and which might be helpful in any consideration of the movement's attraction and of the consensus upon which it was built in the first years of its rule. The aesthetics of fascism used both a pseudo-classical ideal, if not consistently, and the instrumentality of that part of established religion which ever since the Baroque had represented the "beauty of holiness."

THREE

Racism and Nationalism

RACISM AND NATIONALISM seem to belong together. Indeed, by the second half of the nineteenth century racism was nearly identical with right-wing nationalism. Racism gave new dimensions to the idea of rootedness inherent in all of nationalism, while at the same time sharpening the differences between nations, providing clear and unambiguous distinctions between them. Yet, nationalism did not have to be racist, racism was just one among several alternatives from which nationalism could choose. And though, ever since the turn of the century, many nationalism allied themselves with racism, racism as a modern ideology originating in the eighteenth century stood on its own two feet, building upon anthropology, history, and—last but not least—a reawakened aesthetic consciousness. Racism used history, anthropology and aesthetic sensibilities in order to set a standard of human looks, beauty and behavior. Anthropology, history and this new aesthetic consciousness were all concerned with the search for roots; they could fulfill a longing for immutability and certainty in a world of rapid social change, help get one's bearing and to prove one's superiority.[1]

What seemed to propel racism outside a national framework was its general applicability: any national or ethnic group could and did make use of it. That is why it is dangerous and wrong to confine racism to its most obvious recent manifestations in Nazi Germany or apartheid South Africa. A tendency to trivialize racism has been much more common, to make use of the term in contemporary polemics in order to designate all those acts which create or maintain disadvantage. Racism as a political slogan could lead to such absurdities as the United Nations first declaring that Zionism is racism, and then repealing this assertion, as if racism's finality was not one of its chief and most fateful characteristics. Such a conflation of the term in the end hurts the victims of racism, it trivializes an ideology whose historical roots and evolution are not vague but can be chartered with singular precision, and which, as we shall see, obtained its success precisely because it was so sharply focused.

Racism is a totality encompassing the whole human personality, its looks, behavior and intellect—it is a world view as complete as other ideologies which evolved during the nineteenth century, such as socialism or conservatism. Indeed, with its claim to immutability and to a truth which transcends the individual, racism itself, with its own iconography, can be called a civic religion, and like any system of religious belief it created its own world of myth and symbol. The racial myths are familiar enough, they concern the far-away origins, the hardships and triumphs of the race, leading to redemption when the race wars are won. Racism appealed and appeals to the same longing for immutability and redemption which constituted the appeal of traditional religion, and of so many modern ideologies as well.

But racism possesses one great advantage over many other world views: where they tended to leave room for a variety of interpretations, and even projected a certain vagueness which left space for differing interpretations, racism leaves nothing to chance. Racism is always focused—whether it legitimizes itself through science or through pseudo-historical scholarship, it does not tolerate any ambiguities. That the quest for certainty, clarity and decisiveness preoccupied racist regimes in twentieth-century Europe is no coincidence.

Adolf Hitler's constant and unremitting boast that no ambiguities will be tolerated, that there must be certainty in all things, while it hardly described his own rather inefficient government, was fulfilled in the designation and extermination of the supposed racial enemy. The need for a leader and the creation of racial élites gives racism a further and even sharper focus. Hostile commentators between the two world wars emphasized the eclecticism and vagueness of racism, but that is not how it struck many contemporaries who saw in it a discrete and refined system. To be sure, racism is a scavenger ideology in as much as it took bits and pieces from other systems of thought and bent them to its own will: legitimate anthropology, Darwinism, as well as actual history (Hermann the German, after all, was a real historical figure, if different from the myth racists created). Eclectism, however, must not be confused with vagueness.

Racism and nationalism did not join because racism was ill-defined but because an integral or all-inclusive nationalism developed in such a way during the nineteenth century as to meet and to marry this world view. Indeed, without such a marriage European racism would have remained impotent. Through nationalism racism was able to transform theory into practice; it was dependent upon nationalism, while nationalism itself could exist without any necessary reliance on racism.

Here nationalism was by far the more flexible ideology, making alliances with almost every political or social movement, conservative, liberal or socialist. This may account for the fact that some extreme nationalists, even when they embraced racism, could still show ambivalence about its strict application, which held true, for example, for the conservatives in Germany between the two World Wars.[2]

Racism like nationalism had its symbols as part of its iconography, but for the most part these were not abstract—like flags or national anthems—but concrete, centered upon the human form. The human body itself became the predominant racial symbol, and a great deal of racist literature was devoted to an explanation of how one could recognize on sight one's own as over against those of a different race.

Racism centered upon the construction of stereotypes as living and familiar symbols, and that was one of its greatest strengths. Some kind of reality, however tenuous, must inform every symbol, but racism made a conscious effort to link symbol and reality in a straightforward manner. Racism at its origins defined itself against black populations, where the differences from Europeans seemed unambiguous. The very construction and appearance of the human body, its size, shape, muscles and bones, were made to bear witness to the superiority or inferiority of a race and its culture. Body structure expressed racial difference. Once again, racism encompasses a totality, in this case body, soul, and life-style. While the anthropological and biological origins of racism were important—the emphasis upon heredity which one could not escape—aesthetic considerations were equally important in the making of the racist stereotype which must be easily recognizable, familiar, and project an all-inclusive image.

The human body as a racist symbol was dependent upon a certain standard of looks and comportment. Such a stereotype catered to a deep need of modern European society. Both these points need elaboration because they have a direct bearing upon the appeal of racism, and upon its relation to nationalism as well. Anthropology and the many other eighteenth-century sciences concerned with bodily structures, such as Lavater's physiognomy, originated at the same time as a new aesthetic ideal.[3] The rediscovery of Greek sculpture popularized by J. J. Winckelmann in his writing during the last decades of the eighteenth century set the tone, even if it was modified by subsequent taste. Winckelmann's praise for Greek sculpture was eagerly received throughout Europe. Here was a transcendent beauty which, exemplified by the statues of Greek youths, reduced human beauty to a general, easily understood, principle. And this principle, in turn, catered to the deep need of an emerging industrial society for both a dynamic and order, for progress which nonetheless must be kept under control. The aesthetic which racism adopted was centered upon harmony and proportion, as well as upon disciplined and controlled strength, projecting moderation as a cardinal principle of beauty. Moderation, however, was paired with activism, with virility, in the name of progress which modern society wanted and needed. For Winckelmann the muscles which were clearly visible on the bodies of his Greek youths projected energy and virility, while their posture and face radiated composure and self control. He summed up his various descriptions of the harmonious structure and muscular build of such youths by likening them to the quiet surface of an ocean which, nevertheless, throws up waves.[4]

This was a masculine symbol, distinguished from so-called feminine passivity, for the woman with her lush contours was the mother of the race and must seek her fulfillment solely in this role. Women as public symbols were either mothers of the family or mothers of the nation, such as Germania, Brittania or the sedate Marianne after the revolutions of the early nineteenth century.[5] Masculinity symbolized the active life, the hope for the victory of the race over its enemies and the subsequent construction of the ideal racist society. Gender division was basic to racism. Woman was not an inferior race—after all, she performed vital functions for the existence and well-being of the race—she was excluded from public life, but a racial equal. Nevertheless, racism was aggressively masculine and so were most of the symbols through which it represented itself. The far-away past in which the race was rooted—whether through the ancient Germans or in England's case, the ancient Saxons—was patriarchal, and the roots of the race were thought to determine its future as well.

Racism from its origin to modern times adopted a neo-classical male aesthetic, encouraged by anthropologists who liked to contrast natives and Europeans based on their resemblances or differences from the idealized Greeks. Here Peter Camper's table of 1791 showing the progression of skulls and facial expressions from monkey, to black, to average European to the Greek ideal type, provides an outstanding example, and Robert Knox's famous facial angle of 1862 also reflected an ideal of perfection as symbolized by the Greeks.[6] An ideal type was born who was to set an easily recognized standard of looks and bodily structure for the members of the "superior" race.

Though national varieties of this ideal type exist—as, for example, between France, Germany and England—its basic bodily structure remained intact even if the hair and eye color differed. It is only lately that scholars have examined in detail the actual bodily structure of the racial ideal,[7] for this not only reflected a standard of beauty at a time when the cult of beauty became a pseudo-religion for the European middle classes, but in addition catered to a highly visually centered age. It is no coincidence that during the second half of the eighteenth century, once the linkage between body and mind had been firmly established, we witness a stepped-up concern with people's outward appearance, whether it was through the new science of anthropology, the reading of the human skull (phrenology) or the human face (physiognomy); all these new eighteenth-century sciences—compelled not just by science but also by an aesthetic ideal, as we have mentioned—attempted to judge the inward by the outward man. After all, most of our political and national symbols, from the national flag to national monuments and national anthems also originated in the late eighteenth century. To be sure, the drive to domination and the search for roots is basic to racism, but the way it was mediated, how racist ideology chose to present itself, is equally important for an understanding of racism's appeal in the modern age.

Nationalism could annex many of the ideas and the stereotype I have discussed because it too was based upon the principle of separateness—if not necessarily of superiority—from other political, social or cultural groups and upon self-representation through symbols. Modern nationalism, even if it was tolerant and respected the culture of other nations, always contained elements which might lead to a greater exclusiveness. If racism constructed an ideal type, nationalism was sooner or later in search of the proper "national character". At the hand of Madame de Staël or Hegel, at the beginning of the nineteenth century, national character was anchored in a cohesive national culture and was not connected to any one stereotype.[8] But in an age of a general quest for symbols, the nation itself felt the need to take on life, not just through occasional national festivals but through the participation of every one of its members, and it did so partly through the projection of ideal types.

Sharing the general aesthetic I have mentioned, the national stereotype also concentrated upon the male body, sharpening gender divisions. For example, at the end of the eighteenth and the beginning of the nineteenth century, gymnastics came into fashion as a kind of body sculpture meant to create men worthy of their nation. This was the aim of Friedrich Ludwig Jahn's *Deutsche Turnkunst* (*German Gymnastics*, 1816), but even before this, during the French Revolution, gymnastics had been included in a few National Festivals.[9] The basic manuals of gymnastics, like that of Guts Muths (1793), link gymnastics with male beauty, ". . . for who does not value the letter of recommendation which beauty provides?"[10] The national stereotype was similar to that of racism wherever a nation insisted upon its identification.

If nations identified a national character in a consistent manner, then nationalism and racism drew much closer together. This happened mostly in the last decades of the nineteenth century whenever a more integral nationalism tried to dominate. Nations, it is important to note, however, were not dependent upon finding a national character for their self-representation, while such symbolism was central to racist ideology.

The national stereotype, in addition, did not have to be aggressive; it could, for example, be a peasant harvesting, while the racist stereotype always looked out for the enemy. Gymnastics, however, were not advocated solely as body sculpture or in order to symbolize a virile nation, but were regarded as a useful tool for military service as well. Once the search for a national character started, and a national stereotype was proposed (even if this was only the so-called clean-cut Englishman or the all-American boy), an exclusiveness was asserted which had the potential for aggression against those who were different. Here too looks and appearance took in the whole personality.

The difference between racism and nationalism is sometimes difficult to determine, because both work with almost the same ideal type, gender divisions, and separateness. And yet this difference does exist. Nationalism as patriotism can tolerate ethnic difference; it does not have to be self-assertive or preoccupied with looks and appearance. Moreover, throughout its history there have been men and women who while loyal to their nation regarded it as merely a step towards a concern with all of mankind. This was far from racism, and ignoring the reality of such a nationalism can be dangerous. After all, nationalism has proved itself the most powerful ideology of modern times, and condemning it without distinction, or identifying it automatically with racism, deprives us of any chance to humanize an ideology whose time, far from over, seems to have arrived once more. But it would be equally blind to ignore the aggressiveness and ideas of superiority which are latent in any world view which tends to emphasize exclusiveness and totality.

Racist symbols stood for an attitude of mind, a moral universe. The aesthetic of the racial stereotype exemplified the proper moral posture, based upon harmony and self-control, upon moderation in all things, while at the same time projecting a certain dynamic. It represented the race as it wanted to see itself: beautiful, strong and moral. At the end of the nineteenth century as had been the case with Winckelmann's Greek youths so much earlier, the moral posture which the ideal type symbolized continued to correspond to the social and moral standard which normative middle class society advocated. For example, as John Ruskin pointed out in his various writings, wholesomeness was the order of the day. The Greeks, which he saw through Winckelmann's eyes, neither fasted nor over ate, they spent much of their time out-of-doors and therefore they were full of animal spirits and physical power, incapable of every morbid condition or emotion. The integral nationalism of Germany and France towards the end of the nineteenth century increasingly concretized the ideal of a national character in this manner, once more sharing its model with that which racism projected. The English national character was no exception here, it shared many features with the racial stereotype: the construction of the male body, the "quiet strength," and the proper morality. The existence of such a stereotype as a national symbol can demonstrate how closely a more benign nationalism could approach racism, even though the "clean-cut Englishman" was tempered by a commitment to fairness and to parliamentary government—both incompatible with or uncongenial to racism. Here, within the nation itself, national and racist stereotypes could reflect similar social if not political ideals.

Racism depended upon the existence of its enemies; it had always defined itself as at war against hostile and inferior races. Darwinism only added a sharper edge to an already present antagonism. Racism's ideal type needed a counter-type, as we saw in the last chapter, someone whose looks and appearance were made to differ sharply from the accepted norm.[11]

Blacks had been stereotyped from the beginning of racial theory, while Jews were the only sizeable minority living in Europe who, before emancipation—and in eastern Europe until much later—dressed differently, spoke a different language from the rest of the population, and whose religious practices seemed chaotic and mysterious. Blacks were not a visible presence in Europe itself until well after the Second World War, nevertheless early in their regime the Nazis first isolated and then killed the few hundred black youth who did exist. These were the so-called Rhineland bastards, whose mothers were German women but whose fathers were black soldiers who had briefly occupied the Rhineland after the First World War. Once again, for both blacks and Jews, racism worked with a concrete difference which, though it might apply to only a small fragment of the group, could be seen and built upon. The Jews unlike blacks were always present, and the Jewish ghettos in eastern Europe as well as those inside European cities where Jewish immigrants from the east had settled (such as Whitechapel in London), were used by racism as proof that a counter-type existed, and to give credence to their assertion that assimilated Jews were merely the outposts of a conspiracy directed by "true Jews" from inside the ghettos. All Jews shared the same outward appearance exemplifying their soul. Sander Gilman has shown how for blacks and Jews racism constructed an "ugly" bodily structure which symbolized their essentially destructive nature.[12] This meant that they were unable to create or to live in an ordered society, and for that reason alone must be considered sub-human. Jews, in Nazi Germany, for example, were declared *Gemeinschaftsun-fähig* (incapable of creating or sustaining a community), and this like their supposedly misshapen bodies was believed to be inherited.[13]

The counter-type took on a life of its own during the nineteenth century as it became an object of medical study and investigation. The "outsider" was medicalized as he became part of normative society's preoccupation with visible symbols of health and sickness. Physicians projected upon those who did not fit the established social norms characteristics diametrically opposed to those of the healthy male: they were diseased and infectious. For example, the image of Jews and homosexuals ran parallel in much of the medical literature at the *fin de siècle*. There exists a considerable body of writing which holds that both Jews and homosexuals have a tendency to hysteria with the attendant nervous distortions of their bodies. Moreover, both were feminized at times, given characteristics—such as their tone of voice and their body movements—thought more appropriate to women than "real men."[14] Above all, such "outsiders" lacked control over their passions, that moderation which was inherent in the normative stereotype. Here again racism and social prejudice supported each other—the perceived needs of normative society and racism's concentration upon the unambiguous distinction between friend and foe.

Nationalism did not need such a counter-type for its existence; after all, Jews were often welcomed into their respective European nations, and it is open for discussion whether nations which possessed empires looked upon all their subject-peoples as counter-types. But, once again, some nationalisms did make use of the counter-type in order to sharpen their own sense of community. Nationalism imagining itself under siege tended to become racist, projecting a counter-type and, like that of the Jews, locking it into place as the eternal enemy. However, while by no means all nationalisms followed this model, the ideal type as symbolizing the national character, and the counter-type as its foil, were at times present even in those nations which eventually, in the Second World War, were to fight the racist regimes in Europe. It was astonishing to witness how, for example, in the United States, the constant condemnation of Nazi racist policy made no perceivable difference in racist attitudes toward blacks within the nation, or to that anti-Jewish racism which surfaced now and then in Congress, and continued to inform United States immigration policy. Examples of this nature could be gathered from other nations as well, a reminder of the affinity which existed latently, and sometimes even in practice, between some explicitly non-racist regimes and racism.

Here racism may, once more, reflect the texture of modern society. Does modern society need an enemy as a foil who would serve to strengthen its self-image? At the very least such enemies always existed, constructed into counter-types in word and pictures. Foreign enemies were, of course, a tempting target: however because of the fluid relationship between nations it was often impossible to conceptualize them in racist terms; they could, after all, be tomorrow's allies. The supposed internal enemy was better suited as opponent in the race war—a counter-type like the Jew whose conspiratorial activities could beguile foreign powers and turn them into the enemy of the superior race. The Nazis for example, saw the Jew as the driving force behind all of their foreign enemies: England was said to be in the hands of Jewish capitalists, while French and Jewish interests coincide, both out to destroy Germany. As Adolf Hitler wrote in *Mein Kampf*, wherever in the world attacks against Germany take place, the Jews are their author, in fact they are out to destroy all non-Jewish states.[15] Here, principally the Jews, but in addition all those marginalized by or existing at the margins of existing society, provided easily accessible symbols for the war which had to be waged: Jews, homosexuals, gypsies and vagrants, habitual criminals and the insane.

The Nazi regime, as the most successful racial state in history, would seek in the end to exterminate precisely these socially unacceptable "counter-types." Their fate had been predetermined, it was

inherent in racism itself, put into practice by a heightened nationalism, helped along by normative society's apparent need for outsiders
in order to define itself. A heightened nationalism, especially after the
First World War, sometimes added its political enemies to the traditional list of outsiders. The "anti-national" communists or socialists
were pictured as the opposite of the ideal type—once again, dirty,
misshapen and shifty.

When nationalism allies itself with racism discrimination is no
longer the issue, but instead war has to be waged against the "outsider" defined as both the enemy of nation and race. Racism was the
catalyst which pushed German nationalism over the edge, from discrimination to mass extermination. German nationalism like all
nationalism had alternative traditions to that of racism, and however
chauvinistic after the First World War much of German nationalism
turned out to be, mass murder was not usually part of its agenda. Thus
it seems absurd to write about National Socialism and to omit or to
downplay racism, which became the fashion among many social and
so-called Marxist historians after the Second World War.

The association of National Socialism and racism was significant
for another reason as well, for racism by its very nature possessed a
dynamic which was directed against the *ancien régimes*—its emphasis
on virility, on war against an enemy, its projection of a racial utopia
based upon clear and visible distinctions, made it difficult for racism
to support the maintenance of the status quo. The racist movements
in Europe sought to come to power by creating conditions of civil war,
and the accusation that all existing regimes were degenerate was a
staple of their propaganda.

A dynamic political movement was much more attuned to racism
than a conservative political party. Such movements, especially after
the First World War, were directed against the existing political order
and promised radical change. The term "political" is important here,
for as we mentioned, racism supported existing manners and morals,
and sought to eliminate the socially dangerous counter-type. This
distinction added greatly to racism's appeal: the racist revolution

would leave intact and indeed purify normative society and change the political élites which, in any case, were usually blamed for the nation's misfortunes.

The racist utopia was populist, it stood outside the present political system. Modern right-wing nationalism as it developed during the nineteenth century tended to focus upon the people themselves rather than upon political structures. National Socialism, for example, looked beyond the state to the Volk for its legitimization, as did right-wing movements in France like the *Action Francaise*. While modern nationalism usually supported the state, as in Wilhelmian Germany or the Third French Republic, a radical nationalism in alliance with racism fueled a revolution from the Right rather than from the Left, a populist rather than a socialist revolution. National Socialism—indeed all of fascism—belongs to that revolution though, of course, not all fascism was racist. Racism therefore cannot be simply written off as reactionary, just as nationalism was a revolutionary force during much of its early history.

The present-day tendency to trivialize racism disguises its role as the catalyst for action. Wherever there has been a firm alliance between nationalism and racism—whether in the first modern racist government in Algiers in 1897 which lasted only one month, and which intended to water the tree of liberty with Jewish blood,[16] or the Nazis—the story is always the same. Racism has a definite world view and its own specific symbolism, a fact that has often been masked through the alliance it made with nationalism—though nationalism itself, as we saw, does not have to be racist. Racism then is a totality, it cannot be divided up into its parts; it is a civic religion with its own agenda which includes getting the nation battle-ready by destroying the existing political élites and subsequently defeating and eliminating the so-called inferior race. While racism works through stereotypes in order to achieve its ends, such stereotypes are also present both in nationalism and our own society in general. The very existence and success of stereotypes as symbols should and must be an alarm signal which warns us that racism is waiting to strike. Nationalism has made racism a reality, and we must recognize that it is all too easily infected. Coming to understand the relationship between racism and nationalism should lead us to try and humanize national-ism which, as patriotism, has at times managed to resist the racist temptation.

FOUR

Fascism and the
French Revolution

REEXAMINING THE RELATIONSHIP between two cata-
clysmic events of modern history, fascism and the French
Revolution, can throw new light upon the changing concept
of the nation and its political style. The French Revolution as a
historical event did not play a crucial role in fascist thought or imagination. It was not considered as an ancestor which had influenced
the movement, and if fascists thought about the French Revolution
at all, it was for the most part either to oppose it as a symbol of
materialism and liberalism, or to contrast it to their own true revolution. The French fascists, to be sure, had greater difficulty in coming
to terms with a revolution that was part of their own national history
and that had provided France with some of her most important military victories. And yet, for all such denial and ambivalence, the
French Revolution did provide an important background for the
fascist conception of politics. The French Revolution put its stamp
on a novel view of the sacred: it created a full-blown civic religion
that modern nationalism made its own, and fascism, whatever its
variety, was, above all, a nationalist movement. Moreover, some
fascisms, almost in spite of themselves, did show some continuity of
mind with the French Revolution.

At this point in research, it may well be impossible to prove any direct connection between the French Revolution and fascist political practice or ideology. Fascist leaders were conscious of the Revolution and its leadership within a polemical rather than historical context. The relationship between fascism and the Revolution involved a general reorientation of post-revolutionary European politics, rather than specific points of contact—a reorientation adopted at first by modern European nationalism, but subsequently by many other political movements as well. The basis of this reorientation was Rousseau's concept of the general will, that only when men act together as an assembled people can the individual be a citizen.[1] The general will became a secular religion under the Jacobin dictatorship—the people worshiping themselves—while the political leadership sought to guide and formalize this worship. Fascism saw the French Revolution as a whole through the eyes of the Jacobin dictatorship, and it was this aspect of the Revolution that exercised its influence upon it. The parliamentary phase of the French Revolution was nonexistent as far as the fascists were concerned, and it is of interest only for contrast in any comparison between the two movements, providing the opposite pole of the political spectrum. But one would learn little from such a comparison about either fascism or the French Revolution. During the Jacobin dictatorship, the unity of the people was cemented by common citizenship, by the worship of a supreme being, but also through appeals to an awakening national consciousness. The nation was no longer in the custody of a dynasty, but belonged to all of the people. The worship of the people thus became the worship of the nation, and the Jacobins sought to express this unity through the creation of a new political style based upon a civic religion.

This new politics attempted to draw the people into active participation in the new order and to discipline them at the same time through rites and festivals, myths and symbols, that gave concrete expression to the general will. The festivals of the Revolution, which reached their fullest expression under the Jacobins, had their own sacred space, such as the Champs-de-Mars or the Tuileries, and they contained processions, competitions, songs, dances, and speaking choruses. Symbolic gestures were also important, as at times people fell into each other's arms in order to document the overriding theme of revolutionary and national unity. The *mise-en-scène* mattered as well: allegories of fraternity taken from the classics might surround the crowd, as well as temples and pyramids. There was joy in color and form while even nature was far from forgotten; the Revolution endowed the early rays of the sun with symbolic and political meaning.[2] The general will became a new religion expressed through an aesthetic of politics. Though revolutionary festivals took a variety of forms, they pointed to the new age of mass politics.

The chaotic crowd of the "people" became a disciplined mass movement during the Revolution, participating in the orchestrated drama of politics. But apart from political rites and festivals during the Jacobin dictatorship, an increasing conformity saw to it that the new order would not degenerate into chaos: dress, comportment, and even songs were enlisted to support that effort, and so were a multitude of organizations to which people were supposed to belong. Eventually, the revolutionary armies further strengthened the authority of the revolutionary state. Such conformity was placed in the service of the passion for liberty, closely associated with patriotism and the cult of reason.[3] This new politics attempted the politicization of the masses, which, for the first time in modern history, functioned as a pressure group and not just through episodic uprisings or short-lived riots. The age of modern mass politics had begun.

Stressing this aspect of the French Revolution should clarify its importance for fascism, especially as nationalism took up the new politics with its carefully organized festivals, rites, myths, and symbols. Modern nationalism from the very beginning presented itself as a democratic movement through which the general will of the nation would be put into practice. The drama of politics was meant to awaken the passion of the people for their nation. Just as some Frenchmen bewailed the decline of republican passion in the fourth

year of the Revolution, so democratic nationalism thought itself
dependent upon a continuing revolutionary spirit. This nationalism
was largely tamed after the lost revolutions of 1848, co-opted by established states and dynasties. Yet some of the revolutionary impetus of
nationalism survived, in the form of a democratic nationalism based
not on hierarchy and privilege but upon the general will of the people.
This nationalism provides the link between the French Revolution
and fascism: the nationalization of the masses was a common bond
between the French and the fascist revolutions.

However much fascist movements and democratic nationalism
differed from nation to nation, the instruments of self-representation
and the need for popular participation were common to both. Moreover, all fascisms shared the utopianism which was said to have
inspired the masses during the French Revolution: the longing to
create a new man or a new nation.[4] Many other comparisons will be
made in this essay, such as the fascination with death and the use of
martyrs, or the preoccupation with youth, beauty, and war. But all
such specifics are part of the general reorientation of European politics that we have mentioned already, and that began with the French
Revolution. The Revolution, as it were, set the tone and the example
for a new mass politics whose real triumph came only after the First
World War. This was not a consciously adopted example, and many
who took it up after the Revolution in order to organize the masses
hated the Revolution, and saw the rites and ceremonies of the Jacobins
only as a part of the Terror. This makes tracing any continuity difficult indeed, and yet, as a matter of fact, Jacobin politics were adapted
to quite different ends. Early German nationalists, for example, who
stressed the importance of festivals, of a political liturgy which
centered upon the myths and symbols of the nation—using processions, folk dances, speaking choruses, and the singing of hymns—
seemed to have few ideological contacts with the Jacobins, and yet the
democratic impetus, and the means through which it expressed itself,
constituted a bond between the two movements.

Nationalism was the inheritor of Jacobin politics, a modern, democratic, and, at first, revolutionary nationalism as opposed to the nationalism that supported the existing political and social order. This democratic nationalism which fought against the *ancien régime* for a more meaningful national unity was perhaps the most important single link between the French Revolution and fascism. Popular sovereignty was affirmed and controlled through giving the people a means of participation in the political process—not in reality, but through a feeling of participating, of belonging to a true and meaningful community. Whether in fascist mass meetings or the great festivals of the Revolution, men and women considered themselves active participants, and for many of them this was to prove a more important involvement than representative government could provide, removed as it was from any direct contact with the people. Revolutionary ardor or ideological commitment needed to express itself in a more direct manner. But such enthusiasm—an often messianic political faith—grips masses of men and women mostly in times of crisis, and this inheritance of the Revolution was operative mostly in turbulent times, as the Jacobin dictatorship and fascism itself demonstrate.

For all that, this inheritance is difficult to disentangle from others, not in its ideal of "the people" or the organization of festivals, but as a source for the aesthetic of politics. Italy was a Catholic country and Adolf Hitler grew up in Catholic Austria, and Catholic in this context meant the Baroque with its theatricality, its love of symbols and gestures. Hitler was much influenced by the revival of the Viennese Baroque at the end of the nineteenth century, with its grandiose buildings, its festivals, and the royal parades on the famous Ringstrasse.[5] Gabriele D'Annunzio's use of Christian themes in his festivals during his rule over the city of Fiume was obviously indebted to the Catholicism of the Baroque, creating rites taken over by Italian fascism.

Some of the festivals of the French Revolution had themselves borrowed from Christian liturgy, and modern, democratic nationalism depended on it to an even greater extent. Thus the holy flame, so common in nationalist festivals, derived from the holy flame above the altar in Catholic churches, while declarations of faith were made, not to God, but to the nation. The dialogue between leader and crowd was in its stylized responses indebted to that between the priest and the congregation. Such borrowing from the Christian liturgy was especially important in Germany, where the new national consciousness was set upon pietistic foundations, and where practically all the early leaders of the nationalist movement came from a pietistic Lutheran background. For example, Ernst Moritz Arndt, the poet of German national unity, held in 1814 that prayers must accompany national festivals.[6]

German nationalism used Christian terminology to express itself, a trend which was to reach its climax in national socialism. There was (as we mentioned in the introduction) reference to the "resurrection of the Greater German Reich," "the blood of the martyrs," and constant appeals to providence. Hitler, at one point, called the martyrs of the movement his apostles.[7] The French Revolution had also created a new language for itself, but this had no effect in Germany. People were familiar with Christian terminology, and this was co-opted by the Nazis. Furthermore, the Nazis imitated the interiors of churches as appropriate for their own kind of worship. The Jacobins had done the same, holding one of their important festivals in the Cathedral of Notre Dame.[8] No takeover of churches took place in Nazi Germany; instead, Christian forms were consciously used in order to construct a rival religion.

The so-called "sacred chambers" (*Weiheräume*) in factories and big businesses that were reserved for party festivities were often arranged like a church: where the altar stood Hitler's bust was substituted, placed between banners of eagles decorated with swastikas, as the symbol of unity between the nation and the Nazi movement. And yet, all this overt borrowing from Christianity must not obliterate the basic importance of the French Revolution even here: for the concept of the general will, of the people worshiping themselves, was the presupposition upon which all this borrowing rested. Popular sovereignty was not merely appealed to in Nazi speeches, but in one ceremony during the party day at Nuremberg, Hitler advanced toward the holy flame as one of a crowd, emerging only at the last moment.[9] The creation of a political liturgy based upon the aesthetic of politics was a consequence of the belief in the artificial construct of "the people": they had to be mobilized, shaped, and disciplined, and the way in which this was done was influenced—if not directly determined—by the French Revolution. The Revolution signaled the break between the old politics of dynasty and privilege, and the new democratic politics supposedly based on the will of the people.

The overt attitude of National Socialists toward the French Revolution was one of hatred: it symbolized all that had gone wrong with Germany. Historians used to explain what they regarded as the aggressive nature of German nationalism, and therefore of National Socialism, through the fact that Germany had been untouched by the ideals of the French Revolution, and that subsequently it had missed the benign influence of the Enlightenment. Thus Germany came to differ from Western Europe. Such a view of German history can no longer be upheld. German nationalism, even as it fought against Napoleon, at first internalized ideas of freedom and humanity which the French Revolution projected. Love of fatherland and freedom were the slogans under which the German Wars of Liberation against France were fought, and freedom for many of those involved meant freedom both within the nation itself and for other nations wanting independence.[10] To be sure, as the struggle became more intense, opposition to the French Revolution and what it stood for increased, and proclamations of freedom rang increasingly hollow, or meant merely national independence; now only the fatherland counted. But just as the ideal of liberty exemplified by the French Revolution was repudiated, its influence reasserted itself through the idea of popular sovereignty and its consequences, which German nationalism, embattled against the reaction, accepted.

German nationalism, like all modern nationalism, involved the mobilizing and control of the masses. To achieve this, it constructed a world of illusion which in its content bore no resemblance to the

French Revolution. This world, which the Nazis adopted as their own, was a rural, not an urban world (like that of the Revolution), one in which a mythical German past had remained alive, pointing to a better future. Most nations represented themselves through preindustrial symbols like the native landscape, projecting a feeling of continuity and harmony in contrast to the modern age. Hitler boasted that with the rise of National Socialism "the nervous nineteenth century had come to an end."[11] The images and the rhetoric of nationalism were opposed to that which the Jacobins had projected. The storming of the Bastille was made into a metaphor symbolizing the perils of modernity.

All nationalism claimed to provide stability in a restless world, seeing itself as a civic religion with a claim to timelessness. National symbols looked backward rather than forward; these were no Goddesses of Reason who lacked a past.[12] While the Festivals of Revolution had a short memory, honoring the death of Marat or of the revolutionary martyrs, the martyrs of movements like National Socialism were immediately assimilated to heroes who had fought for the fatherland in the medieval past or during the Wars of National Liberation. Nationalism had a different sense of history than the French Revolution; it looked to conventional, non-Enlightenment sources for its inspiration. And though the revolutionary festivals in the countryside also built upon ancient peasant traditions,[13] the thrust of these festivals was not directed toward recapturing the past in order to control the future.

The content of most nineteenth- and twentieth-century nationalism was different from that of the French Revolution, but its method of politics and self-representation was similar. For example, Robespierre might have felt at home in Nazi mass meetings, except for their huge dimensions and the kind of precedent and imagery used. He would have recognized the rhythms of such meetings, their songs and speaking choruses, as a political statement, and their play upon light and shadow would not have been strange, for the Revolution was fond of annexing to its own festivals sunrises, sunsets, and dawns.

The Nazis were particularly disturbed by the Revolution's break with the past, its repudiation of history, which seemed to them a logical consequence of the Enlightenment. Indeed, the triumphant Revolution had forgotten history; for example, the Pantheon, which was at first opened to great men of all nations and ages, was finally restricted only to those who had followed the turns and twists of the Revolution.[14] The Nazis and the fascists in general saw socialist and Bolshevik revolutions as the logical consequence of such a break with history: rootless and opportunistic, devoid of principles. All these revolutions were, so they claimed, controlled by the Jews, eternal strangers and anti-nationals. Hitler in *Mein Kampf* criticized just such a revolution. A revolution that is a true blessing, he wrote, will not be ashamed to make use of already existing truths. After all, human culture and man himself are merely the end-products of a long historical development for which each generation has furnished the building blocks. The purpose of a revolution is not to tear down the whole building, but to remove what is unsuitable and to build again upon the space thus vacated. Here was the model of a revolution that was pitted against that which France had provided. Such was Hitler's most consistent position toward the Revolution, even if, at times, he admired its destructive power, which had served to put an end to the old order and had led to a new beginning.[15] This was, after all, what he himself wanted to achieve. But, in the last resort, the French Revolution, manipulated by the Jews, according to Hitler, had produced evil rather than good.

Nervousness was the disease most feared in the nineteenth century as leading to a general degeneration, not only of individuals, but of the state. The fascists were haunted by fear of degeneration, a word they applied liberally to their enemies. The answer to such fears, in their eyes, was the maintenance of respectability and racial purity. Keeping control over one's sexuality was vital to Adolf Hitler, who was obsessed with the spread of syphilis.[16] A clear division of functions between the sexes was basic to moral and physical health. The accusation that the Nazi ideologist Alfred Rosenberg in his *Der Mythos des*

20. Jahrhunderts (1930) leveled against the French Revolution was telling in this context. The collapse of the *ancien régime*, he wrote, had as its necessary and natural consequence the establishment of the overbearing influence of women, many of whom took on functions that had been the preserve of men. Had the ideals of that Revolution not included the liberation of women, whose forerunners, according to Rosenberg, were two demimondaines, Olympe de Gouges and Theroigne de Mericourt?[17] Rosenberg linked women's liberation to prostitution, and this within the framework of a confusion of sexes. The accusation of immorality leveled by the nationalist right against the French Revolution in most of Europe was more than just the reaction of prudes. It symbolized the destruction of the social and political order.

But here, once again, bitter opposition should not disguise certain similarities that point back to that general reorientation of European politics I have mentioned before. The Jacobins also insisted on clear and unambiguous distinctions between morality and immorality. Those who supported the Revolution and those who opposed it should be clearly distinguished. Robespierre loved to divide the enemies of the Revolution into various groups,[18] and to create order even among those destined for execution.

The uncompromising distinction between enemy and friend, supporters and those who must be eliminated, was drawn in the name of the general will of the people. Even as the guillotine was kept busy, it was claimed that the people themselves wanted the Terror put on their daily agenda.[19] Hitler made the same claim somewhat more theoretically: the people themselves saw in a ruthless attack against the enemy proof of a just cause, and in the refusal to exterminate him a sign of weakness.[20] He made these remarks in the context of the nationalization of the masses, as he called it, crucial to the reawakening of Germany. The emphasis upon unambiguous distinctions, in politics as well as social life, formed a common bond between Jacobins and fascists. The either/or cast of mind, which put a premium upon decisiveness, was a means to impose a new and untraditional leadership upon the nation. Such leadership was dependent upon the successful nationalization of the masses, and this meant decisiveness, clarity, and conformity, projected in action as well as through the revolutionary or national cult.

The general will of the people, if not mediated through representative government, needed coherence, and political as well as personal conformity were essential to the existence of such a direct democracy. The myths and symbols—the whole of the civic religion with its cult as the objectification of the general will—focused and directed the faith of the people. Jean-Jacques Rousseau himself had recommended to the government of Poland the institution of games, festivities, and ceremonies in order to create republican habits of mind which would be impossible to uproot.[21] But what about the leader himself as focusing and directing the faith of the people? Here the legacy the French Revolution left to fascism was at best ambivalent.

During the Jacobin dictatorship, the public leadership function was exercised through speeches and proclamations. Robespierre and other members of the Committee of Public Safety were compelling speakers, but they were never the center of a cult or an integral part of the myths and symbols of the civic religion. They were closer to Rousseau's original concept of the general will, which foresaw a legislator but no charismatic leader as the object of popular adoration and enthusiasm. The deeds of the Revolution were carried out in the name of abstract principles, such as freedom or reason, and not in the name of one man. To be sure, martyred leaders became part of the revolutionary pantheon. Jacques-Louis David cast his painting of the assassinated Marat in the form of a timeless monument.[22] However, David never painted a living leader of the Revolution; for example, no such monument was erected to Robespierre. Jacobins were willing to celebrate collective deeds, but accepted individual heroes only when they were dead.[23] Leadership during the Revolution was, after all, collective leadership; the ideal of equality was maintained in theory and not yet objectified by one leader acting on behalf of the nation. Napoleon would change all that in a direction leading, not forward to future fascist leaders, but backward to monarchy and empire.

Fascist ideals of leadership could find no comfort here. The only connection between these ideas and the Revolution was, once again, the political liturgy, which could serve to support and to frame the leader, even if at times, as we have mentioned, it was used to demonstrate that the leader was one among equals. The theory of democratic leadership adopted by Hitler and Mussolini emerged as a consequence of the growth of urban and industrial society. Gustav Le Bon's *The Crowd* (1889) was a milestone on the road to modern dictatorship—a work, as I have mentioned before, known by and important to both Hitler and Mussolini.[24] Here it is necessary to say more about that book which was inspired by the crowds mobilized by General Boulanger between 1886 and 1889 in his bid for dictatorship, one of the first modern mass movements with a truly cross-class appeal. The Boulangist movement sparked a concern with the role of the masses in politics, illustrated by a spate of works dealing with collective psychology.[25] Le Bon stressed the effect of what he called "theatrical representations" upon the crowd, but also the necessity of providing a leader through whom the crowd attains its identity.[26] Such a leader must himself be hypnotized by the idea whose apostle he has become. Here Le Bon refers to the men of the French Revolution, together with Savonarola, Luther, and Peter the Hermit, as having exercised their fascination over the crowd only after having themselves been fascinated by a creed.[27] Le Bon had observed well. This was the kind of leadership needed in an age when the mobilized masses could sway politics in a manner which had not been possible earlier—with the exception of the French Revolution. Here again the Revolution prefigures a reorientation of European politics that, properly speaking, became effective only in industrialized Europe.

The use which the fascist leaders themselves made of a political liturgy, and the appeal of democratic leadership, varied from nation to nation. While Hitler made thorough use of this manner of self-representation, Mussolini seemed to have greater difficulty grasping its importance for the integration of the masses into the fascist movement. However, this was a matter of degree, for fascism also wanted to become a civic religion. Though much was borrowed from D'Annunzio's rule over Fiume, Mussolini was also influenced by the political cult of the Revolution and the educational and integrative function it had served. Moreover, unlike Hitler, he borrowed from the Revolution the idea of a new calendar, in which the year One was the year of the final attainment of power.[28] What better signal could be devised to show that the old order was finished and a new age about to commence? The civic religion of nationalism, wherever it took roots, had little choice but to draw, however indirectly, on the only serviceable past within reach: the example of the Jacobins, with their attempt to unite, through mass rituals and easily understood symbols, the people, the state, and the nation. Mussolini would let the development of a speech depend upon the eyes and voices of the thousands who packed the piazza.[29] He posed for a photograph beside a statue of Augustus, and on another occasion was presented with a Roman sword; but such episodes are only part of a fully fledged political cult, with festivals like those celebrated by the Revolution, or like Nazi mass meetings.

While Italy was well on the road to a civic religion in the first ten years of fascism, later the cult of the Duce became more personal, as it came to be projected upon one man and the state, rather than upon the leader as a symbol of the ideology of his movement—an ideology now supposedly shared by all the people. Indeed, the cult of the Duce was kept almost separate from the Fascist party.[30] Hitler, on the other hand, in the long term, attempted to restrict the impact of a single individual upon the ritual. The ceremony itself should have an independent life, he believed, because this would ensure the continuity of the Third Reich even after his death; for his successor would not possess his own magic and the use of the liturgy would disguise this fact.[31] Mussolini never exalted a political liturgy in this manner,[32] nor did he have the illusion that it might function to keep the leader all-powerful through giving him the appearance of a priest at the altar of a Baroque church.

Politics as a theater filled with passion had come into its own in Italy with Gabriele D'Annunzio's rule over the city of Fiume. The succession of festivals in which D'Annunzio played a leading role was supposed to abolish the distance between leader and led, and the speeches from the balcony of the town hall to the crowd below (accompanied by trumpets) were to accomplish the same purpose.[33] D'Annunzio used secular and religious symbols side by side in order to create a civic religion. His was a fully worked-out political liturgy intended to keep Fiume in a state of continual excitement and euphoria, uniting the city against its enemies and projecting it as a symbol for a new Italy. The French Revolution was involved in such a political theater only in a most indirect way. D'Annunzio's rule over Fiume was the first time in the post-revolutionary age that the aesthetics of politics had been used once again as a principal means of governance. But the immediate inspiration for such politics was the poet's own fertile imagination, inspired by the artistic movements of his age.

Mussolini did take from Fiume some of his way of doing politics and many of the fascist rites and ceremonials through which the collectivity fused with the leader.[34] However, eventually the Duce was at the center of such politics, becoming less the symbol of some transcendent principle—such as the Volk's soul or the race—than a political leader, the living creator of a new state. Nationalism in Italy had retained a liberal core and until the 1930s had avoided fusing with racism, or with that mysticism of the Volk which was to bedevil Germany. The state, not the Volk, played a dominant role in Italian nationalism, and here important groups such as the army saw the nation as symbolized by the king rather than by Mussolini. The Mirabeaus, Andre Chéniers, and Davids, who helped to shape the festivals of revolutionary France, would have found no peers in fascist Italy, where the political liturgy did not excite such attention, and the names of those who organized fascist rites—men like Italo Balbo, Augusto Turati, or Achille Starace—were noted for other services rendered to the Fascist state. Germany, on the other hand, had its Albert Speer and Joseph Goebbels, who managed the aesthetic of politics.

We have found links and differences between the French and the fascist revolutions, not by examining specific attitudes, but through more general principles. The political liturgy, the aesthetic of politics, forms the core of continuity between the two revolutions, together with the quest for totality and the either/or mentality as the spur to decisiveness in politics. Basic to all of these links was the democratization of politics, the rule of the general will, that informed the nationalism upon which fascism was built. Fascism and the French Revolution, each in its own way, saw themselves as democratic movements directed against the establishment. Fascism as a movement had a revolutionary thrust, and even in power—having itself become the establishment—made full use of an anti-establishment rhetoric directed against the bourgeoisie.

There are two further connections between the French Revolution and fascism that bear mention: the preoccupations with death and youth. Funeral symbolism played a large role in revolutionary festivals, often acted out around an empty tomb.[35] These were the tombs of the martyrs of the Revolution, whose actual funerals were grandiose *mise-en-scènes*, at whose end stood the Pantheon. The Revolution attempted to redesign cemeteries as places of eternal sleep rather than Christian resurrection. Architects experimented with tombs containing the ashes of great men to be placed at the center of such cemeteries.[36] The cult of the martyred dead, or of those who had played an important role in the Revolution, was celebrated during Jacobin rule and the Directory. Fascism celebrated a similar cult of the dead. Italo Balbo first organized fascist funerals in Italy as mass events combining religious with patriotic ceremony.[37] Such funerals organized by Balbo, provide a continuation of the fascist ceremonial once displayed by D'Annunzio.

The fascist cult of the dead was not confined to the martyrs of the movement, but included the fallen of the First World War. Both Italian fascism and National Socialism regarded themselves as the true inheritors of the war experience, guardians of the cult of the fallen soldier. Fascist Italy built some of the most spectacular war cemeteries—such as that at Redipuglia in the Alps—using Christian symbolism, as, for example, the three crosses of Calvary, to proclaim the resurrection of those who gave their life for the fatherland. All nations who had been at war gave singular honor to their war dead, but in fascism such remembrance was close to the center of its political ritual, never to be lost from sight. The martyrs of the movement were assimilated to the fallen soldier of the First World War; both had sacrificed their lives for the nation. Italian fascism's cult of the dead in contrast to that of Nazi Germany, has up to now not received much attention, and therefore statements about it must be tentative. But in a movement which saw itself in the light of the First World War, and which was pledged to continue the fight for Italy's victory, sacrificial death was bound to occupy an important place in the rhetoric and ceremonial of the party.

There can be no doubt about the pride of place held by the memory of the war dead and martyrs in National Socialism. Some of the most spectacular ceremonies at the Nuremberg rallies were devoted to this cult, including perhaps the central ceremony where Hitler stood alone in front of the eternal flame against the background of massed party formations. Christian symbolism was once again part of this cult: for example, the bullet which killed Albert Leo Schlageter, considered a Nazi martyr, was kept in a silver reliquary.[38] State funerals were carefully programmed ceremonies of great splendor. Thus, when the body of the assassinated Nazi leader of Switzerland, Wilhelm Gustloff, was transferred to his home in northern Germany in 1936, the journey took fifteen hours. There was a ceremony at every station on the way, and the partially open coach with the coffin and guard of honor was flanked by two coaches reserved for wreaths.[39] State funerals, though infrequent, were an integral part of the cult of the dead which the Nazis practiced.

State funerals were celebrated with great pomp throughout the nineteenth century, but these were funerals of rulers, generals, and members of the government. The French Revolution and fascism democratized state funerals: not birth or privilege, but service to the cause, warranted such display, regardless of the person's social origin or standing. France took up this revolutionary tradition with the founding of the Third Republic; for example, the funeral of Victor Hugo in 1885 has been called one of the first fruits of the mass age, with its procession past the catafalque standing under the Arch of Triumph and ending at the Pantheon, which was opened for the first time in thirty five years.[40] The precedents for such a funeral were those of Marat or Mirabeau, and, although Napoleon III had refined and elaborated the practice of state funerals, these did not have the same overall national and educational purpose. Yet here, once more, there was no straight line connecting the two movements, but a gray zone, which complicates the tracing of influence. For example, the actual pomp and circumstance of state funerals began, not with the French Revolution, but with the Baroque. The theatricality of the Baroque, and its fascination with death, led to a surfeit of funeral pomp, with interminable processions and elaborate decorations: the catafalque came into its own as a kind of stage for the corpse. Though fascism, like the French Revolution, preferred a simpler, classical style for its decorations, Baroque funeral pomp remained a fixture in the Catholic regions of Europe. The tradition of the Baroque, familiar to fascist leaders, obscures the influence of the French Revolution. Nevertheless, while Baroque funerals were religious rites without any political purpose, both the French Revolution and the fascists integrated such funerals and the cult of the dead into their political style, as part of their own self-representation.

Why this preoccupation with death by revolutions seeking to usher in a new and dynamic age, be it the Republic of Virtue, the Thousand-Year Reich, or the drive to create a new fascist man who would put everything right? The fascist call to sacrifice made use of the Christian dialectic of death and resurrection. The transcendence of death was closely linked in fascism to the fallen of the First World War, as documented by the design of military cemeteries with their crosses and frequent representations of soldiers touched by Christ.[41] The Nazis, for example, took the cult of the fallen soldier and applied it to their own martyrs. Death and life were not contraries, but linked to one another. For some Italian fascists, death had to be accepted; it was sober and devoid of sentiment, a test of individual discipline. But, for the most part, fascists held to the traditional idea that sacrifice for the nation transcended death. Thus fascism sought to abolish death, just as it attempted to make time stand still. Such an emphasis in its ideology is hardly astounding in a movement dedicated to perpetual war.

The French Revolution could not make use of the Christian theme of death and resurrection. Instead, death was defined as perpetual sleep. Indeed, the redesign of cemeteries was part of the attempted de-Christianization of France. The cult of the martyrs helped to legitimize the Revolution, and the funerals of so-called "great men" in the Pantheon were seen as a means to educate the public in virtue.[42] These were men of the past like Rousseau, Voltaire, or Descartes (whom the Revolution could claim as its ancestors), the martyrs of the Revolution, and a few of its leaders. This cult of death was obviously different from that of fascism: it lacked the dialectic of death and resurrection. Only through the preservation of his memory in the minds of his countrymen could the martyr of the Revolution or the "great man" be assured of eternal life. With fascism, on the other hand, the dead return to inspire the living.[43] As soldiers fell in the wars of the French Revolution and Napoleon, there was a slow return to the idea of the sacredness of their last resting-place, as Christianity reasserted itself as a doctrine of consolation.[44] Though the nature of death was different, both the French Revolution and fascism practiced a cult of death in order to legitimize their revolution through its martyrs, to justify the call for sacrifice now or in the future, and perhaps also because they were under the spell of the apocalyptic vision that the scourges of God had to be overcome before time could be abolished. What Ernst Bloch called the "hidden revolution" was never far below the surface even of those revolutions which rejected it.[45]

The cult of youth is easier to analyze: both revolutions sought to present themselves as youth movements filled with energy, resolve, and beauty. Yet, here also, there were important differences in practice and theory. Fascist movements were youth movements in fact and in theory, but the militants of the French Revolution were often family men, settled in life.[46] To be sure, young men went off to war, giving rise to songs and poems which extolled their youthful qualities as soldiers of the Revolution. Though the Marseillaise called all citizens to arms, according to the third verse it was "our young heroes" who fell in battle, while the earth stamped out new heroes to take their place. Fascist worship of youth hardly needs underlining. It is documented by the statues surrounding the Forum Mussolini in Rome, or the figures crowning the Führer's rostrum at the Nuremberg party rallies, showing a Goddess of Victory flanked by three figures of naked youths. But here, again, the connection is indirect, indeed even less certain than in the case of the cult of death. The cult of youth was a product of war, not of the French Revolution, while its revival at the *fin de siècle* directly influenced fascism.

It is easier to find general rather than specific links between fascism and the French Revolution and I have tried to sketch some of them here. If they are to be summarized, it might be simplest to state that the French Revolution marked the beginning of a democratization of politics that climaxed in twentieth-century fascism. I have attempted to analyze the legacy of the French Revolution as it applied to both National Socialism and Italian fascism. But this legacy differed, just as the two fascisms were different in many respects. National Socialism was the true inheritor of the aesthetics of politics. Though Mussolini also made use of the new mass politics, his dictatorship was more personal than that of Hitler, who tended to cast his power in symbolic form. But Italian fascism forged its own link to the Revolution, absent in Germany. The French Revolution had regarded itself as a new departure, creating a nation of brothers, while some of its radicals had talked about creating a new man. That was precisely what Mussolini had in mind: that fascism should create a new type of man, no longer a product of the present order.[47] He never told us exactly what this new man should look like or how he should behave, though this can be inferred from the new fascist style. The new man proclaimed that fascism must pass beyond the present into a yet uncharted future.

This seems one reason why some Italian fascists did not stop at the usual condemnation of the French Revolution, but called upon fascism to surpass it with a new kind of democracy to be run by producers. The fascist ideal of the new man inherits from the hated Enlightenment the concept that a new man can be created through education and experience.[48] The Nazis, and especially the SS, also envisaged a new man, but he was to exemplify ancient Germanic virtues, a man from the past unspoilt by the present. The primacy of historical myth in National Socialism could not tolerate a revolutionary concept of man. Their different concepts of a new man was the nearest both Italian fascism and National Socialism came to providing an official guide to utopia. But here, once more, differences between the two fascisms affected their view of the French Revolution. Mussolini, at least nominally, was opposed to utopias, to concepts standing outside history, and in his article on fascism in the *Enciclopedia Italiana* he linked the idea of utopia to Jacobin innovations based upon evil and abstract principles. Fascism was supposed to be a realistic doctrine which wanted to solve problems arising from historical development. For all that, the new man could not be allowed to exist outside the fascist state, but was an integral part of this state on the road to utopia. In spite of the repeated attacks upon utopianism, the fascist state itself tended to become a Republic of Virtue.[49]

The French Revolution was condemned, not only for its utopianism and materialism, but also for its passion for absolutes, as Jacobin thought was characterized by another article in the *Enciclopedia*[50]— surely an odd condemnation from a movement which believed in absolutes, from the myths and symbols of the nation to the infallibility of the Duce. The Jacobins were also attacked by Italian fascists for being too rigid and formalistic, but even this attack focused upon their love for absolutes. This meant, for one historian writing in the *Enciclopedia*, the attempt to purify France through the shedding of blood on behalf of abstract principles, such as the Supreme Being or the Republic of Virtue.[51] Once more, fascism itself was mirrored in this condemnation—it, too, wanted to enforce public virtue and was not averse to the shedding of blood, if not on behalf of the Republic of Virtue, then on behalf of a virtuous Nation.

Were such accusations due to the fact that fascism could not see the mote in its own eye, or do we see one revolution attacking a rival? While the first hypothesis was certainly true, the latter was of greater consequence. Hitler, as we have seen, constructed his own model of revolution, quite different from that of France; Mussolini, too, claimed originality for his revolution, which wanted to create a new man and a new nation through its own momentum, based upon its peculiar mixture of left- and right-wing doctrine. Perhaps because of the liberal tradition of the Risorgimento, and the syndicalists and futurists who joined with fascism, Mussolini's revolution was closer to the French model than that proclaimed by Nazi Germany. The Nazi condemnation of the French Revolution was on the whole straightforward: it was liberal and materialist, the work of Jews and Masons.

But what did French fascists themselves make of their own national revolution? Many of them had passed through the Action Française, with its exaltation of the *ancien régime* and hatred for the Revolution that had so wantonly destroyed it. We cannot describe here the attitudes of each French fascist movement to the Revolution; in any case, this would mean telling a repetitive tale accusing the Revolution of having begun a process which culminated in the corrupt Third Republic. Nevertheless, we can find ambivalent attitudes toward the Revolution on the part of some French fascists, different from those in Italy or Germany. George Valois, one of the founders of French fascism, saw the French Revolution as the beginning of a movement, both socialist and nationalist, which the fascists would complete.[52] Unlike George Valois, who never ceased to flirt with the left, the young fascist intellectuals who edited the journal *Je Suis Partout* in the

1930s and 1940s did not find their roots in the French Revolution, but were ambivalent about its heritage. This *équipe* reveled in their youth, worshiped energy, and cultivated an outrageous polemical style directed against republican France. *Je Suis Partout* published a special issue on the French Revolution in 1939, dedicated to those who had fought against the Revolution, especially the peasants of the Vendée, who were said to have sacrificed their lives for the truth, and to Charlotte Corday, who had assassinated Marat.[53] There was nothing ambivalent here, nor about the headline claiming war and inflation to be the driving forces behind the Revolution. The Revolution, so we hear, had opened the door to speculators long before present deputies had demonstrated once more the link between corruption and republican parliaments. And yet there was a certain admiration for Robespierre, "genie inhumain et abstrait," himself unique in his incorruptibility.[54]

However, once more Robespierre, the Jacobin, is condemned for his passion for absolutes, his "religious passions"—and this from Robert Brasillach, the leader of this *équipe*, who could be said to exemplify just such a passion.[55] Brasillach, as one of his contemporaries put it, was himself a sentimental romantic, who was attracted to the aesthetic of politics, greatly admiring the Nuremberg party rallies.[56] This did not prevent him during the Second World War from accusing the Gaullists of possessing the religious spirit of a militant Robespierrism, which left no room for open-eyed realism.[57] These strictures were echoes of Mussolini's criticism of the Revolution, and in this case what we have called the mirror effect was present as well: the Revolution was accused of attitudes, many of which were, in fact, shared by fascists. Brasillach and his friends had broken with the Action Française precisely because it was too sober and stodgy, not passionate enough, and because it looked to the *ancien régime* rather than to a future revolution. Their revolution meant hatred for capitalism, Jews, and parliamentary democracy, a love of youth, and a fascination with violence.

Speaking about the French Revolution, Brasillach exclaimed that it had set the world on fire and that it had been a beautiful conflagration.[58] Revolution itself was praised, even if its content was denied. Similarly, Drieu La Rochelle praised the truly virile republicanism manifested by Jacobin authoritarians during the French Revolution.[59] For these young fascists the French Revolution served as an example of how to bring down the old order, manifesting the beauty of violence and of manliness. But even here they were not consistent. Thus, in the special number of *Je Suis Partout* on the Revolution, Brasillach condemned the Jacobin Terror and called for a general reconciliation—with the Vichy government in mind.[60] There was always the pull of conservative attitudes toward the Revolution, and it was the historian Pierre Gaxotte of the Action Française who wrote the leading article, claiming war and inflation to be the motors of the Revolution, in the special issue of *Je Suis Partout*. There, he roundly condemned all revolution: a revolution without the guillotine, without looting and denunciation, without dictatorship and prisons, was said to be an impossibility.[61] And this was written in a journal of which Robert Brasillach was the driving force.

The Jacobin lurked close to the surface among these French fascists and, as in the case of Mussolini, mirrored some of their own commitments and practices. The "abstract" was rejected in favor of a greater realism, but what was more abstract than a national mystique which demanded unquestioning loyalty, or a view of men and women through their stereotypes? For was not the so-called new man, after all, an ideal type?

The Jacobin Terror was at least momentarily rehabilitated by Marcel Déat's Rassemblement National Populaire (RNP) when, as the Germans occupied all of France, the collaborationists wanted to show themselves worthy of being trusted by the Nazis. Now a leader of the RNP wrote that, as in Robespierre's time, terror must be the order of the day. The sworn enemies of the national revolution should pay with their lives for treason or resistance.[62] But such praise for the

Terror merely grasped a convenient precedent and hardly touched upon the influence the French Revolution itself may have had upon Marcel Déat and his political party.

The rejection of the French Revolution as a model for change was general among fascists, although, as we have seen, this was graduated in the Latin nations rather than one-dimensional as in Germany. But, when all is said and done, the most important influence exercised by the Revolution upon fascism was its inauguration of a new kind of politics designed to mobilize the masses and to integrate them into a political system—through rites and ceremonies in which they could participate, and through an aesthetic of politics which appealed to the longing for community and comradeship in an industrial age. As Adolf Hitler put it, when a man leaves his small workshop, or the big factory where he feels small, and enters a mass meeting where he is surrounded by thousands of people who share his convictions, he becomes convinced of the righteousness of the cause, gaining personal strength through fighting within an all-encompassing confraternity.[63] This was a language the members of the Committee of Public Safety might have understood.

Tracing the connection between the French Revolution and fascism means emphasizing degrees of difference, nuances, and inferences. No body of research exists that might encourage more authoritative statements about the link between the two movements, starting with the influence of the Revolution upon important fascist leaders. We would also have to know what, if anything, those who organized fascist rites and ceremonials actually borrowed from the Jacobins: only in the case of Nazi Germany can it be said with some certainty that the earlier movement provided little or no detailed inspiration. For all that, important connections existed, and even the manner in which fascist movements rejected the French Revolution can cast some light upon fascism itself. In the last resort, the political culture of fascism was indebted to the French Revolution in general, as the first modern movement to make use of a new kind of politics in order to mobilize the masses and to end the alienation of man from his society and his nation.

Every fascism had its own character, and Italian fascism received much of its dynamic and sometimes revolutionary fervor not from the distant past, but more directly from the Futurist movement that was at one and the same time artistic, revolutionary, and political.

FIVE

Fascism and the Intellectuals

I T USED TO BE THOUGHT by a good many historians that fascism was a movement opposed to intellectualizing, and that unlike other social movements it was imposed by a willful minority upon a confused majority. Such a "revolution of nihilism" could not be expected to capture the true enthusiasms and dreams of men. Benedetto Croce, for example, regarded fascism as a childish "adventure," a drunken activism, whose very nature placed the movement outside the mainstream of history.[1] Fascism was seen as an aberration from the dominant current of European history and thought.

This view is relevant to the problem of "fascism and the intellectuals," for if fascism were merely a pragmatic, activist response to the immediate historical situation, the intellectual would have no real place either among the duped masses or in the cynical political leadership. If prestigious intellectuals like Ezra Pound and Giovanni Gentile became fascists, this could not be explained by their intellectual heritage or position but rather as another aberration—in Pound's case, insanity.

The refusal to consider seriously the fascist commitment of a good many intellectuals calls for a definition not only of "fascism" but also of "intellectual." If, with André Malraux, we define an intellectual simply as one who traffics in ideas, then a pragmatic, activist fascism would exclude such a person. The functional definition of an intellectual as the guardian of ultimate values within society would also make his fusion with fascism difficult, for that movement was supposedly devoid of the values which intellectuals prized. Above all, the tendency to define intellectuals as wedded to the ultimate values of rationalism, individual freedom, and Kantian morality has stood in the way of understanding the involvement of intellectuals with fascism. Croce is not atypical in having realized the menace to individual freedom which fascism represented, without ever having understood the movement itself.

The intellectuals with whom we are concerned fit into a broad definition: they regarded themselves as guardians of ultimate values in society and saw in fascism a means to realize these values. They defined their own task as primarily educational, at the same time being conscious of their importance as an intellectual "class" in confronting the problems of the age. Moreover, they did not lack a sense of history but saw in fascism a movement that recaptured the values of a past they prized: not of the bourgeois age of the last century but of Graeco-Roman times—or more genuine spiritual values. It is typical that a young anti-fascist intellectual like Carlo Roselli understood fascism and fascist intellectuals far better than Benedetto Croce, the liberal of an older generation. Roselli regarded materialist socialism as dead and advocated a new socialism representing "innate ideas" of liberty and justice. The intellectual must come to the masses with the truth, through ideas truly held.[2] Mussolini, he wrote, sensed the death of the older materialism, but his dishonesty rendered him a mere adventurer.[3] Roselli shares with the fascist intellectuals his call for spiritual unity and his admiration for classical values. But the socialist anti-fascist and his enemies had still more in common: the call for a national revival on the basis of a spiritual impetus, the rejection of politics of pragmatism and compromise, and the concept of intellectuals as heralds of a new, non-materialistic age. The socialism of

Roselli, which was duplicated in other European nations, reflected the same concern that informed the fascist intellectuals: the more rationally ordered society became, the more non-rational became the needs of the individual in that society.

The trend toward irrationality was heightened by the nature of the historical reality within which the fascist commitment of these intellectuals was set. Liberal-democratic society was, in fact, working badly or not at all in nations like Italy and Germany. Political stalemate was added to economic crises: parliaments were ineffective in the face of rising unemployment and poverty. It is important to bear these facts in mind; for men of anarcho-syndicalist background like Massimo Rocca or Dino Grandi in Italy, the actual situation in which the country found itself was crucial in determining their allegiance to fascism— whatever additional reasons they gave for such a commitment.

The interplay between ideology and the historical fact is difficult to assess for each individual case. However, it seems clear that most intellectuals' commitment to fascism was based on a very real dilemma: after 1918 the society in which they lived did not seem to function well or even to function at all; its political and economic instability (which seemed to verge on collapse) had to be transcended. The men we are discussing fled into an ideology which promised to restore culture as well as society; as intellectuals they judged the totality of society and refused to break it down into its constituent parts. This totality was symbolized by the temper of cultural activity—if the arts were restored, then society as a whole would be able to transcend the present. Idealism formed the core of their outlook and kept them from joining with Marxism, while the Marxist protagonists did their best to hold these intellectuals at arm's length.

Ezra Pound, the self-styled fascist, felt that poetry had an important part to play in society, and the Belgian fascist leader Léon Degrelle called men like Mussolini "poets of revolution."[4] When José Antonio Primo de Rivera spoke of the Falange as a "poetic movement," he was not merely echoing Belgium's Degrelle or the Flemish fascist leader Van Severen; he reflected a tendency of all fascism.[5] The role of poetry in the development of modern nationalism is well known and needs no elaboration here. Poetry, music, and art played an important part in the fascist movement as expressions of the non-rational needs of men, which must be satisfied if men were to achieve the necessary spiritual unity and take up the activism that would over-come the bourgeois age.

Economic and political reality did concern the intellectuals, but they believed that their idealism would solve the problems which plagued their times. To be sure, in Italy many intellectuals who came to fascism started with a pragmatic attitude toward the movement, for here ideological debates did not arise until well after the seizure of power. But even in Italy, fascism held that the creative individual, because of his attitude of mind, would solve the specific problems facing the nation. In Germany the retreat into mystique in order to transcend the present had deeper roots. But all fascists believed that, in the last resort, the spiritual unity of the nation would resolve all difficulties. Most fascist intellectuals defined this spiritual unity as a resurgence of creativity viewed in aesthetic terms: the dawn of a new world of beauty and of aesthetic form. The shift from "aesthetic poli-tics" to the idea of the state as the motivator of aesthetic rejuvenation distinguished fascist from anti-fascist intellectuals; in other respects, the world view of the anti-fascists was close to fascist idealism.

Fascism itself was apt to describe the nation in aesthetic terms. Consequently, cultural matters played a large part in the literature of the movement. No doubt this view of the nation as a repository of culture attracted the allegiance of many intellectuals. The young French fascist Robert Brasillach was typical in his opinion that a great political movement must also be an aesthetic one, with a "life style" appropriate to its ideology. Brasillach praised the culture of the court of Louis XIV, the Soviet cinema, and, especially, the Nazi mass meet-ings and their liturgy, "the most remarkable of modern times." Brasil-lach, in common with fascist intellectuals of other nations, saw in this fusion of mass politics and aesthetic form a "collective beauty" analo-gous to the spectacles of the Middle Ages or of ancient Greece. Within such a context, the Third French Republic was an anti-aesthetic regime whose art and culture were part of fragmented reality.[6]

Not only in France, but in Germany and other nations as well, the organic unity of life and politics which fascist movements stressed included an emphasis upon cultural forms. This catered to the preoccupation of intellectuals with such matters while, at the same time, providing them with a rationale for their place in the movement. Moreover, this new world of beauty and aesthetic form was directed by the nation, which gave it a harmony and unity for which such men longed. The national state was the ultimate expression of all human desires, so it seemed to both the philosopher Gentile in Italy and the poet Gottfried Benn in Germany, because fascism transformed the nation into an aesthetic as well as an ethical state. This belief glorified the state as the embodiment of human creativity and human idealism. It is important to stress that the attraction of fascism for intellectuals took place within the context of nationalism: a state that drew together into one spiritual unity the creative souls of its citizens—not the drab state of *raison d'état*, but a state whose very nature was identical with the cultural expression for which these men yearned.

Fascism at first was linked with artistic movements which were not necessarily conservative or sentimental. Some factions of National Socialism sympathized with the Expressionist "chaos of the soul"; Mussolini's regard for Marinetti and the Futurists needs no documentation. The obvious attraction which fascism exercised on creative intellectuals is often overlooked. It gave them a place in the movement and made it possible for them to combine their creativity with a desire to infuse society with their concept of ultimate values.

To sum up: many intellectuals in post-First World War Europe believed that the liberal and bourgeois age had collapsed and that the misery which followed the war was the result of that collapse. Moreover, because of the development of liberal-bourgeois society, poetry (by which they meant all creativity) had fallen into a shallow materialism and sentimentality, and this decline was part and parcel of the corruption of society as a whole. Since creativity was at the roots of the unfolding of the human personality, the elimination of the present must stress the restoration of cultural values. These intellectuals found their answer in fascism and its national mystique. Though the postwar world brought the crisis of liberal-bourgeois society to a head, the position of the fascist intellectuals must also be seen in the context of a prewar literary tradition and as influenced by the contemporary development of Marxism. The fact that the intellectuals were a part of these historical developments must have made their entry into fascism a great deal easier.

The literary tradition of the *fin de siècle* had stressed the irrational, the problems of the individual in a restrictive society. Fascism claimed to reestablish the true creativity of man which had been stifled, just as an earlier generation of men of letters had searched for the genuine beneath the façade of bourgeois society. The fascist contention that human creativity could only stem from the depths of a spiritual impetus symbolized by the nation appealed to such longings and, at the same time, to the longing for authority.

The role of socialism in rejecting the intellectual is equally important. Initially, many artists and writers supported the socialist labor movement, but this movement repudiated the intellectuals and alienated them, as a growing orthodoxy became increasingly suspicious of their allegiance to a working class to which they could not claim to belong.

Marx himself had been hostile to intellectuals and that feeling grew to ever greater proportions within the socialist movement. The beginning of the twentieth century witnessed a veritable persecution of intellectuals in the German Social Democratic Party and the collapse of the enterprises with which they had been associated. Socialist parties in other West European nations also seemed wedded to a materialism which repudiated the intellectuals.[7] Art was regarded as a social "product" and, in consequence, realism of subject matter was bound to triumph over the creative imagination. Writing about the future of poetry in 1937, Christopher Caudwell asserted that there was no neutral world of art free from determining causes. These causes were the conditions prevailing in the real world in which the artist must live and whose tensions he must accurately reflect. The artist must not leave his soul in the past.[8] But intellectuals wanted to be more than a mirror for social and economic determinism; they might reflect the tensions of society, but they also wanted to transcend them through their own creativity. There was no room for their poetry within traditional socialism. Rather than work to introduce an idealist element into Marxism as Roselli and others attempted, many intellectuals turned instead to the literary and aesthetic appeal of the fascist movement.

Fascism seemed to combine this appeal with a critique of bourgeois society which socialism had already presented. The word "decadent" best characterized the postwar present for these men. Here, once more, an already traditional critique fused with the literary tradition of the *fin de siècle*. At that time also the outwardly prosperous establishment seemed merely a disguise for inward decay. For many fascist intellectuals the supposed decadence of the present provided the springboard for their commitment to the fascist utopia. A society in which spiritual unity replaced both the class struggle and human isolation, in which order was reconciled with the irrational mainsprings of creativity, presented a world in which ultimate values would surely triumph. Giovanni Gentile believed fascism to be a personal interpretation of the new spirit striving toward the ethical state.[9]

The disillusionment and despair of decadent reality haunted these intellectuals. Louis-Ferdinand Céline's *Voyage au bout de la Nuit* (*Journey to the End of the Night*, 1932) is typical of this mood. Wherever his travels led the hero of the novel, from fighting in the First World War to Africa, to the United States, and back to France, the picture never changes. The world is not what one thought it to be in one's idealistic youth, nor is it what it seems to be, for underneath all the hypocrisy it is devoid of compassion and love. Naked struggle, human selfishness, and lust for material gain are the only realities. Typically, Céline's famous novel centered on the fate of the poor in such a society: "The poor man has two fine ways of dying in this world, either through the complete indifference of his fellow men in time of peace or by the homicidal fury of these same fellow men when war comes."[10] Decadent materialism was responsible for this state of affairs. His half-crazed *Bagatelles pour un Massacre* (*Trifles to Assist a Massacre*, 1937) is filled with the images of putrefaction with which fascism in general was obsessed in the face of its enemies. Marxism was closed to him. Why, he asks, is there no communist work of literary excellence? Communism cannot produce any great works because it has no soul, but is devoted to bourgeois ideals.[11] The root of all evil, however, is capitalism, which has even managed to overcome the movements aimed at eliminating it—and capitalism is the handiwork of the Jews.

Ezra Pound reached the same conclusion in his "Usura Canto"; capitalism was introduced by Jews and ". . . thereafter art thickened. Thereafter design went to hell . . ."[12] The search for clarity of form became a search for the "genuine," the genuine outside decadent society. Céline wrote that at least Hitler did not lie like the Jews; he was no hypocrite. The Führer tells me, Céline continued, that "might makes right" and I know where I am: there is no "syrup" as with the Jews—no general "indefinite wobble," as Pound would have called it.[13]

Before the Second World War Céline was loath to join any political movement. He believed in the inevitable triumph of the impotent, the megalomaniacs, and the decadent, all of which were symbolized by the Jew. His *École des Cadavres* (*School for Corpses*, 1938) ends by affirming the necessity of racism but, at the same time, asserts that the Aryans were too cowardly and lazy to get rid of the Jews. However, after the defeat of France, Céline's attitude changed and he now took advantage of the Nazi victory to attempt to translate his racism into reality. In 1941 he called for the formation of a political party (*parti unique*) which would unite all racists and anti-Semites. Two years later he threw his support to Jacques Doriot, who accused the Vichy government of proceeding too slowly in constructing a fascist France. Finally, in 1944, when the deportation and murder of Jews was in full swing, he reprinted a part of the *Bagatelles* which held that pogroms were fully justified; "they are a blessing of heaven." The Nazis realized his worth, and together with some others appointed him as expert on the Jewish question to the army of occupation.[14]

Céline was not merely a collaborator with the occupying power, he was genuinely involved in using the occupation in order to bring about an end to that degeneracy which before the Nazi triumph he had thought to be inevitable. The Jews were his foil: a near-paranoiac, he believed in the Jewish world conspiracy against the Gentiles. Céline heaped praise upon the *Protocols of the Elders of Zion*, and in the *Bagatelles pour un Massacre* left little doubt that he accepted the genuineness of this clumsy forgery. In his hands (to use Norman Cohn's phrase) the *Protocols* became a warrant for genocide, not merely by means of the printed word but also by attempted political action. Intellectuals like Ezra Pound or Gottfried Benn also turned to the Jew as contrasted with the Aryan in order to work off their own paranoid tendencies. Many an intellectual found his way to fascism because it seemed to provide a weapon against the conspiratorial menace of modernity. The fascists did not merely make use of Céline's theories; he himself joined the cause, though his proposed anti-Semitic and racist party never materialized. Toward the end of the war, and afterward, he again withdrew into his earlier pessimism and fatalism about the future of France. Céline's politics, his attitudes, grew out of despair with decadent reality. This despair, the opposition to bourgeois hypocrisy, and the search for sincerity, were all common to intellectuals who came to fascism and to many anti-fascist intellectuals as well. André Gide, no fascist or anti-Semite, praised the *Bagatelles pour un Massacre* for its bluntness and rejection of polite formulations.[15] Gide failed to see that Céline's work would lead him directly into fascist political action.

The German poet Gottfried Benn, like Céline a physician by trade, found ultimate fulfillment in his commitment to National Socialism. His earlier works were filled with imagery of a disease-ridden and decadent civilization—much like Céline's, whom, by the way, he regarded highly. Benn's personal and artistic development traversed many stages and both Futurism and Expressionism played their part. What seems to have remained constant, at least until 1933, was a theoretical nihilism which denied the possibility of metaphysical truth. At times Benn sang Dionysian hymns to the cult of the ego (Nietzsche exercised a considerable influence on his thought), while directly after the First World War he defended the Berlin Dadaists when they were accused of bringing contempt upon the armed forces and distributing indecent publications.[16] Surely not an auspicious beginning for a future follower of National Socialism. But his attitudes had changed by the time of the National Socialist seizure of power, and in a famous speech on "The New State and the Intellectuals" (1933) he praised history as the absolute value which had put forth a new biological type in order to do battle against the decadent age. Man's inner struggles were waged not to maintain the consciousness of the ego (as he had held in 1920) but on behalf of an absolute: the Aryan had been sent by history to play a messianic role.[17] National Socialism produced "a new world of the soul, deeply exciting in determining the expression of man's inner self."[18]

Benn's evolution toward National Socialism explains one element in fascism's attraction for some intellectuals. It involved not only the longing for the genuine (Benn was seeking the great barbarians of the twentieth century) and the desire to eliminate decadence, but also the restfulness which the movement promised to a troubled soul. The intellectuals who fell prey to the appeal of fascism were not content to remain on the fringes of society or politics, to be united with those "rootless intellectuals" who had made and were making the greatest contributions to European thought. They abhorred rootlessness, and the fascist emphasis on the rootedness of the creative individual in the national soul made a strong appeal to them. National Socialism provided Benn both with excitement and with a firm intellectual *point d'appui* which he had hitherto lacked. "There are moments when this whole tortured life sinks into nothingness, when only the horizon seems to exist, its infinity, the seasons, the earth, in simple words—

Volk."[19] The very discipline of a firm, simple, and organic ideology fulfilled a need not only for Gottfried Benn but also for a poet like Ezra Pound who had not passed through Expressionism. Yet there may well be some truth in Ladislao Mittner's contention that the feeling of impotence in Expressionism led to dreams of violence, to a tyrant conceived in the imagination.[20] Certainly a good many intellectuals who had been Expressionists followed National Socialism in Germany and Benn only provides the most famous example.

The desire for discipline was always combined with a vision of creativity as springing from man's irrational nature. The cultural elitism which Camillo Pellizzi saw in the *"gruppi di competenza"* shared such ideas; while Céline put the emphasis on man's "soul" and Benn heaped scorn on a "rationally thought-out culture."[21] Aesthetic principles replaced devotion to conventional morality. Such attitudes led to a love for the extreme, the direct, and the primitive; degenerate and corrupt society had to be transcended. But, in the end, these writers and poets called a halt to their adventure; they, like most men, longed for an authority to which they could relate themselves and they found it not only in an emphasis upon strictness of literary form but also in the arms of fascism.

The Marxist road was barred, and the simple fascist explanation for the supposed decadence of the age had its appeal. Capitalism was symbolic of the rationalization of life, and these intellectuals wanted to opt out. Drieu La Rochelle, perhaps the most interesting French fascist, believed that art had become scientific because it could no longer be artistic in a decadent world.[22] Like their predecessors in the nineteenth century, and many anti-fascist intellectuals, these men sought for the genuine beneath the surface rationalizing of life. They found this genuine element within their own souls and in a closeness to nature—once more, hardly new discoveries. Walter Benjamin has given a good characterization of the attitudes toward which they were brought by their analysis of present society. These men attempted to solve the dichotomy between "genuine" nature and modern technology in immediate and mystical ways. They were not content to take the more circuitous route of attempting to fashion better human institutions.[23] Intellectuals were led by their hatred of society and its institutions to a retreat into the supposed inner life of the spirit. Fascism as a political movement could benefit from this mystical and therefore ill-defined approach by making the appropriate compromises with existing institutions on its way to power. The intellectuals, however, built this contempt into a system of absolute values which transcended reality.

The search for the "genuine" was not supposed to be a return to romanticism, however. The decadence of the age, wrote La Rochelle (1939), means that sentimentality has taken the place of the creative drive.[24] John Harrison was undoubtedly right in asserting that the literary men of the English world who sympathized with fascism wanted more austere, more direct forms, and a hard intellectual approach. Yeats, Pound, Wyndham Lewis, and T. S. Eliot all opposed romanticism in the name of the classical tradition.[25] Like Charles Maurras before them, they plucked out the identity of beauty and order from the ancient heritage: a reassurance that culture would not be debased through democracy. Order meant authoritarian rule, and this would correspond in the political world to the strictness of form which they desired in literary style; for example Gottfried Benn, in 1934, praised strictness of form in contrast to pristine and unformed nature. An absolutism was needed which would exclude all chaos in art and lead to unwavering moral decisions. These decisions had to be in favor of harshness, struggle, and leadership, opposed to compromises and prevarication in art as well as in politics. A dictatorial leadership was required to give shape to the amorphous mass of democracy symbolic of decadent society—"sensitivity without direction," as Ezra Pound characterized that form of government and society.[26] Drieu La Rochelle, in his novel *Gilles* (1939), described a democratic French politician as a man who showed as much indulgence toward you as you did toward him; who reassured rather than led. The typical bourgeois politician believed in liberty and justice in the same way that a merchant treasured his rents and property.[27]

The longing for a *point d'appui*, for form and direction, led such men into advocating dictatorship. The French fascist Lucien Rébatet put the case with admirable succinctness: "We have suffered a deep disquiet ever since the [French] Revolution, for we no longer know a leader [*chef*]...I aspire to a dictatorship, a strict and aristocratic regime."[28] Gottfried Benn could have written this passage, and so could Ezra Pound. Elitist ideas came into play here, were in fact basic to an understanding of the fascist intellectuals. Fascism had little of the proletarian vocabulary of Marxism, and many fascist leaders openly stressed the elitist nature of the movement. Their self-conscious concept of intellectuals as guardians of ultimate values made such writers and artists inherently sympathetic to such ideas. Moreover, their concept of culture and form was already elitist in nature: they were the most creative individuals and they knew the prized ancient traditions. Elitism combined in their ideology with the call for strong leadership.

True leadership must be committed to the unflinching implementation of spiritual values. Whether it be the classical values (defined by Wyndham Lewis in his fascist period as simple, rational, and aloof)[29] or the living cosmos of a pre-civilized age (as seen by D. H. Lawrence, at times sympathetic to fascism), the leadership of a chosen few was essential to lead mankind into the golden age. The longing for authority of intellectuals in modern society is a common enough phenomenon. In fascism, as they analyzed the movement, this authority would be based on the ultimate values to which they were committed and which, indeed, they were already advocating through the written and spoken word.

The open-endedness of much of European fascism, its ideological fluidity under authoritarian leadership strengthened its attraction. German National Socialism was an exception here, for it was built on a more clearly defined ideological base. German idealism and volkish thought had long histories behind them, and many German intellectuals must have found this ideological orientation familiar, even traditional.[30] However, the specific German tradition (in which Austria must be included) gave to this fascism a provincial cast which contrasts with fascism in Italy. In the West, at any rate, the fascist movements, and the intellectuals who were involved, looked to Italy rather than to Central Europe for inspiration. It is therefore dangerous to extend the ideological foundations of the German fascist experience to other countries.

Typical of the difference between fascism in Central and in Western Europe is the assertion of the leading German National Socialist philosopher, Alfred Bäumler, that with the Nazi seizure of power the period of Hegelian striving was at end. Hitler had transformed Hegel's "idea" into reality.[31] In Italy even Gentile, the philosophical idealist, called for a continual progression of the "new spirit" (meaning fascism), which should not be allowed to harden into a credo or a system of dogma.[32] Camillo Pelizzi argued that "the fascist state is more than a state, a dynamo" (1924).[33] French fascist intellectuals were apt to reject Hegelianism itself as blurring and reconciling differences in a bourgeois fashion, opting instead for a simple Nietzschean dynamic. Yet, even among the French fascist intellectuals, we find the longing for a *point d'appui*, though it is muted in comparison with other European fascisms. For example, the young fascist Robert Brasillach in his *Le Marchand d'oiseaux* (1931) praises the binding force of nature and the peasant as contrasted with the vagabonds in the city.

This difference between Western and Central European fascism is important in our context, for it explains how some intellectuals could seek in the movement a repudiation of Germanic romanticism and sentimentality and infuse it with a diversity of spiritual values, instead of seeing in fascism a singleminded concentration on the ideals of blood and soil. As far as some of them were concerned, race played a lesser part in producing the leadership than did a vision of Plato's philosopher king. We must not forget that racism and anti-Semitism until the late 1930s played a minor role in taming the "dynamo" of West European fascism.

Yet there existed an incipient conflict between the intellectuals' longing for authority and their equal love for the dynamic that would end the degeneration of their time. Drieu La Rochelle's fictional hero Gilles, not untypical for French fascism, finds mental peace in fighting on Franco's side in the Spanish Civil War. There Gilles discovers that gods fall and are reborn, a process which can only take place through the shedding of blood.[34] For many intellectuals, fascism released an ever-present urge for action that could now find full play. This often became a commitment to brutality in the name of the spiritual values that must be realized. Gentile justified the brutality of teachers toward students: it would force students to affirm their own personalities.[35] Gentile associated the necessity for brutality with the quest for spiritual unity, which was all that really mattered.

These intellectuals found joy in immediate action rather than in long-range planning, in immediate decisions rather than in judgments *sub specie aeternitatis*. Because Charles Maurras refused to act during the fascist and war veteran-inspired Paris riots of February 1934, many French fascist intellectuals broke with the *Action Française*. This predeliction for the immediate could be documented in other nations as well. Such a desire formed an obvious contrast to the politics of compromise which characterized decadent democratic society. Julien Benda, understanding this tendency among the intellectuals of his time, characterized as "treasonable" the attempt to confer moral sanction on physical force.[36] This represents, of course, a treason not confined to fascist intellectuals; but the moral power which they lent to the activist struggle was regarded not merely as an unfortunate necessity but as an integral part of the system of absolute values. Such activist ideals could also serve to deepen the allegiance to authoritarianism, for leadership was necessary to win the battle.

However, the yearning for leadership must always be connected with the quest for the genuine of which we have already spoken. The Greek ideal of an ordered society was specified, side by side with a new paganism. The influence of Nietzsche received full play, for he had already praised the Greeks and the barbarians as the prototypes of the superman. This primitivism was rendered still more appealing through the experience of war, which had led a whole generation of

European writers into ecstatic praise of naked brutality and the shedding of blood. Here indeed, in their view, was a Nietzschean reflection of life as it truly existed, and not as the bourgeoisie thought it to be. Writers such as Ernst Jünger transposed the warrior to peacetime society: a new type had emerged who, as the "worker," would make a *révolution sans phrase*, and for whom freedom and obedience were identical concepts.[37]

The preoccupation of the fascist movement with the war attracted intellectuals who had found the "genuine" life experience in that catastrophe. Oswald Spengler's vision of the barbarians roaming the countryside is symptomatic as the expression both of an age which was finished and of the seeds of a new culture to come. For Drieu La Rochelle, the modern was characterized by barbaric simplicity and brutality, while Gottfried Benn was attracted to all that was primitive and archaic—only a return of this kind could produce the necessary will to power.[38] Robert Brasillach, writing about Alfred Rosenberg in Germany and his own French fascists, eulogized the "teachers of violence in France and the teacher of violence in Germany": both shared the wish to destroy a society built on bad ideas, and a respect for the heroes to come.[39]

The longing for primitivism dissolved into hero worship. This truly resolved the conflict between the love of activism and violence, on the one hand, and the longing for security and authority on the other. The nineteenth-century tradition of heroes and hero worship gave a respectable intellectual background to such a longing. The hero symbolized the "new type" of man who would change the world. As Gottfried Benn put it: "History sent a new biological type to the front."[40] The "new man" whom fascism put into the foreground of its efforts was infused with a Nietzschean will. Jünger conceived this type as a group, a leadership elite; in fact, a new "people." But others saw him as an individual symbolic of what other individuals could become. The hero, in this case, resolved not only the conflict between violence and authority but also the dichotomy between individualism and leadership. For creative intellectuals this was important.

Fascism, unlike socialist orthodoxy, did not exclude the cult of the individual, provided that the individual could be seen as the executor of some organic national force. The "new man" whom fascism wished to create symbolized the new society. He had released within himself the creative forces of his own soul and through strength of will would usher in a new world. Intellectuals had a special mission in transforming the old into the new man, for education played a vital part in this process and education was a traditional field of activity for intellectuals.

In all this, it is important to keep the chronological factor in mind. The intellectuals were attracted to a fascism which seemed open-ended and whose ideology, within its organic framework, gave it a "superb openness to artistic creativity." The "anti-idealist" congress of young fascist intellectuals in Italy (1933) was typical of this feeling. They opposed the Hegelian idealism of Gentile in favor of Niet-zschean ideas. These young Italians were at one with equally young French fascists in their belief that Hegelian idealism blunted the necessary dynamic and eventually led to a pedestrian, economic view of the state, from which "it is absolutely impossible to aim at fascism."[41] This heroic dynamic, as they saw it, seemed present in Italian fascism until the early 1930s and in Germany until 1934. Then Hitler outlawed Expressionism and began to suppress all forms of creativity which did not conform to the tradition of volkish art and literature. Even so, some intellectuals who had joined the Nazi movement, as well as members of the SS—dedicated to a "silent revolution in permanence"—opposed the fossilization of dogma and specific programs.

They dreamed instead of a real revolution, a true uprising of the German people, which would lead to fundamental change within the nation. Typically, such a commitment to revolution was used by an Expressionist writer like Arnolt Bronnen to justify his conversion to National Socialism. He greatly admired a faction of the S.A. (the Sturmabteilungen, a para-military Nazi organization) for wanting a revolution, though this longing was little more than a desire to release a pent-up dynamic. Bronnen lost his innocence soon after Hitler attained power. His reaction to this disillusionment was typical of that of many other intellectuals who had joined the Nazis for similar reasons: half-hearted gestures, pathetic in their futility against the "revolution betrayed."[42] The attitude of men like Bronnen toward Hitler remained ambivalent throughout the Third Reich. The hero of earlier days was not easily deposed in their confused minds. In Germany, unlike Italy, there was no real protest against the movement in power in favor of the "true movement" as it had existed earlier.

National Socialism, as we have seen, never emphasized the thrust toward revolution which Italian fascism inscribed on its banners after the First World War. Mussolini himself may not have taken this radical vocabulary seriously, but the dynamic "open-endedness" which many earlier fascists had prized was more deeply embedded in the Italian than in the German movement. In Italy the protest of young intellectuals in the name of a fascist dynamic against a fascism grown old in power can be seen in at least two youth journals.[43] Marinetti, the Futurist, did not turn on Mussolini but instead in 1937 denounced Hitler for having condemned Futurism, Impressionism, Dadaism, and Cubism in favor of a "photographic static"[44]—an unimaginative realism which sanctified the status quo. However, for both the great fascist powers the dynamo which Camillo Pellizzi had praised had come to a standstill by the end of the 1930s.

This did not occur in the fascisms that remained out of power. Especially in France, where the splintered movement was largely in the hands of a Paris coterie of intellectuals, the problem of the fossilization of dogma never arose at all. Small wonder that these Frenchmen misread National Socialism and were disappointed when the German movement refused to carry through their kind of pseudo-Nietzschean revolution. Marc Augier was one of the founders of the fascist-collaborationist journal *La Gerbe*. He joined the SS and felt that the Germans had reached the ultimate stage of Nietzschean thought and were standing on the threshold of a new and grandiose world. But Augier left the SS. Hitler turned out to be too exclusively

German for this French fascist and did not have the vision to lead an anti-capitalist crusade to free the masses.[45] The "teacher of violence in Germany" could not, as Brasillach had thought, stand on an equal footing with the "teachers of violence in France." The eternal truth that National Socialism was supposed to exemplify was rooted in an unchanging history and race, which tamed the appetite for destruction and served to stifle any open-ended dynamic.

Professor Hans Naumann in Germany spoke of making sacred once again the eternal "holy bonds" which had cemented human relationships of old: the shared native countryside, the family, and the common ties of blood.[46] Mussolini at times equated reason of state, the traditional and unchanging needs of power politics, with the idealism of the fascists.[47] All this was far removed from the barbarians roaming the countryside, or the "new man" some fascists wished to create who, at least in Germany, could degenerate into that sentimental nationalism which most of these intellectuals condemned. The restfulness of a coherent ideology for which men like Benn longed had become separated from the excitement these intellectuals craved.

More seriously, the intellectuals' ideal of culture came into conflict with the fascist concept of hierarchy, which they misunderstood, and with the needs of fascism as a mass movement. Fascism believed in a hierarchy of function and not of status: potentially all members of the nation were equal. The elite stood out because of its service to the nation, not because of any intellectual superiority. The masses were not the enemies of culture, for they could be lifted into the category of "new men" (although privately fascist leaders like Mussolini expressed cynicism about the masses). To be sure, intellectuals could become part of the functional elite as educators, but even then they were still faced with the needs of fascism as a mass movement.

This meant that the cultural ideals for which these intellectuals stood were compromised by reality: the bourgeois life which they despised was in fact integrated into the fascist mystique. All these intellectuals might have agreed with Thomas Arnold's judgment on middle-class culture: "Can life be imagined more hideous, more dismal, more unenviable?"[48] The mass meetings which for Brasillach had symbolized aesthetic politics continued, but the cultural thrust of the movement took on a decidedly bourgeois cast. Fascism was annexing the tradition of middle-class reading and art, emphasizing the sweetly sentimental and conservative as the true products of human creativity. Italy did so perhaps to a lesser extent than Central Europe, but even French fascism sometimes lapsed into the despised genre. As a political mass movement, fascism had to appeal to the prejudices and predelictions of its constituents, whatever ideals the intellectuals attempted to put into the movement. Here they were caught: on the one hand, they wanted the security and thrill of participating in a mass movement; on the other, such a mass movement tended to compromise with the cultural ideals of people deeply bound by bourgeois tastes and morals.

Fascism in Western and Central Europe made middle-class morality the base of one of its appeals. The traditionalism which became part of fascist ideology praised precisely that sentimentality which many fascist intellectuals had condemned as bourgeois degeneracy. This development is most obvious in National Socialism's rejection of cultural experimentation. National Socialism felt that it could rely on popular taste in its battle against modernity in art and literature. Hitler wanted to substitute "eternal art" for modern art, and this meant that art must not create anything new but must instead reflect the general life of the people, which sought artistic expression. The people came first, so art must reflect their soul and thus appeal to them. When Goebbels abolished art criticism and substituted mere art reporting, he did so because the public had to be given a chance to make its own judgments, to form an opinion about artistic matters through its own feeling.[49]

The result was culture defined in terms of the popular taste of the non-intellectual classes. Sentimentality triumphed over strictness of literary form and romanticism over the classical tradition. The intellectuals found themselves part of an organic world view which had tamed their activism and which defined the genuine in terms of popular artistic tastes. Some, like Ernst Jünger, turned their backs on the movement, but most maintained their allegiance to fascism, though it had lost its élan.

In fact, fascism now repudiated the intellectuals, as the socialist movement had repudiated them earlier. For the fascists, artistic creativity was now defined as merely a reflection of reality, and the results of fascist artistic endeavor moved closer to socialist realism. Hitler's emphasis on "clarity and simplicity" had not meant a preference for strictness of form but rather a belief in an art and literature simple enough to call for the support of the populace. This tendency had always existed in fascism, but the intellectuals had chosen to ignore it, believing that it would vanish in the mystique of a national spiritual unity. But that very mystique led to a renewal of the old bourgeois culture. This fact became obvious only as fascism developed into the 1930s. Fascist professions of faith before this time might easily have led to a misunderstanding. It has, in fact, been claimed that in Italy the repudiation of the intellectuals was a conscious move of the Fascist Party to consolidate its power.[50] The peasant who provided fascism's heroic prototype proved to be not the Nietzschean Prometheus but a comfortable bourgeois.

In analyzing the relationship between fascism and the intellectuals, it is important to see the ideological commitment of the intellectuals within the diversity of fascism as it developed. The basic ideological presuppositions of the movement existed from the beginning in most fascisms, but they changed in emphasis and direction. Those fascist movements which came to power had to show political flexibility and find a solid base of support in one part of the population. Fascist intellectuals ignored the pressures of existing reality on fascism, thinking that the fascist revolution would break sharply with the corrupt present but remain uncontaminated by its imperatives. But fascism's own mystique was merely a profession of faith and, as it turned out, gave the movement flexibility in making alliances within an existing reality which the intellectuals deplored. Fascists came to believe that theirs was a spiritual revolution, which through a new type of man would renew the nation and the world; in reality, this revolution became enmeshed in the very middle-class values it was supposed to fight. The acceptance of the century-old tradition of popular taste— conservative and opposed to all art and literature which it could not understand—spelled an end to meaningful participation by the intellectuals in the movement.

The attempt to ignore realities in favor of some higher value which brooks no compromise is not confined to fascist intellectuals. The neo-Kantian socialists suffered from the same failing; their idealism had put an end to a meaningful participation in or alliance with the existing socialist parties. Drieu La Rochelle's hero had called for unity between young communists freed from Russian influence and young bourgeois freed from the trammels of liberalism. A "Third Force" would be created: a victorious fascism.[51] Instead, fascism became a mass political party, which stifled creativity in the name of its truth and showed a willingness to assimilate the values of the bourgeois age which those advocating a "Third Force" could not readily accept. Drieu La Rochelle himself found it difficult to join such a political party. At first (in 1936) he played an important role in the fascist party of Jacques Doriot (PPF), only to leave it again two years later and rejoin it once more after the fall of France. The suicide of Drieu La Rochelle at the end of the Second World War was not merely the result of despair in the face of the Allied victory, but to a still greater extent despair at what fascism had made of itself.

SIX

The Occult Origins of
National Socialism

THE INTELLECTUAL ORIGINS of National Socialism
are no longer shrouded in darkness. The intensity of
German national feeling itself seems no longer sufficient
as a sole explanation for the rise of National Socialist ideology; a
more complex cultural development gave its impress to that movement long before it crystallized into a political party. Ideas that were
both of a national and of a romantic and occult nature were important components of this development, part of the revolt against positivism which swept Europe at the end of the nineteenth century. In
Germany this revolt took a special turn, perhaps because romanticism struck deeper roots there than elsewhere. The mystical and the
occult were taken both as an explanation and as a solution to man's
alienation from modern society, culture, and politics. Not by everyone, of course, but by a minority that found a home in the radical
right. As such, mystical and occult ideas influenced the world view of
early National Socialism, and especially of Adolf Hitler, who to the
end of his life believed in "secret sciences" and occult forces. It is
important to unravel this strand of Nazi ideology because this mysticism was at the core of much of the irrationalism of the movement,
and especially of the world view of its leader. Such ideas coursed

underneath the banality and respectability of National Socialism, though they themselves were also a reaction to bourgeois society. Protest against bourgeois society and its lifestyle was widespread, but here our concern is with a specific protest against bourgeois materialism and positivism by men and women who lived on the fringes of middle-class society; eccentrics who merit our attention only because Adolf Hitler and a few other important Nazis took them seriously. This German reaction to positivism became intimately bound up with a belief in nature's cosmic life force, a dark force whose mysteries could be understood, not through science but through the occult. An ideology based upon such premises was fused with the glories of an Aryan past, and in turn, that past received a thoroughly romantic and mystical interpretation.

This chapter intends to throw light on this ideology and to show its connection with later German history.[1] An obvious link can be seen through some of the men who participated in this stream of thought, men who later became prominent in the National Socialist movement. However, we are primarily concerned with the actual formation of this ideology from the 1890s to the first decade of the twentieth century. This is necessary because historians have until the last decades ignored this stream of thought based solely on intuition as being too outré to be taken seriously. Who indeed can take seriously an ideology that drew upon the occultism of Madame Blavatsky, rejected science in favor of "seeing with one's soul," and came dangerously close to sun worship?

The early formulators of this romantic and mystic world view were men like Paul de Lagarde (1827-1891), Guido von List (1848-1919), Alfred Schuler (1865-1923), and above all, Julius Langbehn (1851-1907).[2] They were popularized by publishers like Eugen Diederichs of Jena, whose influence was manifest in the diverse branches of the movement. It was Langbehn who pithily summarized their common aim: "to transform Germans into artists."[3] By "artist" these men meant not a certain profession but a certain world view opposed to that which they called the "man machine." This transformation, which they felt had been omitted when Germany became unified, would convert the materialism and science of contemporary Germany into an artistic outlook upon the world, an outlook that would result in an all-encompassing national renewal. Such a viewpoint was connected to their belief in the cosmic life force, which opposed all that was artificial and man-made.

Langbehn in his *Rembrandt als Erzieher* (*Rembrandt as Educator,* 1890) supplied the key to this transformation: mysticism was the hidden engine which could transmute science into art.[4] Nature romanticism and the mystical provided the foundation for this ideology. It was no mere coincidence that Eugen Diederichs, who was so instrumental in popularizing this world view, was the German publisher of Henri Bergson. He saw in Bergson a mysticism, a "new irrationalistic philosophy,"[5] and believed that the development of Germany could only progress in opposition to rationalism. The world picture, Diederichs maintained, must be grasped by an intuition that was close to nature. From this source man's spirit must flow and bring him into unity with the community of his people. Such true spirituality Diederichs saw reflected in the late thirteenth- to early fourteenth-century German mystic Meister Eckhardt whose works he published; later Alfred Rosenberg, the Nazi ideologue, returned to Meister Eckhardt for the same reasons. Just as the romantics at the beginning of the nineteenth century had opposed the "cold rationality" of antiquity and had found their way back to a more genuine humanity, so Diederichs hailed this movement as a "new romanticism."[6] Thus, a search for this "genuine humanity" dominated the movement, based upon a closeness to nature, for the native landscape which gave man a heightened feeling for life. When Diederichs organized the gathering of the Free German Youth on the Hohen Meissner mountain in 1913, Ludwig Klages, the Munich philosopher, told them that modern civilization was "drowning" the soul of man. The only way out for man, who belonged to nature, was a return to mother earth.[7] Such ideas led naturally to a deepening of the cult of the peasant. Julius Langbehn summed this up: "The peasant who actually owns a piece of land has a direct relationship to the center of the earth. Through this he becomes master of the universe."[8]

In opposition to peasant life there was the city, the seat of cold rationalism. Indeed, this was nothing new or unique; Jacob Burckhardt had already written that in cities art became "nervous and unstable."[9] Throughout the nineteenth century men had advocated a retreat into the unspoiled landscape, away from a society rapidly becoming industrialized and urbanized. But for the "new romanticism" nature did not signify the sole source of human renewal and vitality. Mysticism played a central role in this movement, connected with the concern for man's soul as an embodiment of the cosmic life-force.

Julius Langbehn cited Schiller's phrase that "it is the soul which builds the body," and added that the outward form of the body was a silhouette of its inner life.[10] The portrait painter Burger-Villingen enlarged upon this when he criticized the phrenology of Francis Gall. Gall's measurements of the skull led to serious errors, he claimed, because they comprised only the external influences of man. The important thing was to grasp the nature of man's fate, which was dependent upon his soul.[11] Thus Burger-Villingen measured the profiles of men's faces in order to comprehend the expression of their souls. For this purpose he invented a special apparatus (a plastometer), which was much discussed in the subsequent literature. Julius Langbehn wrote that researches into man's facial characteristics were a part of historical research.[12]

This remark leads into the philosophy of history of these men, which provided the explanation for the mystic development of the soul from its base in nature, through the cosmic life-force. History, Diederichs wrote, is never factual but merely a thickening of the life stream of events through which, at one point or place, the universally valid laws of life become visible in reality. History could only be seen with the soul since it was the progression out of nature of the inner life substance. It was at this point that the mystic and the occult came to the fore. This belief in a life force was a kind of cosmic religion to a man like Diederichs, who referred to Plato as one of his sources.[13] Yet, in opposition to rationalism, this religion was grasped through the intuition of the soul feeling its closeness to nature.

Ernest Dacqué, whose book on *Urwelt* (the primeval world) was used extensively by all these men, coined the phrase "nature somnambulism"—an intuitive insight into those life forces that determine the physical nature of man. As man got ever farther away from nature, what remained of this somnambulism was wrongly described as soothsaying or as psychological disabilities. Yet all things creative were a survival of this nature somnambulism.[14] Paul de Lagarde put the same idea somewhat differently. Germans, though reaching into the future, should return to the past—a past devoid of all else but the primeval voice of nature.[15] Manifestly, only those people who were closest to nature could grasp through their souls the inner, cosmic life force that constituted the eternal.

In Vienna, Guido von List set the tone for this kind of argument and fused it with the glories of an Aryan past. Nature was the great divine guide and from her flowed the life force. Whatever was closest to nature would therefore be closest to the truth.[16] List believed that the Aryan past was the most "genuine" manifestation of this inner force. It was closest to nature and therefore farthest removed from artificiality—from modern materialism and rationalism. Thus he set himself the task of recreating this past. Given the philosophy of history common to these men, they looked down upon any scholarly disciplines such as archaeology: "We must read with our souls the landscape which archaeology reconquers with the spade." Again, List advised: "If you want to lift the veil of mystery [i.e., of the past], you must fly into the loneliness of nature."[17] List's ideas were brought to Germany largely through the efforts of Alfred Schuler of Munich. This remarkable man, who never published a line, attracted to his person men like Rilke and George. His circle of admirers maintained that Schuler "saw with his soul" and could reconstruct the past by simply using his inward eye. To a small coterie of friends, Schuler lectured on the nature of the city. Urbanism was condemned and equated with the intellectuals' alleged materialism, which supposedly perverted their thought. Against this equation were those adepts whose "idealism" could only stem from the mysterious call of the blood, the true creative instinct.[18]

For Schuler, the inner life-force was equated with the strength of the blood, an equation common to other writers as well. He fulminated against the shallowness of soulless men ignorant of nature and its life forces, an ignorance epitomized, he thought, in the Jewish poet Karl Wolfskehl blaspheming: "People are my landscape."[19] Significantly, Schuler believed this life-force could be manipulated through spiritualism. He tried to cure Nietzsche's madness through an ancient Roman spirit rite. Klages was to lure Stefan George to a séance where Schuler would take over George's soul, transmuting it into a living receptacle of cosmic fire. George, stubbornly obdurate, was appalled by the proceedings, and after the séance demanded that Klages accompany him to a café where settled bourgeois, ordinary people, drank beer and smoked cigars.[20] In Klages's eyes he was henceforth condemned, though any historian analyzing the thoughts of these men might easily sympathize with George.

Schuler and Klages were not alone in believing the inner life-force to be akin to spiritualism. Indeed, the mysticism which, as Langbehn put it, transformed science into art, was precisely this life-force defined in terms of the occult. The ideology of this movement had direct ties with those occult and spiritualist movements that were in vogue toward the end of the century. Such ties were especially fostered by theosophy. The opposition to positivism in Germany fed upon movements which in the rest of Europe were regarded as "fads" rather than as serious world views. In Germany the belief in the life-force or cosmic religion embodied in the blood, which all things Aryan truly represented, led to a world view that gave special status to those who were "initiates" of such mysteries.

The similarity of these ideas to the occult was noted by contemporaries. Franz Hartmann, himself a leading German-American theosophist, remarked upon the similarity of List's ideas to those of Madame Blavatsky, the foundress of theosophy. This he did by comparing List's *Bilderschrift* to Madame Blavatsky's *Isis Unveiled*. For just as List attempted to tear the veil from the true wisdom of the ancient Germans, so Blavatsky revealed the surviving traces of a "secret science" in ancient and medieval sources. Their principles, she maintained, had been lost from view and suppressed; in like manner, List claimed that Christianity had tried to wipe out the language of the ancient Germans, thus destroying their true nature wisdom.[21] List believed that this lost language could be found in the mystic writings of the Kabalah, mistakenly thought to be Jewish, but in reality a compilation of ancient German wisdom that had survived persecution. Madame Blavatsky made identical use of the Kabalah; she, too, rejected its Jewish origins, considering it a survival of true and secret wisdom.[22] Hartmann himself, attracted by such parallelisms, became one of List's leading supporters.

But we can go further than this. Madame Blavatsky's *Isis Unveiled* was concerned with a study of nature. She attempted to study nature as she thought the ancients had studied it, in relation not so much to its outward form but to its inward meaning. Thus she also saw nature as being eternally transmitted through a life-force which she thought of as an omnipresent vital ether, electro-spiritual in composition.[23] This vague idea directly influenced men of the 1920s like Herbert Reichstein, who believed that the first Aryan was created by an electric shock directly out of this ether. They called their theory "theozoology."[24] Her approach was, in general, similar to those exponents of the life-force we have discussed; she, too, felt that seeing with one's soul was the reality, and deplored scientific methods.

There is, however, a still closer relationship of these two bodies of thought through their use of imagery. For Madame Blavatsky, fire was the universal soul substance, and this led Franz Hartmann to state that it was the sun which was the external manifestation of an invisible spiritual power.[25] For the men we have discussed, the image of the Aryan coming out of the sun was common. The painter Fidus, so closely associated with the German Youth Movement, used this motif constantly. This popular painter believed that it was not enough for the artist to faithfully reproduce nature. Painting, for Fidus, was a transmission from the extrasensory world.[26] His paintings included studies of astral symbolism, as well as designs for theosophic temples. It was he who painted the official picture to symbolize the Hohen Meissner gathering. Best known, however, were his paintings, bordered by theosophic symbols, on themes such as the "wanderers into the sun"—girl and boy wandering hand in hand, surrounded by growing plants, their nude boyish bodies translucent before a blazing sun.

Eugen Diederichs was also deeply concerned with such symbolism. He founded, in 1910, the so-called Sera circle in Jena. Its symbol was a red and golden flag with the sun as centerpiece. The main activities of this circle centered in the youth movement: excursions, folk dances, and above all, the old Germanic festival of the "changing sun."[27] Here Germanic custom and spiritualist symbolism were intertwined. For Diederichs also the sun was the creator of life, a reaffirmation of the prime importance of those cosmic forces that underlay all reality.[28]

Langbehn himself maintained that "a theologian should always be somewhat of a theosophist" to compensate for the formalism inherent in his profession. He saw a similar value in spiritualism in general. His criticism of contemporary occultism was not that it was wrong, but that it was misdirected, searching through professional mediums for spirits where there were none.[29] Such a linkage between theosophy and the volkish world view will remain throughout the movement's history. This can be conclusively demonstrated through *Prana*, which called itself a German monthly for applied spiritualism and which was published by the theosophical publishing house at Leipzig. The editor was Johannes Balzli, the secretary of the Guido von List Society, founded to spread the "master's" teaching and to finance his publications. Franz Hartmann, himself an honorary member of that society, was one of *Prana*'s most frequent contributors, as was C. W. Leadbetter, the stormy Anglican curate whom Madame Blavatsky had taken with her to India and who later became Annie Besant's Svengali. Guido von List himself contributed to its pages, while Fidus provided most of the illustrations. The word "Prana" was taken to mean the power of the sun, the visible symbol of God, and "all present." This in turn was to be the sign of the "new Germany."[30]

In *Prana's* pages we find ideas on food and medicine that were common to this movement. Medical science was universally deplored in favor of spiritual healing, and the eating of meat was said to impede not only spiritual progress but the understanding of nature and the life force.[31] Theosophists linked the flesh of animals to their undeveloped intelligence; eating meat would thus induce animal coarseness in humans. *Prana's* writers further elaborated this idea, adding that meat could not increase life for it was lifeless and thus led to death.[32] The medical and vegetarian vagaries of Adolf Hitler were intimately linked with the mystic, Aryan ideology found in the pages of *Prana*, though *Prana* was not the only journal that reflected this mixture of thought.

That such ideas marched into the 1920s with renewed vigor can be seen in the case of Arthur Dinter, who rose to prominence as an early National Socialist in the twenties. As a National Socialist deputy he played a leading role in the overthrow of the socialist government of Thuringia in 1924 and subsequently became the editor of the *National Socialist*, published in Weimar. His celebrated racial novel *Die Sunde wider das Blut* (*The Sin Against the Blood*, 1918) attained a large circulation. Though a companion novel, *Die Sünde wider den Geist* (*The Sin Against the Spirit*, 1921), never proved as popular, it combined the racial ideology of his first book with episodes that could have been taken directly from Madame Blavatsky. For Dinter, the racial ideas of a man like Houston Stewart Chamberlain made sense only when they were integrated with his own spiritualistic experiences. Dinter made liberal use of such theosophist concepts as the astral ether, the sun, and the idea of rebirth (Karma).[33] For Lanz von Liebenfels, another of *Prana's* favorites, the term "Ariosophy" meant a combination of such ideas with a world view centered upon the Germanic past.[34] Small wonder that the industrialist who was the principal financial contributor to Guido von List's Society was also an ardent spiritualist.[35]

This, then, was the mysticism that transformed science into art. When these men called upon Germans to be artists, they wanted them to recognize that their true soul was an expression of the cosmic spirit of the world based upon nature. Possession of such a spirit meant recalling that which was truly genuine, the Germanic past, as opposed to modern and evil rationalism. Langbehn, so often cited by his successors, felt this to be the only true individualism in a world of mass man. This individualism would lead to the creation of an organic human being in contact with cosmic forces. These forces were conceived in spiritualist terms, though Langbehn's touchstone was not Madame Blavatsky but Swedenborg. To him this mystic was the ideal German type.[36] In a similar manner Diederichs came to see the identical image reflected in Meister Eckhardt.[37]

Such a philosophy of life did not need spiritualistic mediums in order to penetrate the "secret mysteries." Indeed, for List the past came alive in the very human shape of Tarnhari, who called himself the chief of the lost German tribe of the *Völsungen*. The tribal traditions, which he related from his fund of ancestral memories, confirmed List's own researches. Tarnhari promptly produced several works of his own in which he told "family stories going back to prehistoric times." The stone of wisdom had come alive. It is symptomatic that this impressed Ellegard Ellerbeck, later one of the ornaments of National Socialist literature. As he wrote to List, "reading yours and Tarnhari's works I realize again that Ar [Aryan] lives laughingly."[38]

One idea implied in all of this must be stressed. Only he who had ties with the genuine past could have a true soul, could be an organic and not a materialistic human being. Such ties were conceived of as being inherited. The genuine spirit of the ancestors was cumulative in their progeny. For Guido von List, as for his successors, only the Aryan could grasp the "mysteries" of life which governed the world.

These ideas allowed Langbehn to stress once more not only the virtue of a settled and ancient Germanic peasantry but of a hereditary monarchy as well. A hereditary monarch was not merely someone elevated from the masses like the president of a republic. In the government of the nation, such a monarch would be aided by the "natural aristocracy." This aristocracy did not derive solely from an inheritance of status; every German could be a part of it if he threw off rationalism and became again an "artist"—the organic man.[39] Such a man was Rembrandt, in Langbehn's opinion; writing his book *Rembrandt as Educator,* he hoped to influence Germans through a striking example. The end result was to be the creation of an organic state where there would be neither "bourgeois," nor "proletarians," nor "Junkers," but only "the people" linked together in a common creativity (now become possible), and united in a bond of brotherhood. Classes would not be abolished; as Langbehn put it: "Equality is death. A corporate society is life."[40]

In his first book, *Ritter, Tod und Teufel (The Knight, Death, and the Devil,* 1920), H. F. K. Günther, later to become a chief racial expert of the Third Reich, sketched such a social ideal. Human rights have today preempted the place of human duties. These duties, formerly expressed in the loyalty of the knightly gentleman to his king and generalized throughout society in the web of reciprocal loyalties between landlord and peasant, must once again become the cement of social organization. To Günther, "the community, the public good, demands that every profession fulfill the work which is its due."[41] Manifestly, such a social ideal, found in all these men, continued the impetus of romanticism. It was reminiscent of that Bavarian deputy who earlier in the nineteenth century believed that "Love" would cure the tensions between laborer and employer. In an immediate sense it was a part of the ideal of an organic society which reflected organic man. Langbehn was explicit in his insistence that true individualism could only be realized in such a social order. He considered liberal individualism a part of materialism, dissolving society into incompatible units rather than knitting it together.[42] Paul de Lagarde summarized this in one of those phrases that made him so popular: "That man is not free who can do as he likes, but he is free who does what he should do. Free is he who is able to follow his creative principle of life; free is that man who recognizes and makes effective the innate principles which God put within him." The prospectus of an elite boarding school run by the Nazi Party in order to train future leaders repeats this redefinition of individualism, word for word as stating the attitude towards the party and state with which its pupils must be indoctrinated.[43]

Such freedom led to an organic view of man and the state. Not only was liberalism mistaken, but socialism as well. Social democracy, Diederichs claimed, was mechanistic; a true people's state was viable only if it reorganized society in a more meaningful manner, according to the aristocratic principle, the only environment in which men could unfold their real inner selves.[44] Langbehn concluded that this corporate structure fulfilled the aristocratic principle and was also in tune with the Germanic past. Significantly, this ideal urged these men to advocate only one concrete social reform: each worker should be given his own plot of land.[45] Again, the reform's justification was not sought in terms of material welfare within the framework of the movement's general ideology—factory work removed man from the all-important contact with nature.

Yet these men desired the transformation of their ideology into deeds. It is of great significance that while Diederichs used the word "theosophy" in the first prospectus of his publishing house, he came to be critical of that movement—not because it was spiritualist, but because it was too purely speculative in nature. The feeling about infinity must lead to deeds, and to his important journal he gave the name *Die Tat* (*The Deed*).[46] Paul de Lagarde had already made it plain that while something was accomplished through the understanding of true ideology, it was even more important to transform such ideals into serious practical action.[47] It was an "idealism of deeds" such men desired, deeds which helped to create a nation resting upon this idealistic foundation. Through such a concept, ideas of force came to play an important role in this ideology. For Langbehn, art and war went hand in hand. Shakespeare's name meant, after all, shaking a spear, and this for him was proof of the connection between art and war. Moreover, in German, spear (*Speer*) and army (*Wehr*) are words that rhyme. Thus in the Germanic past, true individual development had gone hand in hand with war.[48]

The lineaments of this "idealism of deeds" clearly emerge in the poetry of Avenarius, the first author of Diederichs's publishing house. Happiness was not the goal of life. What was important for the poet was the strength and wealth of the soul, and this strength depended upon the degree to which nature reflected itself within it. This whole feeling must be grounded in honesty and rootedness. But such ideals, in turn, must be sharpened through conflict with the nonbelieving world around them. Struggle becomes, therefore, a necessity. Avenarius as a poet gave due honor to the good fight honestly waged; poets must sympathize with the use of force. As one of the commentators of his poetry declared: "His is a true Germanic personality which is proud and straight, knows the bitter hate against all which is cowardly and fraudulent. Such ideas are a reminder not to let the soul degenerate through mildness."[49]

The "idealism of deeds" postulated the use of force to establish and defend a Germany based upon this romantic and mystic ideology. It was to be used not to destroy the existing social structure but to create and perpetuate the organic state. One employed force against the enemy—that materialistic and rationalistic culture which had undermined the weakened and retreating Aryan by divorcing him from nature's life force. The Jew, the creature of urbanism and materialism, typified this enemy within the gates. To Langbehn, Berlin and the Jew were the components of a conspiracy inimical to German revival, just as later a National Socialist writer exclaimed that volkish thought would triumph in the provinces, not in the cities. Berlin, above all, was the domain of the Jews.[50] Perhaps such considerations led to the anxious question in an issue of the National Socialist *Weltkampf* concerning Madame Blavatsky's Jewish origins, to which the comforting (and true) answer was given that she was of Baltic extraction.[51]

To their hatred of the Jews these men added an ambivalent attitude toward Christianity. Ludwig Klages continued a trend that derived from Guido von List, who had linked victorious Christianity to the virtual extinction of the ancient Germanic nature wisdom. He regarded it as his life's task to resurrect this wisdom. Klages believed that the course of a victorious Christianity was plotted from "a center" inimical to the Aryans.[52] Thus a universal Christian conspiracy against the truth was placed next to the universal Jewish conspiracy—a conspiracy documented by the Protocols of the Elders of Zion. With Lagarde and others, this developed into a Catholic-Jesuit conspiracy linked, so they asserted, to the Jewish world conspiracy itself.[53] Men like Diederichs and Langbehn were in a quandary, however, for they did not deem it wise to reject Christianity altogether. Protestantism as the German form of Christianity, in opposition to the Catholic conspiracy, was their solution to the problem. Their distrust of Christianity led them to reject Christ conceived as a historical figure; instead they tried to assimilate him to their concept of the life force.

This could be done, as did Schuler, by holding Christ to be merely the most important of the "initiates" into the Germanic wisdom. For List, all the great "initiates," Buddah, Osiris, and Moses, were Saxons.[54] More popular, however, was Houston Stewart Chamberlain's and Langbehn's idea of Christ as the Aryan prototype. Diederichs believed, as did Lagarde (and indeed, all of the men discussed), that St. Paul, the Jew, had made Christ into a Jewish figure, imprisoning him within the confines of theological thought. Instead, Christ was at one with the cosmic spirit, a spirit best understood not through scripture but through such mystics as Diederichs's favorite, Meister Eckhardt.[55] He spent much of his energy propagating this kind of Christianity. The chief adviser to his publishing house was

Alfred Drews, who in his *Die Christus-mythe* (*The Myth of Christ*, 1909), published by Diederichs, attacked the historicity of the Christ figure. Similarly, Munich's volkish publisher J. F. Lehmann spent his time furthering an identical evangelism, agitating against the theologians of the organized churches who were as inimical to the "idealism of deeds" as were the Jews themselves. Indeed, such a view of Christ rendered the Old Testament null and void; Arthur Dinter suggested that it be banned from the schools.[56]

Langbehn combined this view of Christ with the ideal of force. Germans, he wrote, should model themselves upon the medieval bishops who advanced, sword in hand, against their enemies. Such Christianity fitted into a German and mystical context, which symbolized a humanity that knew the necessity of force. "Humanity wants what is best, the fighter accomplishes what is best."[57]

Here also art and war must be combined. Yet this concept of Christianity rested on slight foundations. Diederichs, for one, realized this when he wrote that the very word Christ made him "nervous." He never tried to disguise the heathen quality of his Sera circle.[58] By fusing Christ with the life spirit of the Aryan, these men wanted to create a national religion. One of the attractions of Swedenborg for Langbehn was the fact that Swedenborg posited a separate heaven for each nation and thus recognized the importance of the national factor in religion.[59] Luther, however, was their real hero, for these men saw in him a truly national religious figure who rejected theology, so they thought.

These are the principal facets of an ideology that was to pass into the National Socialist movement. This was the "race mysticism" about which men like Günther and Rosenberg wrote. Out of this mixture of the romantic and the occult the Aryan arose: sometimes out of the sun, sometimes through a historical process, but always as a true, organic individual—a part of nature and of the life-force that springs from nature. Guido von List sang of the Aryan during the ice age engaged in building his spiritual and bodily strength in the hard fight with nature, arising quite differently than other races who lived without struggle in the midst of a bountiful world.[60] For the element of struggle was always a part of this ideology; art and battle go together. This, however, was not the Darwinian struggle for the survival of the fittest, but rather the good fight of the Aryan who was eternally of the elect. The effectiveness of Dacqué's book in overcoming the "English disease," Darwinism, was noted by a National Socialist journal of the 1920s. Darwinism was of one cloth with political democracy; both dissolved the organic unity of man as part of nature, and Darwinism did so through survival of the fittest.[61] The Aryan was the sole organic man, and his task was not a struggle for survival against equals, for he had none. Instead, his was an inner struggle to recapture his unique heritage and an outward struggle to rid himself of Jews and theologians. Alfred Rosenberg had this in mind when he wrote of the "romanticism of steel"; the revolution against capitalist bourgeois society could only have reality if it served the permanent values of blood in revolt.[62]

The men we have singled out for analysis were some of the chief purveyors of this thought. There were a host of others. A list of organizations sponsoring the meeting at the Hohen Meissner makes this amply clear. The German Youth Movement has entered this story at every turn. Undoubtedly, the *Wandervögel* were one of the prime transmitters of the movement's thought. They too rejected intellectualism for the mystique of contact with nature. Excursions brought out the "real man" as opposed to the artificial man of modern material culture. For Karl Fischer, the founder of that movement, romanticism was an expression of national feeling with an explicit racial base. Hans Blüher, the controversial historian of the *Wandervögel*, reminisced that in the movement's early days consciousness of race sufficed to join soul to nature.[63] Closely associated with the youth movement were the country boarding schools, founded by Hermann Lietz (1898). These schools, which later had a great influence, institutionalized many of the ideas we have discussed. One admirer said correctly that "in Lietz's hands the regenerating natural forces of agriculture and rural life were made to work for the education of men."[64] Lietz believed that the emphasis in education should not be on book learning but on building character through contact with the landscape of the fatherland and knowledge of the Teutonic inheritance. The end product of this educational process was to be an aristocracy of men and women who would not "bend their knees" before the Moloch of capitalism and materialism. Instead, they would stand for an ideal that represented, in Lietz's words, a "purer religious world of thought and feeling." For the sake of this ideal, such leaders would take up the fight against the "dark" instincts of the masses.[65]

This religious world Lietz saw in terms of a Christianity which, as for the others, was divorced from Christ as a historical personage. In Paul de Lagarde he saw the theologian nearest to his position. Christ must be rescued from St. Paul and emerge again as a hero image: thus young Germans could be inspired to an active, heroic life. For this task the ancient German and Grecian religious myths were more valuable than the Old Testament, which Lietz also rejected.[66] Lietz developed these ideas into an explicit racism. At first he took Jewish students into his school, but he gradually banned them from his educational system. Toward the end of his life, after the German defeat in World War I, he began to write about the necessity of freeing Germany from the "Jewish spirit" and from all those who were moved by it.[67]

Typical for Lietz's attitudes was the change he made in the English system of student self-government, a system which had originally impressed him and had, in a sense, inspired his work. He substituted for this the "family" system—each teacher was supposed to be the "father" of a small group of students. The differences of class and status were to be displaced by an "organic state."[68] This led to a break with some of his associates who believed, as Lietz did not, in the reasonableness of the majority and thus wished educational decisions to be made by students and faculty jointly. The ideal of the organic state was thus mirrored in the structure of the schools themselves. As he wrote toward the end of his life, only the organic, that which is in tune with nature,[69] will last. Here too Lietz was close to the ideology we have discussed. It is small wonder that the list of books which he recommended for reading aloud to students during the evening hour set aside for that purpose included racial-nationalistic novels and ended by recommending the books published by Eugen Diederichs. Diederichs, in turn, longed to publish Lietz's works, while Lehmann actually published books which furthered his cause, and sent his sons to one of Lietz's schools. Nor is it astonishing that one of his leading collaborators became one of the most prominent of National Socialist educators.[70]

Again, in this case, personal continuities were not as important as the furthering, indeed the institutionalizing, of a cultural atmosphere. After the First World War, many country boarding schools were founded, some by prominent men like Prinz Max von Baden. Their aim was a national, spiritual renewal based on the principles Lietz had set forth. To be sure, some substituted a broad non-national humanitarian outlook, while others adopted Lietz's ideas without giving them an explicit racial base. Yet the atmosphere was set; its romanticism and "idealism of deeds" colored the thought of those generations who had passed through the country boarding schools and the youth movement.

Transmitted in this way, the romantic and mystic ideology with which we have been concerned drew ever-widening circles into its sphere of influence, even if among these many later rejected National Socialism. Among those influenced were some of the best literary minds of contemporary Germany. Stefan George came under the influence of Schuler and Klages at the same time that he composed some of the "cosmic" poems of his *Der Siebente Ring* (*Seventh Ring*, 1907). Claude David has no hesitation in saying that the hand of this group of men is seen in some of Rilke's *Elegies*.[71] Still more actively involved with the movement was August Strindberg. He participated in the ancient Germanic rites which Lanz von Liebenfels, with List's assistance, performed in one of his Hungarian castles.[72] Strindberg's novel *Tschandala* took over a word which List and Liebenfels had used to designate the lower races.

In Germany the recovery of the unconscious, in reaction against the dominant positivist ideologies, laid part of the groundwork for the German form of twentieth-century dictatorship. This reaction combined the deep stream of German romanticism with the mysteries of the occult as well as with the idealism of deeds. What sort of deeds these turned out to be is written on the pages of history.

SEVEN

Fascism and the Avant Garde

F ASCISM CONSIDERED ITSELF an avant garde: a group of
men who were leading society into the post-liberal age. The
classical definition of avant garde as being at one and the
same time opposed to bourgeois politics and bourgeois tastes is a
part of fascist rhetoric, of that populism upon which the fascist
movements sought to build their appeal. If we define avant garde as
an alternative discourse to the bourgeois consensus, then fascism
would have seen itself as such an alternative. Basic to an understanding of the relationship of fascism and avant garde is the fact that
fascism was both a new movement and in a hurry; that it had no
longer period of gestation like socialism, that it was founded only
after the First World War. Fascism was obsessed with the thought
that it had to claim instant success, lest the collapse of the old order
benefit socialists or communists. The rawness of the movement, its
apocalyptical tone, meant at once a search for tradition and an
obsession with the speed of time. Fascism stood at the frontiers of
technology and technocracy—Robert Paxton tells us that the tech-
nocrats entered the Vichy government like a conquered country.[1]
The alliance between technology, technocracy, and the authoritarian
state was completed in the interwar period. But at the same time

fascism integrated itself into nationalist traditions, attempting to harness a usable past—the Roman Empire, or the German wars of liberation. As a nationalist movement, fascism aimed to link past and present.

The attempt to combine the technological and technocratic avant garde with a look backward to the national past was thus basic. The obvious contradictions involved would be resolved when the state of the future superseded the decadence of the present. For fascism, the post-liberal age was to substitute youthful vigor for old age, camaraderie for an atomized society. But above all, the post-liberal age would lead to the domination by an élite over nature, inferior peoples, and nations. The theme of domination is of special relevance in defining the relationship between avant garde and fascism, for it enabled fascists to champion one of the principal achievements of modern industrialism and technology, the communications revolution of the twentieth century. This revolution exemplified the sudden and frightening changes of industrialization, the new speed of time, the nervousness and restlessness castigated by so many critics of society, in a word, that degeneration which in 1892 Max Nordau saw exemplified in all of modern art and literature. Fascists, like Expressionists and Futurists, accepted the new speed of time not as exhausting but as toughening the nerves of a virile élite. They saw in the radio, the film, the motorcar, and the airplane a means of domination, an *élan vital* appropriate to the new fascist man.

But unlike the Expressionists, the most up-to-date industrial accomplishments were integrated into a glorified national past, accepted and at the same time transcended through national values. It is in this context that the airplane can illustrate the relationship between fascism and this avant garde, for here the new frontiers of technology and time became part of a new élitism, the search for a new man at the same time eternal and modern. Henry de Montherlant in 1922 summed it up well: The struggle of the airplane against nature is not so much the glorification of technology, but a means to prove one's manliness and youth.[2] Now that the war was over, aviation continued the challenge of combat into the peace. Saint-Exupéry, who did more than anyone between the wars to popularize the mystique of flying, held that man was being judged by the "*échelle cosmique*"—that as an aviator face to face with transcendent values, he could recapture his individuality in mass society.[3] Mussolini, who had written already in 1909 that the human herd could not understand the nobility of Blériot's flight across the English Channel, summed up the élitist politics of flying: "Aviation must remain the privilege of a spiritual aristocracy."[4] The pilot exemplifies the proper will power and soul, a book about *Mussolini Aviatore* tells us, but above all he must understand the fullest meaning of the word "control." The pilot appropriates a piece of eternity, of the sky, and it is this appropriation of immutability that enables him to keep control.[5] The analogy to a political élite is obvious here.

Confrontation with the frightening phenomena of modern aviation meant emphasis upon a new aristocracy in the age of technology (so different from what Saint-Exupéry once called ants in their commuter trains). Aviation here tended to be associated with élitist and right-wing politics, though Bertold Brecht on the left attempted to strip the adventure of flying of its mystique. His radio play *The Flight of the Lindberghs* presented this flight as the conquest of nature by man, the demystification of the world: ". . . when I fly I am a true atheist."[6] There is no appropriation of eternity here, no longing for immutability. Moreover, Brecht rejected the concentration upon the hero, because this might drive a wedge between the listener and the masses. The part of Lindbergh should be sung by a chorus.[7] Nothing could be further from the attitudes and beliefs of the living Lindbergh, and Brecht eventually retitled the play *The Flight over the Ocean*, substituting "The Flyer" for Lindbergh throughout the text. Yet it was the mystique that remained strong and that, through figures like Lindbergh, penetrated the popular consciousness. Saint-Exupéry, for all his élitism and appropriation of eternity, thought of himself as a good democrat; he nevertheless became both the mystique's victim and its popularizer. More typical than Brecht's attitude to aviation and that of other writers of the left was the constant quest for mediation between the speed of the airplane and a harmonious universe where past and present met. It was said of Italo Balbo, Italian fascism's most famous aviator, that "through aviation he has recaptured the chivalry of old."[8]

The use of the term "chivalry" shows the association of past and present, or rather, that of technology with the eternal and immutable values symbolized by the sky. A pilot has to be "called" to exercise his profession. Typically enough, one fascist tribute to Balbo points out that he served in an Italian mountain troop, the *Alpini*, during the war; he was therefore accustomed to dominating heights and suspending distances.[9] Indeed, the famous mass flights across the Atlantic or the Mediterranean, which he led, were supposed to educate a fascist élite and demonstrate to the world that it had conquered the challenge of modernity. But this challenge was met by integrating past and present, setting the act of flying and the speed of time within eternity—the blue skies, the mountains.

National Socialism used the same technique in accepting and modernizing mass production. Here modern industrialization did not appropriate eternity through the sky but through the nation itself, a symbol as impervious to the speed of time as the sky or the mountain. The program called "Beauty of Work," directed by Albert Speer, modernized the assembly line and the factory but at the same time surrounded the work place with national symbols, building communal halls and so-called sacred rooms in which the nation could be worshipped. Song, play, and physical exercise all became part of the work place,[10] in factories which, more often than not, continued to be built along functional, Bauhaus lines. Factories, so we are told even by a Nazi critic of the *Neue Sachlichkeit* ("New Realism") should express their function and not look like Byzantine palaces or Renaissance villas.[11] The Weimar architectural and technological avant garde was already partially integrated into the Nazi revolution.

Such a process of integration, set as it was in the context of the nationalist mystique, emphasized the activism of the movement, its dynamic when opposed to frightened conservatives and complacent bourgeois. Italian fascism, as we shall see, proceeded in a similar fashion, though here the avant garde included literature and the arts. As far as the Nazis were concerned, the architectural, technological, and technocratic avant garde was easier to assimilate than the avant garde in literature and art, which might challenge the framework within which the modern could become a part of the national mystique, dominating man and nature. No doubt the emphasis of the later Weimar Bauhaus upon form rather than content facilitated its Nazi adaptation, while in Italy the young fascist architects influenced by the Bauhaus stated that revolutionary architecture must accompany the fascist revolution.[12] There was no such talk in Nazi Germany.

Yet at first, Nazi student youth praised Expressionism because it seemed dynamic, open-ended, a "chaos of the soul." But Hitler wanted no chaos, and in September of 1934, he put an end to all flirtation with Expressionism.[13] The movement opposed his banal Wilhelminian taste, but he was simultaneously attempting to tame that activism which stood at the beginning of his own movement. Expressionism was outlawed at roughly the same time that the so-called *Röhm Putsch* took place, which disciplined the S.A. Now the functionalism of much of Nazi architecture was sharply distinguished from the Bauhaus, which Goebbels and the *Völkische Beobachter* had at one time admired, and which was still the style of the future in fascist Italy. Even the efforts of Mies van der Rohe to appease the régime failed, though he and others at the Bauhaus had divined correctly that rhetorical hostility was not always accompanied by the rejection of functionalism and simplicity in architectural style. Perhaps today, when we are conscious that the Bauhaus style contained as many elements of domination as of liberation, we are ready to reexamine its relationship to National Socialism.[14] Indeed, the new stadium for the 1936 Olympics had to be redesigned because Hitler objected to the large scale and functional use of glass by its architect, saying he would never enter a "glass box."[15]

The influence of the Bauhaus and the *Neue Sachlichkeit* was evident in the construction of factories and apartment houses. However, in the case of official Reich and party buildings, Bauhaus influence could easily be confused with the neo-classicism of Hitler's taste. Both, as a matter of fact, were protests against restlessness; both attempted to combine functionalism and order.[16] For example, Heinrich Tessenow, whose architectural theories almost certainly influenced Hitler, advocated simplicity of line and materials. Indeed, the clarity and decisiveness which the Nazis advocated in the struggle against their enemies was reflected in their emphasis upon simple building materials and clear lines. These were embedded in a monumental style that once more integrated modernism with symbols of domination, a linkage the Bauhaus had struggled to avoid. The official architecture—but not that of the army or air force, or even of some local party buildings—linked what had been avant garde to national grandeur and representation.

Such cooptations of the avant garde in architecture and technology were important in Germany because they enabled National Socialism to combine its self-image as a decisive and virile movement with volkish ideology. They could dominate time and space because as an élite, National Socialists had appropriated all that was eternal—the mountains, the sky, and the nation.

But in Italy, the avant garde could build upon radical and syndicalist currents within fascism that were absent in Germany. Moreover, Italian nationalism had retained certain Jacobin traditions that were of little influence in the north. That is why Italy gave more space to the avant garde than Nazi Germany, and why most of this essay looks south rather than north. While modern technology and some avant-garde architectural forms were integrated into National Socialism, as we have seen, it is difficult to extend the interaction between the avant garde and the Third Reich much further. Even in film, it was the techniques of the Weimar documentary that were used rather than the content. Music seems to be the exception to this rule. Here the avant garde found space; for example, Carl Orff wrote his famous *Carmina Burana* in 1937, and continued to compose peacefully during the war.

Perhaps modern music is the most politically neutral of the avant-garde arts because its tonality is accessible only to a few, or can be tolerated if a few folk tunes are incorporated into its compositions. Here the weight of history did not strangle the contents of avant-garde art.

Indeed, it is the density of historical tradition that will determine to a large extent the space available to the avant garde. If historical consciousness and the cultivation of traditions forms the key to a régime's public thought, then whatever techniques are accepted, art and literature must look backward rather than forward. Fascist Italy, unlike Germany, made an alliance with the anti-historical Futurists and syndicalists, and in this way could possess an avant garde that deplored the weight of tradition.

Thus a group of young architects proclaimed in Turin in 1934 that as an avant garde they were joining fascist youth in the search for clarity and wisdom, in the unconditional adherence to logic and reason. Tradition itself, so we are told, was transformed and largely abolished by fascism.[17] Indeed, a member of this group, Giuseppe Terragni, in his Fascist Party building at Como (1932-36) with its cubic form went beyond the Bauhaus to the very frontiers of functionalism. At the exhibition to honor the tenth anniversary of the Fascist Revolution (1932), the hall designed by Terragni was dominated by a huge turbine ("the thoughts and actions of Mussolini are like a turbine, taking the Italian people and making them fascist").[18] Terragni did not stand alone in his devotion to fascism and avant garde; for example, Kandinski had the highest praise for the fascist Carlo Belli's defense of abstract art as the only art suitable for the "wonderful new régime."[19]

For over fifteen years, Italian fascism allowed itself to be represented by an avant garde as well as by the traditional "Roman" styles. To be sure, Mussolini's personal taste was entirely different from that of Adolf Hitler; as we mentioned at the beginning of this book, as a man of the world, he had been exposed to a European avant garde that merely frightened the Austrian provincial. There is a continuity between the impatience with ordered society and settled social structures that Mussolini expressed as a young man and his taste for certain avant-garde art and architecture later in life. He always believed that it was movement that characterized the twentieth century: "We want to act, produce, dominate matter ... reach toward the other end ... other horizons."[20] Giuseppe Bottai, a former syndicalist and fascist of the first hour held, typically enough, that fascism's use of the newest technology also meant accepting the newest forms of art and literature.[21] The Futurists in their original Manifesto combined the call for rearmament and colonial expansion with opposition against the monumental in art, advocating all that was "violently modern." They were Mussolini's closest allies in the effort to get Italy to intervene in the war which, while it helped to transform Mussolini from a left-wing socialist to a fascist, did not markedly change Futurist ideals. Their Manifesto of the "Impero Italiano" (*Italian Empire*, 1923) rejected history as irrelevant: "We are the children of Isonzo, of the Piave ... and of four years of fascism. That suffices!"[22] Here the separation of avant-garde technology from literature and art, so obvious in Nazi Germany, evidently failed to take place.

Mussolini himself, for example, seemed to repeat Futurist ideas when at a speech in Perugia in 1927 he demanded that art must not be weighed down by the patrimony of the past, but that fascism must create a new art.[23] The response to the debate about art in Bottai's own *Critica Fascista* in the late 1920s was more cautious: the state must, as far as possible, avoid interference in artistic matters, and the corporation of artists must restrict itself to discussing the economic problems of the profession. Yet individualism should not remain unchecked. Bottai desired the liberalization of the régime in order to co-opt as many diverse groups as possible into the fascist consensus.[24]

Slowly but surely, over a long period of time within Italian fascism, anti-modernist forces forged ahead, trying to end the tolerance for avant-garde architecture, art, and literature. The group "*Novocento*," founded in 1922 and led by Mussolini's long-time mistress Margherita Sarfatti, proclaimed a native neo-classicism as the guarantor of order and a fitting symbol for the nation. Fascist literature must not reflect restlessness, the search for new artistic expression; instead, it must be based firmly upon the Roman tradition. Massimo Bontempelli, the principal literary figure of *Novocento*, coined the term "romantic realism," meaning a realistic character portrayal within a romantic setting.[25] The identical term became popular among Nazis as well, who rejected romantic sentimentality as denoting weakness and femininity, but at the same time retained romanticism as a "*verklärte Wirklichkeit*" (luminous reality).[26] This was the "*realismo fascista*," producing paintings of the "battle of grain" or of people listening with rapt attention to a speech of Mussolini, once again similar to those paintings that dominated so much of Nazi art.

Novocento had wanted to be cosmopolitan, to spread its myths and optimism throughout Europe. Officially, the movement was regarded with some skepticism, as the article "Novocento" in the *Enciclopedia Italiana* of 1934 demonstrates. Indeed, when Mussolini addressed their first exhibition of art in 1926, it was to proclaim that the state cannot give preference to any one artistic movement over another. Yet in that very same year he ordered the Roman ruins excavated and exhibited within the city.[27] Few could have foreseen that this command would present the greatest danger and indeed eventual defeat for the avant garde in Italy. The state was about to take sides. The *Strapaese* (or ultra-nativist) movement was a more successful attempt to produce a committed fascist literature, here through an idealized picture of village and small-town virtues. Catholic and rural, it was closely linked to the Tuscan agrarian squadristas, who had presented a nearly independent force within early fascism. Yet, typically, this volkish Italian fascism disintegrated when it had to direct its criticism to what it regarded as the undue tolerance of official Italian culture.[28] Volkish literature and art were at the fringes in Italy, not as in Germany at the center of the movement's ideology and culture. The Roman and Catholic traditions, combined with the relative openmindedness of Italian nationalism, prevented fascism's immediate lapse into provincialism.

More important than any single literary or artistic movement like

Novocento or *Strapaese*, the Roman revival which had gathered momentum from the very beginnings of fascism was increasingly directed against the avant garde. Mussolini had called for the excavation of the ruins of Rome in 1926. A year earlier, the founding of institutes of classical dance, drama, and music had already documented official interest in a classical revival,[29] and still more important, the Museum of Classical Antiquity on the Campodoglio had been renamed the "Museo Mussolini" (1925). What could better demonstrate the Duce's association with antiquity than this museum, the only one that bore his name, standing as it did in the capitol of ancient Rome?

But it was the construction of the Forum Mussolini in 1932 that proved the most spectacular symbol of the close connection between past and present. The Duce joined the ranks of such builders of Rome as Pope Urban VIII; he immortalized himself by imitating antiquity. The forum, which was to hold 200,000 people, was surrounded by classical statues symbolizing bodily perfection, and it contained a Roman amphitheater as well. By that time, the Italian Architectural Association (which earlier had taken Mies van der Rohe and Le Corbusier as its models) was beginning to advocate monumentalism and the imitation of classical styles.[30]

This neo-classicism was the result of a conscious search for a national fascist style. Marcello Piacentini, the dominant architect of the 1930s, rejected Mies van der Rohe as being too intellectual. The quest for what he called simple and tranquil lines must lead back to regional traditions, either Renaissance or classical.[31] Piacentini's columns and arches (including his Arch of Triumph at Bologna) led to an eclecticism of style most clearly illustrated by Rome Eur (*Esposizione Universale Reale*), the so-called Universal Exhibition of 1942 (whose modernistic architecture and Basilica can still be seen today coming into Rome from the airport), whose buildings represent a mixture of past Italian styles. Modernism and the avant garde were in retreat but not yet defeated; Terragni was asked to design a building for the exhibition in his functional style. What happened in architecture can also be traced in literature, where works close to the *Novocento* and *Strapaese* dominated.

The conflict between the ancients and moderns in fascism illustrates the constant search for clarity within the movement, the attempt to find an artistic and literary equivalent to the designs of modern technology while maintaining the uncompromising struggle against all enemies, and then to combine this clarity and dynamic with ideals of law and order. The Forum Mussolini, like so many National Socialist representational buildings, combined the use of clear and simple materials with grandeur defined as the monumental pointing back to a secure national past. The Futurist critique of Nazi art as being static, like photography, was in reality a criticism of fascist neoclassicism as well.[32] Like so many early fascists, the Futurists had believed that fascism was a movement whose dynamic would carry it into uncharted spaces. Their poetry and Terragni's architecture were designed to occupy such spaces and at the same time to point forward toward the unknown. But fascism would not follow; as a political movement and as a government, it could not enjoy a wild ride into wide open spaces but was forced to retain control.

Admittedly, in its "second stage" after the war, Futurism absorbed a dose of mysticism that could have been used to tame the movement but that in actual fact was never strong enough to fulfill this purpose. However, even Terragni abandoned his avant-garde modernism when it came to designing memorials to the fallen soldiers. Here, at the very center of the national experience, reverence meant homage to tradition.[33] And this is hardly surprising. Nationalism has always emphasized continuities rather than a leap into the future. The traditionalism of fascist thought was in conflict with Futurism, but it was Marinetti and his group who were banished to the side-lines. The conflict between ancients and moderns is well summed up by the Manifesto which the leading composers of fascist Italy, all of them devoted to traditional modes of composition, issued during the 1920s. Ottorini Resphigi, among others, warned against the "biblical confusion of Babel" that was being brought on by the "continual chaotic revolution in music." It was important to recognize that the past was linked to the future, that "the romanticism of yesterday will again be the romanticism of tomorrow."[34]

But that time was not yet, however much this search for order and harmony appealed to intellectuals like Gottfried Benn, Ezra Pound, William Butler Yeats, or T. S. Eliot. Rejecting neo-romanticism as false sentimentality, they saw fascism as a bulwark against disorder, the "formless wobble," as Ezra Pound called it.[35] These writers, among them some of the most important literary avant-garde figures of Europe, searched for immutable forms and found them in the political discipline of fascism.[36] Gottfried Benn, for example, in his speech in praise of Stefan George (1934), called the feeling for aristocratic form the way to transcend the present—through strictness and discipline (*Zucht*) of form, the "German will" triumphs over nature, science, and technology. The state satisfies the longing toward form, and only then should art follow.[37] This avant garde of writers was integrated into the fascist state through its desire for order and unambiguous literary form; Benn himself saw such form as expressing a spirit analogous to commands given the Nazi battalions.[38]

When Benn welcomed Marinetti to Berlin in 1934, he praised form, order, and discipline once again, as against so-called chaos. The avant garde is not mentioned; instead, the leader of the Futurists is approved for having given fascism the black shirt as the color of horror and death, its battle cry "*A noi*," and the fascist hymn, the Giovinezza. Those who had once been of the avant garde—not only Benn but also Ezra Pound, for example—ignored the fact that an avant garde of Futurism continued to co-exist alongside Italian fascism. Marinetti was not mistaken, from his point of view, in despising the Nazis and the kind of fascist discipline that Benn thought essential for true and eternal art. The Futurists continued to oppose neo-classical and romantic styles, along with the accompanying political turn to the Right symbolized by the racial laws. Thus Marinetti, as well as Terragni, took a strong stand against racism while remaining loyal to fascism—the fascism of their dreams.[39]

All these tensions within Mussolini's Italy are exemplified by an ideal that was constantly on fascist lips: that of the "new man" whom the movement was to produce, who was its goal and its hope. We have referred to this new man throughout this book, but in connection with the avant garde we must consider him once more. Mussolini in particular was content to let the so-called fascist man symbolize the hopes and dreams of the movement. Was such a man to be tied to the past or would he be the creator of new values? Would he be the leader of an avant garde? Renzo De Felice has told us that this fascist man was indeed a man of the future, that while the "new man" of National Socialism felt suffocated by modernity, in Italy the future was considered open-ended.[40]

But whether in Germany or Italy, the "new man" continued a stereotype that had its roots in nineteenth-century nationalism. This was based upon an ideal of male strength and beauty, upon an aggressive virility, an *élan vital*, which we have seen attributed to the pilot who dominated the skies. The new fascist man was supposed to be the very opposite of muddleheaded and talkative intellectuals, of the exhausted old men of a dying bourgeois order. The anti-bourgeois rhetoric and imagery was strong here, yet symbolized by an ideal type, who himself represented bourgeois respectability, order, and domination. However much the new fascist man soared off into uncharted spaces, his ancestors were those youths who had fought the battle between the generations of the *fin de siècle*. Like all of fascism, he was a part of the bourgeois anti-bourgeois revolution, of a play within a play. He was a member of that spiritual aristocracy of aviators of which Mussolini had spoken, those who simultaneously confronted the new speed of time while appropriating a piece of eternity in order to keep control. The literary and architectural avant garde was supposed to proceed to new frontiers, while still keeping in mind the nation's need for immutability. If immutability eventually triumphed with the Roman revival, even earlier the difference between Terragni's cubic party building and his traditional monuments to the fallen seem to bear this injunction in mind.

Within this pattern of thought, Italian fascism was certainly more open to the future than German National Socialism; the new man of the south had avant-garde features lacking in the north, where the ideal German was the ancient Aryan whom Hitler had roused from centuries of slumber. Mussolini was much more ambivalent. In his famous article on fascism for the *Enciclopedia Italiana* of 1934, Mussolini described the new man as, on the one hand, restrained by the Italian patriotic tradition, and on the other, transcending space and time. Man must proceed to ever higher forms of consciousness, culture must never crystallize; and yet the great Italians of the past "are the germs which can fructify our spirit and give us spontaneity."[41] When all is said and done, Mussolini did leave the door ajar to the future, while in Germany nationalism and racism blocked all exits. Neither Mussolini nor many of his followers gave up the idea that fascism, while rooted in the past, was not destined to cling stubbornly to these roots. Nevertheless, however uncharted the new spaces, they were to be controlled and dominated by a national stereotype, rooted as a matter of fact in the imagery and the ideals of the attempted revolution of bourgeois youth at the *fin de siècle*.

The very nature of fascism as a successful modern political movement was bound to restrict the space within which the avant garde could live and flourish. Fascism was a nationalist movement, a mass movement, and a movement of youth. The opposition of nationalism to the avant garde must be evident: emphasis upon the past must necessarily be in conflict with the denial of history. To be sure, in Italy the opposition between nationalism and avant garde seemed muted as Futurists joined the interventionist battle, and as the early fascist movement stressed the immediacy of the war experience and the dynamic of youth. But it was only a matter of time before preoccupation with the heritage of antiquity pushed Futurism to the fringes of the movement. However, where fascists had little chance at political power, ideas of youth, virility, and force could assume greater importance than national memories. The rejection of history could be combined with a fascist commitment.

Drieu La Rochelle is perhaps the principal example of such a fascist. He was not attracted to integral nationalism; his fascism was based rather upon the philosophy of youth and force exemplified by a virile élite.[42] Drieu's fictional hero *Gilles*, in the novel of the same name, (1939) was not converted to fascism by an appeal to France's glorious past, but by the attraction of a spiritual renewal based upon the values of virility, authority, discipline, and force.[43] However, while Italian fascism was certainly attracted to all these ideas, it was, after all, a nationalist movement; moreover, it attained power in coalition with the Italian Nationalist Party, which occupied the traditional right in Italian politics.

The incompatibility between the avant garde and political mass movements needs no elaboration. More than ever before, mass movements between the wars felt the need to stress traditional values, a happy and healthy world based upon the national past. The avant garde wanted to lead the masses, but it was doomed to failure and frustration. Fascism did have a place for the creative artist, but his role would be to create a setting for its political liturgy or to popularize the movement and recapture the supposedly glorious national past. Its model was Gabriele D'Annunzio—the power of artistic creativity harnessed to nationalist politics, helping the "First Duce" rule Fiume.[44] Even if the avant garde was able to function in fascist Italy, even if Mussolini himself liked much of what it produced and had to say, the inner logic of fascism as a nationalist mass movement was bound in the end to restrict the space of human creativity.

Not only did fascism exalt youth but its leadership and followers were much more youthful than those of the established political parties. The avant garde at the *fin de siècle* was also youthful as it hurled itself against the manner, morals, and culture of its elders. That revolt, as the years wore on, tended toward a certain rudeness and virility, and also, strengthened by the war experience, found itself attracted to various nationalisms. The war which furthered the nationalization of the masses also tended to further the nationalization of bourgeois youth. Marcel Arland, writing in 1924, declared that the *mal de siècle*

was a superficial sophistication and wit, which made it natural that
youth should appear rude in the midst of such grace, violent amid such
sweetness.[45] Fascists like Drieu La Rochelle mobilized this rudeness
and violence on behalf of right-wing causes.

The French situation differed markedly from that of Germany after
the war. The victorious Third Republic was able to co-opt much of
the nationalist space in politics, retaining, for example, the loyalty and
even affection of its largest war veterans' associations. Thus it under-
cut that integral nationalism which the fascists appropriated successfully in Germany and Italy. Here some French fascists could base
themselves principally upon the exaltation of youth, virility, force, and
camaraderie, the "*équipe*" of which they were a part. Typically enough
in Germany, the Bund, which was the equivalent of the "*équipe*," was
filled with nationalist and even racist content. The thought of a leading French fascist like Brasillach, though he felt nostalgia for the
historical past, often lacked this proper nationalist dimension.[46] This
enabled such French fascism to provide some space for the vanguard,
as Le Corbusier, for example, collaborated in *Plans*, a journal mildly
fascist in character.[47] The *élan* of youth led to brutality but also to a
certain openness toward new artistic forms and content. The originality of style and tone of a Louis-Ferdinand Céline cannot be found
in the literature of the extreme right either in Germany or Italy.

Céline did identify himself with fascist and racist politics, and the
books which he wrote before and during the war reflect this commitment. Admittedly, these books were a theater of the absurd, filled with
irony and self-contradictions. Here virulent racism and fascism were
in the hands of a true avant-garde writer, who integrated them with
novelty of style and thought. The task is not, to my mind, to explain
away Céline's politics, to underestimate, for example, the seriousness
of his attempt to found a fascist party, but rather to explain how
French fascism could stand this embrace. To some extent Céline
wanted order and certainty in the world, and that is why in *Bagatelles
pour un Massacre* (1937) he constantly praised Adolf Hitler, who had
dared to act out his ideology in contrast to hypocritical French politi-

cians. Like Pound or Benn, fascism gave him the comfort of clarity; but unlike these other writers, he did not long for a strict discipline of literary form. On the contrary, he seems to have despised it. When all is said and done, here a youthful and ahistorical fascism was interacting with a genuine avant garde, and the case of Céline, unique among writers, must be put side by side with that of Futurist painters and architects in Italy.

For the most part, the relationship between fascism and youth was determined by the nationalization of bourgeois youth. The German Youth Movement shared with the avant garde the urge for simplicity, for the genuine, and a hatred of the academic in art and literature. But it found its inspiration in medieval dances, folk songs, and folk music. This search of youth for the beautiful was not functional but based upon the artistic forms of the past. Even those on the left of the youth movement, men who later joined the Communist Party like Alfred Kurella and Karl Bittell, remained romantics. Kurella admired the Stefan George circle,[48] and though George's own poetry might perhaps qualify as avant garde, the classicism of the master and his disciples was meant to bring about the triumph of the "secret Germany"—a concept close to the élitism of the majority of the German Youth Movement, who regarded their own nationalism as the wave of the future. If we look at the writers and artists who came from this movement, those who worshipped at the altar of the fatherland by far outnumbered avant-garde artists like Max Beckmann or Expressionist writers like Kasimir Edschmid.

Though some members of the youth movement called themselves anarchists,[49] the majority followed the radicalization to the right of German bourgeois youth already discernible at the *fin de siècle* and gathering strength after the war. As we saw, in France this was not the case to the same extent, and in Italy many of those who glorified youth were attracted to the Futurists. What proportion of bourgeois youth was attracted to left-wing causes in Italy before the victory of fascism remains to be investigated. Certainly here, as in France, the vast majority of veterans supported parliamentary democracy. Mussolini was specifically excluded from the electoral lists of veterans' organizations in the election of 1919, and suffered a shattering defeat.[50] But it may have been precisely the younger veterans who supported the Legionari Dannunziani or the Fasci di Combattimento. Mussolini called them the "marvelous warrior-youth of Italy."[51]

Fascism wanted to lead beyond liberalism and to find alternative methods of discourse, and yet it was dependent upon the bourgeois consensus. Its members were attracted to Futurism and Expressionism, but both these movements were, like fascism itself, anti-bourgeois revolutions, which were profoundly indifferent to social and economic change. To parody the Expressionist dramas of Walter Hasenclever and others, bourgeois society was not likely to die from an unloaded pistol or from fright. Italian fascism maintained the idea of a permanent revolution that had been close to Mussolini's heart ever since his days as a left-wing socialist. But this permanent revolution, though complicating the relationship of fascism to history, was supposed to be a moral revolution, a quest for higher forms of consciousness based upon political domination. "Fascism is a revolution which, contrary to all others in history, perpetuates its political conquests through a continuous moral renewal."[52] The avant garde fitted these aims of fascism. Its crime in fascist eyes was not that it escaped the confines of complacent bourgeois society, but those of nationalism and the political necessities of a modern mass movement.

Yet, if we define modern technology and modern functionalism as part of the avant garde, its link to fascism becomes meaningful. Here Italian fascism was more portentous than National Socialism in unleashing a victorious revolution. Eventually, no analogy to medieval chivalry or ancient Rome could tame the speed of time, the new technology, and the dynamic that accompanied the victory of the new over the old. Fascism prided itself on controlling and dominating this rush to the future, yet it was not destined to play the pilot in the long run; instead, the modern state and its impersonal bureaucracy would fulfill that function. Mussolini, not Hitler, had paved the way when he exalted the Italian state rather than the Italian Volk.

Modern technocracy would eventually displace fascism as the instrument of domination.

Though it seems today that the modern impersonal state determines the rather wide limits within which the avant garde can function, this might prove deceptive. For in time of renewed crisis, the modern state may once more need the support of nationalism and disciplined mass movements in order to retain control. The apparatus of modernity alone—lacking an ideology to connect past and present and without seeming to appropriate a piece of eternity—may no longer suffice.

There will always be an avant garde, but its living space may well be restricted in the future, as it is in the present and has been in the past. The avant garde in and out of fascism is only tolerated as long as it remains within its charmed circle, as long as it does not ally itself with other powerful groups of society and so present a menace to the prevailing consensus. As we saw, there was fear that Mussolini might make such an alliance, but even when he praised the avant garde he was already preparing a Roman revival. Such a statement about the restrictions imposed upon the avant garde can surely be made about all that our society regards as unusual, abnormal, or disquieting. Like Swann and Charlus at the court of Proust's Guermantes, eccentricities are tolerated just so long as they remain amusing.

EIGHT

Nazi Polemical Theater: the *Kampfbühne*

T HE THEATER PLAYED a vital part in National Social-ism; indeed, it was one of Hitler's dominant passions. No German régime in the past did more to further the theater than the Third Reich. In 1936, for example, some 331 theaters, many of them recently built or renovated, played a regular season.[1] The theater was, in fact, an integral part of Nazi ideology, serving to reinforce the political liturgy of the movement. Mass meetings and the theater were intended to supplement each other. For this reason the liturgical *Weihebühne*, the "*Thing* theater" on which the volkish ideology was acted out, assumed special significance, presenting the liturgy of the movement through cultic plays meant to create a living community of faith. The National Socialist myth was acted out in dramatic and visual form as an act of religious worship in which masses of people participated. The *Thing* theater has been investi-gated[2] and there is no need to analyze it once more. However, the *Kampfbühne* (or fighting stage), the other Nazi attempt to harness the theater to their cause needs further exploration, it antedated and outlasted the *Thing* theater, which was created in 1933 and dissolved in 1937.[3] The *Kampfbühne* began its career in 1926, well before the seizure of power, and endured as long as the Third Reich itself.

It is necessary first to describe the diverse forms of the *Kampfbühne* that existed before the seizure of power. Here we shall proceed by types, as all the forms of this theater overlap chronologically. The S.A. and Hitler Youth "*Spiel-Trupps*" (amateur actors) appeared first; then, in 1931, the Gau theater, a mobile stage that played throughout each province, was created. The *NS-Versuchsbühne* (Nazi Experimental Theater) started in 1927, and in 1930 became the *NS-Volksbühne*, performing on a regular basis. Once we have analyzed these various *Kampfbühnen*, both amateur and professional, we can then set them into the historical background of the search for a national theater which, starting in the nineteenth century, became accelerated during the Weimar Republic. Finally, we must take a glance at the fate of the *Kampfbühne* during the Third Reich.

Whatever its diverse forms, the Nazis defined a *Kampfbühne* as a "*Streitgespräch*"—a polemic against the enemy. It was designed partly to "indoctrinate through fun and entertainment," and partly, in the words of one S.A. leader, to encourage "fighters for the cause to emerge from the masses."[4] To be sure, the Nazi ideology was presented to the audience, but always in a crude and polemical fashion, quite different, for example, from the majestic liturgy of the *Thing* theater. The first "Spiel-Trupps" were attached either to the S.A. or to the Hitler Youth, and gave themselves titles like the "Storm Troops" or the "Brown Shirts." These were enthusiastic groups of amateur actors. Little record remains of their plays, and their theatrical presentations are almost impossible to reconstruct. But as far as we can tell, these fell into two parts: fun and entertainment consisting of folk songs and folk dancing; and a "fighting part," which presented "contemporary political sketches" (*Politische Zeitbilder*). Such, for example, was the mixture of fun and action which the "Brown Shirts" of Hesse-Nassau presented as part of the Nazi propaganda program in the city of Wetzlar in 1932.[5] Sometimes such troupes seem to have used *tableaux vivantes* centered upon stereotypes of bankers, trade unionists, and consumers. For the most part the troupes would march on stage in closed formation, before beginning the songs, dances, and plays.

Play troupes like the "Brown Shirts" and "Storm Troopers" were often used in election rallies, especially during mass meetings in cities. Their plays were *Streitgespräche*, used to bring variety to evenings of martial music and speeches. The Hitler Youth carried their plays to such election rallies in cities, and especially to the villages, where they would perform as part of a *"Bunter Abend"* (cabaret theater) of skits, songs, and dances.

What were such plays like? For the most part only their titles have survived, and these tend toward the banal, as in *All Germans Are Brothers.*[6] I have found only one script without a title performed in Berlin by such an amateur group. Yet, for all its crudity, the play may well be typical for many others. It was performed on a bare stage in a hall belonging to the German Veterans Association (*Stahlhelm*). The stage represented the guard room of a local S.A. troop. As the play begins, shots are heard behind the stage and a dead S.A. man is carried into the room. Immediately afterwards a communist is dragged in as the probable murderer. But as the S.A. look through the pockets of their murdered comrade, they find a large sum of money and the address of a Jew. The Jew himself is then brought onto the stage, "whining in his jargon," and is shot by the S.A. as the man really responsible for the murder.[7] Through simple action and stereotypes the lesson is driven home that communists are the dupes of the Jews.

Such amateur players provided the inspiration for a more permanent play troupe made up of professional actors: the Gau theater. From 1931 onwards, such *Gau-Bühnen* presented "cultural evenings" up and down the province, which consisted of folk songs, political poetry, comic sketches, and monologues.[8] However, political plays were also performed with increasing frequency. We know more about the content of these plays than of those of the "Brown Shirts" or "Storm Troopers" because the Gau theater of Pomerania has been extensively documented for the years 1931 and 1932, though no such documentation seems to exist for other Gau theaters. For example, Walter Busch's *Giftgas 500* (*Poisoned Gas 500*), performed during these years, was a play that maintained its popularity. Its subject is described appropriately enough by the Nazi *Illustrierter Beobachter*[9] as the story of a key German invention, which Jewish greed swindled from Polish heavy industry. The hierarchy of villains will remain unchanged throughout Nazi rule—the Poles are bad but the Jews are worse. The plays performed were always highly topical. Thus the German National Party (*Deutsche Nationale Volkspartei*), always a rival of the Nazis, was satirized for its conceit and pretensions. In addition, plays directed against political Catholicism loomed large in a Polish border region. In one of these, a German Catholic priest hates the Nazis so much that he would rather sell good farm land to Poles than let it be farmed by a German National Socialist.[10] The director of the Pomeranian Gau theater maintained that all in all some 15,000 to 20,000 people would watch a play as it wound its way through the towns and villages.[11] Eventually, the *Gau-Bühnen* became a part of the "Strength through Joy" movement.[12]

The amateur play troupes and the Gau theaters traveled throughout the German provinces. But the so-called *NS-Versuchsbühne* was a traditional troupe, staffed by professional actors, which performed in Berlin in theater buildings hired for the occasion. It opened on April 20, 1927, when, to celebrate Hitler's birthday, Wolf Geyser staged his drama *Revolution* before some 3,000 spectators. It consisted of a series of *tableaux vivantes* which contrasted the ideal life in the future Nazi state to that in the Weimar Republic.[13] A few months later, the Experimental Theater performed Joseph Goebbels's *Der Wanderer*, which was an adaptation of his novel *Michael, Ein Deutsches Schicksal in Tagebuchblättern* (*Michael, The Diary of a German Fate*, 1929).[14] But this so-called Experimental Theater seems to have lacked success, for no regular season was attempted for the next three years, only occasional performances.

The provinces had to step in once more, and it was their pressure which led to the establishment of another *NS-Volksbühne* in Berlin in

1930. Perhaps this *NS-Volksbühne* was supposed to travel throughout Germany, but that function seems to have been usurped by the Gau theater established one year later.[15] The *NS-Volksbühne* was an imitation of the older, left-leaning *Volksbühne* and the Christian *Bühnenvolksbund*. It performed regularly and its plays are easiest to reconstruct because they were reported by the party press.

The *NS-Volksbühne* plays were polemical, and, whether classic or modern, were conceived as *Streitgespräche* in spite of their conventional staging. Schiller's *Räuber* was one of the first plays performed, and it was claimed that here the *Räuber* had finally been staged as Schiller himself desired. The character of Spiegelberg, the enemy of Karl Moor and "leader" of the band, was brought to the fore. He became the villain, transformed into a "loud-mouthed Jewish agitator" who, while himself a coward, incites others to the craven murder of Karl Moor. Schiller's play as performed by the *NS-Volksbühne* was hailed by the Nazi press as the first dawn of a new area of Aryan German art.[16] By contrast, in Piscator's performance of the *Räuber* staged five years before the Nazis' version, Spiegelberg wore the mask of Leon Trotsky, and the murder of Moor was pictured as a noble attempt to rescue freedom from the clutches of the gang. The only other traditional plays performed in those early days of the Nazi theater were Ibsen's *An Enemy of the People* and Ernst von Wildenbruch's *Mennoniten*. The Ibsen play, first staged in 1931, was intended to demonstrate the superiority of Nordic aristocracy over majority rule, and the value of personality as opposed to public opinion.[17] The *Mennoniten* was directed against the Napoleonic occupation of Prussia. It dealt with German courage and French intrigue, the chastity of the German woman and the French attempt to contaminate German blood. Waldemar, the hero of the play, could be viewed as a forerunner of Albert Leo Schlageter, who had fought the good fight more recently in the Ruhr and entered the Nazi gallery of martyrs.[18]

Historical analogies were popular in the *NS-Volksbühne* as they were in Nazi ideology. For example, Walter Flex's *Klaus von Bismarck* was part of the repertoire, a drama that attempted to show how in the

Middle Ages the ancestor of the Iron Chancellor fought against the divisiveness of political parties and for the salvation of the Mark Brandenburg.[19] The *NS-Volksbühne* happily annexed such nationalist drama. If Flex's play was directed against divisiveness, others, such as G. von Noel's *Wehrwolf,* used the peasants of the Thirty Years' War to demonstrate that it was right and proper to defend national rights by violent means.[20] Finally the German struggle of liberation against Napoleon was an always popular theme; thus Joseph Stolzing's *Friedrich Friesen* invoked the wars of liberation against Napoleon. However, light entertainment was not neglected, and Ernst von Wolzogen's *Ein Unbeschriebenes Blatt (A Blank Leaf),* a play of "sunny laughter," was featured in the program, although with the apology that such pause in the fight rejuvenates man's energy for a renewed struggle.[21]

The party seems to have fully supported the *NS-Volksbühne.* For example, when in 1930 it played Walther Ilge's *Laterne,* a play which castigated the French Revolution, the entire Reichstag delegation of the party was present.[22] Yet the vast majority of performances in the *NS-Volksbühne* were not devoted to the historical drama or comedy but rather to contemporary plays whose message did not depend upon analogies with the past. The play written by Hitler's political mentor Dietrich Eckart, *Familienvater (Father of the Family),* was typical of the *Volksbühne*'s didactic style. Eckart's play dealt with a tyrannical and corrupt newspaper proprietor and with a cowardly Jewish journalist who does the tyrant's bidding. Between them, the tyrant and the journalist crush a young playwright (presumably the unsuccessful dramatist Eckart himself), who has dared to expose the newspaper's corruption.[23] Walter Busch's *Giftgas 500,* already performed by the Gau theater, was taken over by the *Volksbühne* as well. The plays of a rising young playwright, Eberhard Wolfgang Möller, were especially popular, perhaps because of their more elaborate staging and the lavish use of choruses. Möller brought to the *Volksbühne* plays of Germanic worship similar to those of the *Thing* theater for which he wrote most of his material.[24] Möller's dramas were unique among the committed Nazi playwrights during the Weimar Republic. While the plays we have mentioned had their first and often only performances on the stage of the *NS-Volksbühne*, his works were frequently performed in regular municipal theaters even before the Nazi theater took them over. Thus his war drama *Douaumont* (the principal fortress of Verdun) was a great success at the Berlin liberal *Volksbühne* before it succeeded on the Nazi stage. Möller's themes were broader than those of most other Nazi playwrights. They were a crusade against the love of money. Parliaments were manipulated as finance capitalists, representing gold, not people. Such populism appealed to the left as well as to the right, even though Möller was a committed Nazi.[25]

The Nazis liked best Möller's *Rothschild Siegt bei Waterloo* (*Rothschild Wins the Battle of Waterloo*, 1932), because unlike others this one was centered on the Jews as corrupting the world through money, a racism that became central to Möller's world view. Rothschild is depicted as the "third great power" besides England and France; indeed, he is the true victor at Waterloo. Though the banker asserts that "my money is everywhere and money is friendly, the friendliest power in the world, fat, round as a ball, and laughing," in reality, it has been earned by dishonoring the struggle against the plundering and butchering French. Rothschild is told that "The dead did not die in order that you could earn money through their sacrifice, and in such a shabby way." The moral was clear: the Rothschilds were a sinister power, "which makes cripples of humanity, men into the objects of the stock exchange, profit from life and capital from blood."[26] Finance capitalism as an all-embracing menace, whether symbolized by Rothschild or the Jews in *Giftgas 500*, was a staple of Nazi drama.

What then were the historical sources of the *Kampfbühne* as we have sketched it? Was it an imitation of the Piscator theater, with its agit-prop and polemics? The *Nationalsozialistiche Monatshefte* in 1931 praised the Piscator stage for having had the courage to present polemical plays.[27] The Nazis paid attention to this left-wing theater, perhaps because Piscator's radicalism appealed to their populism; his unconventional staging could be applied to the *NS-Volksbühne*.

However, the Piscator theater, which existed only from 1927 to 1931, was already in decline when the Nazis praised it.[28] They hardly borrowed from Piscator, in any case; certainly they did not follow the revolutionary staging or use of film, but instead placed the Nazi polemics within a conservative theatrical form. The speaking choruses are an exception here, for the Hitler Youth admitted openly to having borrowed them from the Communist Party.[29]

The genesis of the *Kampfbühne* is not linked to the Piscator theater but must rather be sought in the attempt to create a national theater, and, in the *Vereinsbühne*, a lay theater of trade and apprentice organizations.

The debate over the creation of a national theater had a long history. Gottfried Keller, for example, had been inspired by an outdoor performance of *Wilhelm Tell* during the Schiller Year of 1859 to propose the founding of a national theater, in a natural setting, which would combine choirs with folk plays. Such a theater would bring volkish mythology to life (he called his proposal the "Stone of Myth"—*Am Mythenstein*).[30] The conventional stage was to be abolished, and with it the distance that separates audience and actors. The audience should be drawn into a world of illusion which, through the immediacy of the drama, would become their world of reality. The *Thing* theater resulted from this pseudo-religious "völkische drama," and such liturgical plays were staged in open-air theaters from the beginning of the twentieth century onward.

The thrust toward the creation of a national theater also affected the traditional stage after World War I. The call went out to transform the professional stage into a national theater. Its purpose was to fight so-called degenerate forms of art, which symbolized Germany's defeat and revolution. Here then was the immediate precedent for the Nazi *Kampfbühne*, both in its national purpose and in its polemical intent. Thus Richard Eisner used his older journal *Das Deutsche Drama* (*The German Drama*) after 1918 in order to advocate a national theater as opposed to the theater of the Weimar Republic. He founded an organization in 1927 and was able to sponsor some plays—for example, one entitled *Fritjof* exalting Nordic man, and another, *Andreas Hofer*, dealing with the German war of liberation against kings, bishops, and princes. However, Schiller was Eisner's ideal, just as he was the patron saint of the *NS-Volksbühne*.[31]

The *Manifesto* of Erich Brandenburg calling for a national theater in 1919 was more important than Eisner's efforts, even if lacking in aggressiveness. Indeed, Erich Brandenburg demonstrates how the postwar impulse for a national theater was transmitted into the Third Reich. His *Manifesto* called for an emphasis upon space and movement, and characterized all theater as group art. The influence of the modern dance as practiced by Rudolf Laban and Mary Wigman is of importance here; Brandenburg was captivated by "dancing choirs which make a statement," as Wigman put it. The plays performed must be dramas conceived as symbolical action, analogous to cultic rites. Brandenburg contrasted this German drama to the supposed shallowness of the French and the Italian Renaissance stage. Clearly, the *Manifesto* treats theater as a cultic rite that was capable of renewing the nation. The stage was to be extended into the audience in order to abolish the difference between spectator and performer, while the auditorium should be modeled after the Roman amphitheater.[32]

The *Manifesto* was signed by a wide variety of intellectuals, ranging from the humanist socialist Gustav Landauer (murdered before it was printed), Thomas Mann, and Richard Dehmel to Hans Blüher of the youth movement and the future Nazi poet Will Vesper. They all joined Brandenburg's *Bund für das Neue Theater* (Bund for a New Theater). The Bund soon failed, and Brandenburg then pinned his hope upon the lay plays of the youth movement.[33] Meanwhile, he had refined his *Manifesto*, envisioning national drama as an instrument to fight modern mechanization and materialism. The neo-romantic tone, present but subdued in the original *Manifesto*, took over.[34] While Brandenburg took no part in the *NS-Kampfbühne* itself, as far as I can determine, he welcomed the advent of the Third Reich as the opportunity to fulfill the promise of this *Manifesto* and Bund. The time had come for a festive drama, one that would move "between masses and hero, Volk and Führer."[35] The Nazis, without mentioning the *Manifesto*, adopted Brandenburg and praised his agitation for a national stage.[36]

Brandenburg called for a national theater that would transmit its message through drama, group symbolism (such as the *Kampfbühne* used frequently), and the use of movement and space. These were theatrical forms that also preoccupied the Nazi stage. But side by side with such attempts at national theater, amateur groups continued to play as a part of the youth movement. This amateur play movement was an obvious influence on groups like the "Brown Shirts" and "Storm Troopers," and it would remain highly popular throughout the Third Reich. After the First World War the amateur play was becoming increasingly nationalistic and formalized. Whereas medieval mystery plays had captivated the enthusiasm of the prewar youth movement, now Rudolf Mirbt, prominent in the amateur theater movement, recommended dramas like Hans Johst's *Die Propheten* (*Prophets*), which contrasted the Catholic to the German man, and whose hero was Martin Luther. The symbolism and the simplicity of the staging would remain.[37]

In fact, the amateur play had already been used as a weapon of political propaganda. The Free Corps Rossbach attempted to use *Spielschaaren* (troupes of young amateur actors) directly after the war as a way to mobilize the nation against the Poles and the Republic. Gerhard Rossbach himself saw in such troupes a secret weapon in the hands of a poor and unprotected nation, a continuation of military action by other means.[38] But the Rossbach *Spielscaaren* were not imitated, even by other Free Corps, and had little influence on the professional theater.

More important were those amateur play groups that performed folk plays or folk festivals in the villages or in the countryside, known as the *Heimatspiele*, thirty-one of which were officially recognized as worthy of support by the German government after the First World War. The vast majority of these, unlike the Oberammergau *Passion*

Play, were not religious but either patriotic or concerned with a historical episode that had taken place in the locality. Thus, in *Ahide*, some two hundred amateur players reenacted the heroism and martyrdom of Andreas Hofer, the leader of the Tyrolean struggle against Italy, while other plays recreated the Hermannschlach, which the Germans won against Rome, or the saga of Wittekind. Wilhelm Tell, Goetz von Berlichingen, Andreas Hofer, and the *Niebelungenlied* provided the most popular themes for these *Heimatspiele*.[39]

Amateur plays themselves were performed through the Hitler Youth, the "Strength through Joy" movement, and the *Arbeitsdienst* (Compulsory Labor Service). Amateur actors engaged in simple productions, sometimes merely folk plays, at other times *Kampfbüh-nen*.[40] The Nazis were fearful that the amateur theater might lead to dilettantism and perhaps through the enthusiasm that it generated among the young escape their control; so amateur play educational camps (*Laienspielschullager*) were instituted, where lay actors could receive a minimal training for the stage.[41]

The *Heimatspiele* were viewed as a national theater in which the people themselves acted out their traditions and battles for survival. But side by side with the quest for a national theater, which extended from the nineteenth century into the postwar world, we must set the *Vereinstheater* in all its parochialism and artificiality. Eventually, the Nazis gave such plays performed by trade associations a high priority as true expressions of the Volk soul. If the quest for national theater determined the ambition and tone of the *NS-Kampfbühne*, the *Vereinsbühne* is directly related to its content.

The *Vereinstheater* was widespread and popular,[42] and we know little about it (though as the Nazis rightly claimed, every *Verein* had such a theater, even the *Kleintierhalterverband* or pet owners association,[43] but for lack of accessible records, I must confine myself to one such theater. The Association of Catholic Apprentices, founded by Adolf Kolping in 1851, loved to perform plays that were an integral part of the educational program of the "Kolping family." The apprentice was meant to become a modest and industrious craftsman, who knew how to work, to pray, and to shun easy wealth and monetary speculation. Adolf Kolping's motto was that "Religion and work are the golden soil of the Volk."[44] But there was no Protestant harshness to this morality; the Kolping family spent their evenings sharing play and song, and listening to popular lectures on history and natural science.[45]

The plays, like the short stories Adolf Kolping wrote, contained simple messages, such as "Thou shalt not steal," or lauded the triumph of love and devotion over a hard-headed businessman. The villain, the enemy of all "honest work," was the speculator, the capitalist, the Jew greedy for gold and riches.[46] There is hardly a play where the Jew does not appear as the symbol of evil. If we take as our example plays performed between 1874 and 1884, we can see a hardening of the polemic and of the racism which in notable contrast to Adolf Kolping's own stories comes to pervade such plays.

Joseph Becks was the most prolific playwright of these years; a Catholic priest, he had become the president of the St. Joseph's Guild of Kolping Apprentices in Cologne. Kolping himself in his short stories had been careful to distinguish between the evil gold-loving Jew who refuses Christian conversion and the converted Jew who became a noble figure.[47] Becks no longer makes such fine distinctions.

For example, Becks's *Wurst Wieder Wurst* (*The Tom-Fool*, 1880) shows a Jew trying to cheat a master-craftsman. But the craftsman's loyal apprentices trick the Jew instead. The Jew is not only the foil; he inevitably loses throughout these plays. Becks used traditional comedy, which featured the peasant dolt as the foil. This peasant still appears in the Kolping theater, but by and large it is the Jew who takes the peasant's place, though treated with a brutality largely absent in traditional comedy. Becks constantly stresses the Jewish stereotype, and his Jews talk "jargon"—that mixture of Yiddish and German used in most anti-Semitic writing and found again in the *Kampfbühne* as well. Such plays are crude and polemical, very much like the later performances of the "Storm Troops" or "Brown Shirts." For example, a play written by a teacher called Peter Sturn, *Die Schöne Nase, oder das Recht Gewinnt den Sieg* (*The Beautiful Nose, or Justice Triumphs,*

1878) is typical. A Jew in his greed sells his nose to the highest bidder, only to finally buy it back at an exorbitant price. The content of a play entitled *Hyman Levy as Soldier* (1877) does not need elucidation. These plays spread well beyond the Kolping families and even Catholic circles. After the First World War, the *Bühnenvolksbund* took up the heritage of this *Vereinstheater.* Founded in 1919 in order to counter the modern "immoral" and "atheistic" theater, it was supported by such organizations as those of Catholic apprentices (including Kolping), Catholic trade unions, and the Protestant Union of Commercial Employees (*Deutschnationaler Handlungs Gehilfen Verband*). The Catholics were in the forefront attempting to influence national culture in this way.[48] The Protestants were less active in exploiting the stage for their purposes. The Bund began with 700 individual and twenty corporate members; by 1928, it had gained 300 local affiliates and counted between 220,000 and 300,000 members.[49] This was almost exactly half the membership that had joined the rival leftist *Volksbühnenbewegung.*

The plays given in the first years after its founding were anti-French, anti-socialist, and anti-Jewish. The morality presented was the same the Kolping theater had already proclaimed. Thus one hero exclaims: "Happy are those unemployed who have a wife to pray for them and keep them from falling into the hands of the Volksverhetzer [meaning the socialists]!" Philip Ausserer, a Catholic theologian and gymnasium professor in Salzburg, contributed a play, *Die Wiege* (*The Cradle*), in which a Jew deprives a peasant of his farm. Some plays glorified a pious peasantry,[50] always close to the heart of Catholicism. The theme of the peasant deprived of his land by the Jew was a commonplace one in all volkish literature.[51] There were other plays which showed the horror of revolution and, again through the example of a Jew, that "*Hochmut kommt vor dem fall*" (pride goeth before the fall).[52] Such themes are almost identical with those of the later *Volksbühne.*

The physical stereotypes were present as well. Thus we learn from the *Dictionary of the Theater* published by the Bund for amateur players in 1925 how to make a "Jewish mask": dark skin, sharply marked facial lines, thick eyebrows, bent nose. The "usurer" is made up in similar fashion, but as these were always conceived as old men, pale skin and deep-set eyes had to be created.[53] Yet by that time such anti-Semitic plays had largely disappeared from the repertoire. At the same point, the national Bund repudiated an anti-Jewish resolution passed by its Dresden branch and refused the pressure of younger members to haul down the flag of the Weimar Republic at one of its meetings.[54] The *Bühnenvolksbund* had made its peace with the Republic (as had the Catholic associations that sponsored it).

The Bund declined by 1928, perhaps because of the tensions between the younger and the older generations.[55] The last years of the Weimar Republic required a greater radicalization than the *Volksbühnenbund* now desired. The biblical dramas it produced and the shallow comedies (such as *The Gambler of Monte Carlo*)[56] could not meet this need. These were years when people flocked to see polemical plays hostile to the Republic or to plays like *The Threepenny Opera* where the middle classes could safely enjoy being derided and spat upon.[57] Though most people came for amusement, nevertheless this was surely one sign of the transformation of middle-class values into their own negation, something closely related to the later Nazi experience.

The building blocks of the Nazi *Kampfbühne* were laid through the debate about a national theater, by the amateur play movement, the *Vereinstheater*, and the *Volksbühnenbund*. Surely as the *Kampfbühne* increasingly becomes an object of scholarly investigation, other building blocks will be discovered. The tradition of the *Kampfbühne* was continued into the Third Reich mainly by the Hitler Youth, but also by the "Strength through Joy" movement and the Labor Service. Baldur von Schirach in 1936 made the renewal of the German theater a special task of the Hitler Youth.[58] Beginning the following year, theatrical congresses were held. The first, in Bochum, included not only the *Kampfbühne* but also liturgical theater (in the same year in which the *Thing* theater itself was discontinued). Thus Eberhard

Wolfgang Möller's *Frankenburger Würfelspiel* (*The Dice Game of Frankenburg*, 1936) was performed with the participation of the Hitler Youth. This play had been produced originally for the *Thing* theater, and required 1,200 participants. When it opened in 1936 as a *Weihespiel* (a pseudo-religious play) to accompany the Olympic Games, the Labor Service provided the choruses and the crowds.[59] The play pictured the German peasants accusing tyrants who had oppressed it throughout history in front of seven judges; the audience was drawn into the drama as the actors addressed them directly from the stage. But the *NS-Volksbühne* was also represented at Bochum through Möller's *Rothschild Siegt bei Waterloo*, which concluded the Congress. The Hitler Youth now attempted to advance young dramatists from its own ranks, not only Eberhard Wolfgang Möller but also men like Friedrich Wilhelm Hymmen and Hans Schwitzke who wrote historical dramas very similar to those the *NS-Volksbühne* had performed.[60]

But the *Dramatists of the Hitler Youth* (to cite the title of an official publication) also included men like Paul Alverdes, of an older generation. Alverdes, for example, brought to the drama performed by Hitler Youth the memory of his war experiences. In a play written for the Hitler Youth, *Das Winterlager* (*The Winter Camp*), he called for discipline and obedience to the leader, using as his example a dangerous adventure in which Hitler Youth are lost in a snow storm because they had broken the discipline of the group. However, Alverdes returns to his obsession at the end of the play when two war veterans draw the proper moral and refer to their experience in battle.[61] *Das Winterlager* was performed over the radio; indeed, the radio play provided one of the principal forums for the play groups of the Hitler Youth. But they were also sent into the countryside in order to stem the flight from the land and to help preserve peasant culture.[62] Thus the Hitler Youth took up where they had left off in their pre-1933 election propaganda. The *Spielschaaren* performed popular cabaret in the villages, consisting of singing, dancing, and folk plays, but Nazi polemics also remained part of their repertoire. During the Second

World War they would first take a communal meal with the villagers.[63]

If little enough is known about the actual plays these Hitler Youth troupes performed, still less is known about those of the "Strength through Joy," movement, which also encouraged *Spielgruppen* in factories. Such factory groups were called the Vanguard (*Stosstruppen*) and were meant to urge their fellow workers to sing, dance, and stage plays.[64] The Labor Service in its plays does seem to have stressed what one official called the manly, heroic world view as against the attitude of a nomadic and trading people.[65] We are back to the Jewish stereotype so easily presented on the "fighting stage." Such amateur theaters seem to have been the true continuation of the *Kampfbühne*. Although the professional theater did present some of the plays of the *NS-Volksbühne*, I have found hardly a trace of those writers whose dramas were performed before the seizure of power and whom we have mentioned earlier.

However, it is clear that the *Kampfbühne* exemplified the thrust of Nazi ideology and in its roots points to a theatrical tradition of importance. Surely neither the *Vereinstheater* nor the call for a national stage were without influence upon the attitudes of important sections of the population. Surely, too, the polemical theater during the Weimar Republic must be seen as a whole, in its impact upon the right as well as left, though the actual interaction between them may have been slight. We know much about the Piscator theater because it was innovative and important in putting forward a new dramatic style, while the *Kampfbühne* was crude and primitive. However, the latter's enthusiastic S.A. or Hitler Youth play troupes may well have struck a spark because of their very crudeness and traditionalism. Nor was the *NS-Volksbühne* without an audience, though it could never rival the famous older *Volksbühne* itself.

This theater must be placed next to the *Thing* theater as the objectification of Nazi ideology—an important function in a modern mass movement that relied on empathy, participation, and "enlightenment." For the Nazis themselves, the theater belonged to the most elementary expressions of life, as they put it.[66] That alone makes the *Kampfbühne* worth investigating, even if it is largely devoid of literary merit.

The Nazis did innovate within the relatively new media of film and photography. Some time late in the 1920s they began to use projectors to show a rapidly changing series of photographs: "pictures without words." These contrasted, for example, slum housing to the high life of a Reichstag deputy. They were fond of projecting the so-called Jewish faces of the republican statesmen, or showing Isidor Weiss, the deputy police chief of Berlin, whom they hated, in a riding outfit. This kind of kaleidoscope seems to have been a success with audiences. The Nazis also at times used photo-montage, and did not disdain the newest avant-garde film techniques pioneered during the Weimer Republic.[67] However, such innovation was always embedded in traditionalism. The stream of history which the Nazis claimed was on their side had to be kept alive—the past must determine the artistic and literary forms of the present. The crude and simplistic *Kampfbühne* exemplified not only Nazi literature and art but also the Nazi historical consciousness.

NINE

On Homosexuality and French Fascism

THE LITERATURE analyzing fascist attitudes towards homosexuals is growing rapidly after many years of silence. We can now, for the first time, begin to discern the difference between the Nazi and the Italian fascist persecution of homosexuals: the Nazi's tightening and applying laws against them, while in Italy homosexuality was not criminalized, but if need be, could be persecuted for disturbing the public order. However, the racial laws of 1938 made the persecution of homosexuals easier as well, as they could be accused of undermining the racial health of the Italian nation.[1] Racism provided the justification for the persecution of homosexuals under fascism, together with the attempt to maintain ideals of manliness and virility unsullied by the imputation of sexuality which was crucial for fascist self-representation.

But what about homosexual attitudes towards fascism? This question has received little notice and is indeed difficult to address, if only because anti-fascists tried to defame the Nazi leadership through the imputation of homosexuality. However, an investigation of the dialectic relationship between persecutor and persecuted is important for an understanding of the process of annihilation. Robert Lifton's *Nazi Doctors* (1986) can provide a model here, because of its detailed discussion of the relationship between SS doctors and prisoner-physicians at Auschwitz. While in Germany or Italy such a relationship has to be addressed through an analysis of homosexual reactions to their persecution, France under the German occupation was a special case, for, with some exceptions, the Germans themselves did not actively persecute homosexuals in occupied countries but left it to the local authorities who, as in the case of the Netherlands, obtained few convictions.[2] And in France, the Germans overruled the Vichy government when it wanted to ban one of Jean Cocteau's plays.[3] Here, in France, the attitudes of homosexuals could develop without much outside interference, free from many of the pressures of persecution which prevailed in Germany and the territories annexed outright during the war.

Homosexual attitudes towards the occupation were questioned in France after the Second World War when elsewhere the subject was passed over in silence. Anti-fascist intellectuals commented upon what they perceived as the collaboration of some conspicuous homosexuals with the occupation. We do not know the stand of the vast majority of homosexuals many of whom did serve in the resistance, while others adopted a more favorable attitude toward fascism. Here we are concerned with the collaborationists, some of whom occupied prominent or highly visible positions. Moreover, perceptions of homosexuality are sometimes different from reality, as some who through their male orientation seemed to be homosexuals may have been married, or even if single might have rejected gay sex. The very concept of homosexuality sometimes shades over into homoeroticism without observers being able to make the proper distinction.

I shall draw my example largely from the writings of Robert Brasillach, as well as from Drieu La Rochelle, who may have been a special case, though I could have added other examples from the circle of their friends. Anti-fascist polemics, as I have mentioned, often accused fascists of being closet homosexuals, citing as proof fascism's preoccupation with images of manliness. The poet Jean Quéval, for example, writing immediately after the war, attacked Abel Bonnard,

Jean Cocteau and Maurice Rostand, all known homosexuals and collaborators, as pederasts who attempted to draw French youth into the fascist camp, and who painted a rosy picture of French life under the occupation. "Et pourqois d'ailleurs no serait-on pas pederaste a Paris sous l'occupation?" ("and why should one not be a pederast under the occupation?"), and he goes on to cite Jean Cocteau's aphorism, "tous est dans tous."[4]

Jean-Paul Sartre and Jean Guehenno asked without any polemics why so many homosexuals supported the occupation, Sartre emphasizing the case of Drieu La Rochelle.[5] When Andre Halimi came to interview various writers and artists for his *Chansons sur l'occupation* (1976), he asked Jean-Louis Bory if he would care to defend homosexuals against such charges. Bory who was gay himself did not deny the premise of homosexual collaboration, but put it down to the "myth of virility" which signified power and courage. Moreover, "on retrouve par la le cote femelle qu'il peut avoir en effet chez l'homosexuel."[6] ("Moreover, their womanish nature could have affected the homosexuals"). Fascist preoccupation with masculinity struck a deep cord not merely among so-called homosexuals but among a whole range of men. Masculinity in fascism stood for youthful energy, male camaraderie, and the aesthetics of the male body which came to symbolize true manliness.

Such masculinity held a special attraction for the young French rightists of the 1930s, intoxicated by youth, in quest of passionate engagement, and in revolt against what they considered to be a passive and degenerate society.[7] Robert Brasillach defined what he called the "douceur de vivre" as commitment, love for life, and, above all, close male friendships. "C'est l'esprit meme de l'amitié dons nous aurons volu qu'il s'elevat jusqu'a l'amitié nationale."[8] ("It is the spirit of friendship itself which we want to elevate into a national spirit of friendship"). Male friendship and male camaraderie gave body to the ideal of manliness. The Nazi Party, for example, first presented itself as such a camaraderie to its supporters.[9] But what about the sexuality inherent in such a concept of masculinity?

Drieu La Rochelle best exemplifies this problem, for in his thought, as Robert Soucy has shown, the cult of the male body and the cult of friendship were closely linked. Strength of body signified strength of mind as well, and both were made public through male friendships. "For me," Drieu wrote, "the drama of friendship between men is at the heart of politics."[10] The Nazi Party rally at Nuremberg which he attended in 1935 came to symbolize for Drieu the aesthetic of politics, and he couched his appreciation in language which was similar to Brasillach's own description of these rallies: ". . . il ya une espèce de volupté virile qui flotte partout et quin'est pas sexuelle mais très envirante."[11] ("There is a virile male voluptuousness which courses everywhere and which is not sexual but uplifting").

Drieu despised homosexuals who, along with women and Jews, were the infernal triangle of decadence.[12] He was a great womanizer though he thought that true friendship with a woman was never possible. Brasillach was married and the accusation of homosexuality levelled against him at his trial for collaboration was not supported by the evidence brought forward at the time. What Sartre and the other anti-fascist intellectuals called the "pederastic attraction to fascism" was a homoerotic attraction which went much beyond that small circle of men stigmatized by Sartre, Guehenno or Jean Quéval. The aesthetics of politics in fascism appealed to a large and distinguished group of European intellectuals. The idealized male body was an integral part of this aesthetic. Sculptures of nude Greek youth, for example, were thought indispensable to Nazi self-representation. The classical ideal of male beauty symbolized masculine qualities as understood by generations of young Germans, and by Brasillach's anthology of Greek poetry. Here Greece is eternally young surrounded by "perfect men."[13]

The young French Right devalued women. Brasillach's women were "êtres immaterielles,"[14] and even though he wrote one of the most explicit scenes of heterosexual love-making in French literature,[15] they apparently lacked profound meaning in his private life. It seems to me that Brasillach and his *équipe*, who remained together from the Lyceé Louis le Grand, to the École Normale, to their common venture in editing the pro-fascist newspaper *Je Suis Partout*, were on the border between homosexuality and homoeroticism. There are hints of this in Brasillach's writings not cited at the trial, and in the polemical reply by d'Étiemble to the special issue of *Le Monde* at the 25th anniversary of his execution.[16] Drieu wrote that after the First World War one might have thought that he was especially interested in women; in fact, he was much more interested in men.[17] Many other examples of such attitudes towards women come to mind: thus for the writer Henri de Montherlant any woman who enters a man's life threatens to destroy it.[18]

Male camaraderie, regarded by the Nazis as the cell from which the state grew, gave political direction to the cult of masculinity. Brasillach wrote that for their adversaries *Je Suis Partout* was an official mouthpiece of international fascism, "mais nous savions que nous étions surtout le journal de notre amitié et de notre amour de vie."[19] ("But we knew that it was, above all, a testimony to our friendship and to our love for life"). As far as I know, the meaning of *équipe* or even of friendship in French cultural history has never been investigated. However, nationalism, which furthered the *Männerbund* in Germany was not so closely tied to the French *équipe*. While nationalism played an important role in that *équipe* of friends which Brasillach describes in his autobiography, *Notre Avant Guerre* (1941), it was not at the heart of their friendships. After all, the German tradition of the *Männerbund* with its youth movements and Stefan George Circle was missing in France: all of which appealed to the male eros principally in order to regenerate the nation.

Nevertheless, the ideal of friendship in France also had an erotic component, as Arthur Mitzman has shown, analyzing the nineteenth-century fraternal utopia of the historian Jules Michelet and his friends.[20] Michelet himself wrote about male friendship as a means of progress, as the prerequisite for the love of the nation. Family, nurse-maid and even the mother give way in childhood before the attachment to a male comrade, until such friendships are destroyed as man is enslaved by passion, broken by a harsh education and soured by rivalry.[21] Nevertheless, the ideal of camaraderie as an *équipe* of men was apparently not so fully developed in France as it was, for example, in Nazi Germany. There, these *Männerbünde* encompassed not only the cult of male friendship, male eros, or a shared love for life, but above all meant the subordination of each individual to shared ideals which must be put into practice. Perhaps the French *équipe* implied such a self-contained world, but it seemed to lack the firm contours of the German *Bünde*.

However, the definition of masculinity these French fascists and young Germans brought to their ideal of camaraderie was much the same and so was the need for a leader as a role model for their group. Drieu wanted a leader, "un homme a son plein, l'homme qui donne et qui prend dans la meme éjaculation."[22] ("A real man, a man who gives and takes at the same time"). Such a leader symbolized Drieu's longing for discipline and power. Brasillach, in turn, praised leaders who were "masters of violence."[23]

This love of violence was part of the cult of virility, yet it was never supposed to be anarchic but disciplined instead. Precisely such a concept of disciplined power was symbolized by the Greek sculptures of naked youths. "The Füherer tells me," Céline wrote, "that might makes right, and I know where I am,"[24] while for Ezra Pound fascism put an end to all uncertainty.[25] Male camaraderie reflected qualities of leadership, self-control and a carefully moderated strength ready to use force if need be, all of which were thought to have been a Greek heritage.

It seems to me that one of Germany's principle attractions for such French fascists was that here they found a firm ideal of the *Männerbund*. The passages from Brasillach's writings used against him at his trial, declaring his love for German soldiers with whom he wants to shake hands and whom he wants to embrace,[26] reflect not homosexuality but an idealization of such a *Bund*. The power of male eros, together with love of the nation, played a crucial role in defining the *Männerbund*, and this was bound to prove attractive to youths for whom idealized male friendships in school and university had been at the center of their lives.

Ideals of male friendship, the aesthetics of politics, and the search for a true *Männerbund* determined the attitudes of prominent homosexuals to fascism, attitudes that were not specifically homosexual but shared by many others as well. Certainly, this relationship cannot be characterized solely through the use of the term homosexual, but was informed instead by a homoeroticism which had always played a role in male friendship, camaraderie and nationalism.[27] All of these concepts need further investigation as to their role in homosexual attitudes towards fascism, including the ideal of masculinity which informed all of them. For example, was the *Männerbund*, as conceived by French youth, a means to test their manliness? Such a test became an obsession to many a youth after the First World War, a time when, for example, Christopher Isherwood in England saw himself quite often confronted with the question, are you really a man?

This interpretation which makes the attraction of the ideals of manliness and camaraderie central to the attitudes of these intellectuals towards fascism seems to omit what has been represented as the true dividing line between those who were pro-fascist—which in the French situation meant willing collaborators—and those who joined the French resistance. Anti-Semitism was said to have determined the divide between the Left and the radical Right in France ever since the Dreyfus Affair,[28] more important than the fascist ideal of masculinity and the beauty, camaraderie and virility for which it stood. There is no doubt that in general the strength of anti-Semitism was a crucial factor in determining such political allegiance. However, this argument is irrelevant to the fact that homoerotic attraction played a key role in determining the political attitudes of a certain group of young men once they were confronted with a movement which took the masculine ideal as one of its prime symbols.

The ideals of camaraderie, friendship and of male intimacy involved can tell us something about the effectiveness of the widespread use which all of fascism made of so-called male virtues and the male image.[29] This is why within a larger framework it is important to analyze the attitudes of some homosexuals towards fascism, which were noted at the time and which transcend the specifically sexual, pointing to basic fascist ideals like the cult of masculinity and the aesthetic of politics.

TEN

Nazi Aesthetics:
Beauty Without Sensuality and the
Exhibition of Degenerate Art

B EAUTY WITHOUT SENSUALITY: this title refers not only to the specific relationship between National Socialism and art but also summarizes the background which led to the Exhibition of Degenerate Art in 1937 and the great success that this exhibition enjoyed at the time.

The National Socialist view of art was based upon the idealized people and sentimental landscapes which had informed nineteenth-century popular taste, and upon neo-classical themes which were Adolf Hitler's favorites. National Socialism annexed neo-romantic and neo-classical art as its own, defining it as racially pure, an art that could easily be understood and whose pictured men and women exemplified the Germanic race. This was the official art of the regime which dominated the annual German Exhibitions of Art in Munich whose paintings were often selected by Hitler himself.

There was deeper purpose to the acceptance of such art: it symbolized a certain standard of beauty which might serve to cement the unity of the nation and project a moral standard to which everyone should aspire. What was and is called respectability was supposed to inform personal and public morality which true art must support and reflect. The men and women depicted in Nazi painting and sculpture thus stood for the proper morality and sexual behavior. Beauty without sensuality was demanded of artists and sculptors—a beauty which must reflect generally accepted moral standards which the Nazis championed as their own. For it was the strength and appeal of National Socialism that it did not invent anything new in its effort at self-representation, but simply annexed long-term traditions and popular tastes.

The Exhibition of Degenerate Art was put on in the same year as the Exhibition of German Art and featured paintings and sculpture which reflected the Nazi view of life under the Weimar Republic, as concrete evidence that the Nazis had saved German society. The Weimar Republic was viewed as an onslaught upon all the moral values people held dear: marriage, the family, chastity and a steady harmonious life. Weimar culture was "bolshevist culture," manipulated by the Jews, as the inscriptions at the exhibition and its catalogue make clear. The destruction of respectability and the destruction of society and the nation were linked.

The Exhibition of Degenerate Art must not be seen simply as Nazi propaganda for it played upon basic moral attitudes which have informed all of modern society. After all, respectability has lasted, and while the Nazis through the Exhibition of Degenerate Art used modern art as an example of those forces which would destroy it, even today modern art is condemned if it transgresses the normative morality in too shocking a fashion. That the Exhibition of Degenerate Art stands in a continuity, however tenuous, is demonstrated by the removal in 1989 of Robert Maplethorpe's homoerotic photographs from a Washington gallery because they were supposed to offend against decency and popular taste. Beauty with sensuality presented a danger to society because of what it symbolized, namely the revolt against respectability as a principle of unity and order: the destruction of the immutable values upon which society supposedly rested. If we are to understand the true significance of the Exhibition of Degenerate Art we must refer back to some of the relevant history in order to see how respectability coped with its enemies and what was at stake, for the exhibition itself is like the tip of an iceberg which has not yet melted.

Adolf Hitler himself pointed out at the 1934 Nuremberg party rally what art—and morality—were chiefly about, remarks that were reprinted in the catalogue accompanying the Exhibition of Degenerate Art: "Anyone who seeks the new for the sake of the new strays all too easily into the realm of folly." What was at issue, rather, was art as the expression of supposedly unchanging values in a society in search of such values. The modern age seemed to threaten the coherence of life itself. The acelerated pace of industrial and technological change at the turn of the nineteenth and twentieth centuries meant a certain disorientation, a "simultaneity of experience" with which people must cope. Already by mid-century we hear complaints that railroad travel had destroyed nature as the landscape performed a wild dance before the trains' windows. Just so, the invention of the telephone, the motor car or the cinema introduced a new speed of time which menaced the unhurried pace of life of an earlier age. Such concerns were reflected in the heightened quest for order against nervousness and instability.

Respectability ensured security and order, the maintenance of values, apparently taming the chaos that seemed always to threaten society. Respectability had been a political issue from the very beginning: it reflected people's lifestyle, their attitude toward all that was "different" and to themselves as well. The enemies of respectability, it was said, could not control themselves; they were creatures of instinct with their unbridled passions. Such accusations are scarcely to be found before the age of the French Revolution, but from now on they become common: whether it was Englishmen at the time of the Napoleonic Wars claiming that the French were sending dancers to England in order to undermine the islanders' morality, or whether it was First World War propaganda which sought by means of words and pictures to impute to the enemy every kind of "sexual perversion"—it was always morality and its enemies that were involved. During the course of the nineteenth century, an increasingly clear distinction was drawn between "normal" and "abnormal" sexuality, and between "normal" behavior and what was branded as "immoral." It was above all doctors, using categories of health and sickness, who threw their weight behind society's constantly threatened moral norms, lending them legitimacy and thus defining the stereotypes of what was "abnormal."

Those whom society treated as outsiders were now furnished with all those characteristics which ran counter to the image which society had of itself. The mentally ill, Jews, homosexuals, and criminals were all said to be physically unbalanced. Nervousness was regarded as the chief enemy of bourgeois, mainstream morality with its emphasis upon steadiness and restraint—an illness that lead from onanism to sexual excess. Nervousness was designated as a serious illness by such famous doctors as Jean-Martin Charcot in the 1880s, and, in common with the iconography of illness in general (exhaustion, contortions, and grimaces), was thought to symbolize the opposite of the normative standard of beauty. The Exhibition of Degenerate Art was built upon such views of the outsider and used modern art to construct a so-called cabinet of horrors.

The term "degeneration" summed up the fears which haunted society from the *fin de siècle* onwards. Degeneration was in its origins a medical term used by physicians during the second half of the nineteenth century in order to identify those who had departed from the so-called normal human type because their nerves were shattered, inherited abnormalities or the practice of moral and sexual excess. Such conditions started a process which would inevitably lead to destruction. Degenerates could be identified by their appearance: bodily deformities, red eyes, feeble and exhausted. Max Nordau in his book *Degeneration* (1892) did most to popularize the term as he applied it to modern literature and art. Modern artists, whether Expressionists or Impressionists, were incapable of reproducing nature because they had lost the faculty of accurate observation and instead painted distorted and irregular forms mirroring their own nervous deformities and stunted growth. Not only humans but nations as well could degenerate, a process thought to have started because of the falling birth rates in nations like France. Thus those who refused to conform to the moral dictates of society and its norms were labelled degenerate, and as they themselves were doomed to destruction they might destroy society as well.

In Hitler's view the artists in the 1937 exhibition symbolized degeneracy: "And what do they fabricate?" the exhibition catalogue quotes Hitler as asking. "misshapen cripples and cretins, women who can arouse only revulsion, [. . .] and this as the expression of something that the present age has fashioned and which has left its mark on it." Against this background of attempts to define the boundaries of bourgeois morality, Hitler's pronouncement resurrects the nineteenth- and early twentieth-century iconography of the outsider as described by physicians like Max Nordau. Moreover, it had the identical purpose which was to advance a certain concept of beauty as a readily understood symbol of society's values.

Looked at closely, nervousness itself was a product of modernity: The home of all these outsiders was always the city, further proof of the fact that the outsider scorned the tranquility of eternal values: for him, time never stood still. One of the most despicable Nazi propagandists, Johannes von Leers, expressed it in this way, no doubt speaking for many others in doing so: the city was the refuge of immorality and crime, and it was here that the "Jewish conspiracy" tried to gain control over German hearts and minds in order to drive them insane with frenzy and lust. For all its exaggeration and racial hatred, this view was still indebted to the nineteenth-century tradition of respectability with its emphasis on controlling the passions and on the consequences of losing that control. There is a continuity here which we shall constantly encounter: The National Socialists' attitude toward sexuality and art cannot be separated from the general history of respectability.

The ideal of beauty played a dominant role as a symbol of morality extending far beyond the realm of art. Beauty helped to maintain control over the passions. Friedrich Schiller, for example, in his series of letters *On the Aesthetic Education of Mankind* of 1795, wrote that beauty ennobled the otherwise merely instinctive sexual act, transcending it by virtue of its eternal values. But what is "beauty"? This question penetrates to the very heart of society's morals. For beauty, in neo-romantic or neo-classical art, like the iconography of the outsider already mentioned, becomes the self-portrayal of society, the view it liked to have of itself. Morality and its symbols (of which beauty was positive and nervousness negative) were a political issue of the first order in an age when society believed itself on the very brink of chaos as a result of the new pace of change and the Great War. In this context the term "degenerate art" is merely part of a general sense of anxiety. Hitler himself boasted that with his seizure of power the "nervous nineteenth century" had finally come to an end.

Beauty without sensuality presented a special problem as far as the representation of the ideal male was concerned, for his beauty was inspired by Greek models. Thus during the late nineteenth century, but especially under the Nazis, he was often represented in the nude. For the Nazis such men, through their harmonous form, the play of muscles and their controlled strength, symbolized the true German upon whose commitment the Third Reich depended. The evolution of bourgeois morality went hand in hand with the rediscovery of classical sculptures. As described by J. J. Winckelmann in his *History of the Art of Antiquity* of 1764, male Greek statuary were paradigms of beauty for all time. Winckelmann made Greek art acceptable to the middle classes by raising the statues of naked youths to an abstract plane and turning them into a stylistic principle. Their beauty was conceived of as somehow sexless, a conviction shared by others, too, at a later date and inspired by the belief that the almost transparent whiteness of these figures raised them above the personal and sensual.

This was a male ideal of beauty: women, by contrast, were turned into passive figures such as Germania or Queen Luise, herself stylized as the "Prussian Madonna." From the moment when bourgeois morality was first established, the male and female ideals of beauty differed radically, a circumstance which largely determined the political role of women as a national symbol. The masculine was regarded as dynamic, promising to bring about a timeless order and to cure an ailing world. Thus, for example, Friedrich Theodor Fischer, the nineteenth century's foremost German writer on aesthetics, assigned to beauty and manliness the task of preventing chaos. And yet, for all the differences between male and female symbolism, they had one important point in common, in that both transcended sensuality. Nonetheless, while the male was often depicted nude, the woman, by contrast, was almost always fully clothed, at least to the extent that she functioned as a national symbol.

Male symbolism could not be stripped of all physicality. Quite the opposite. The beauty of Greek youths—lithe and supple bodies, muscular and harmonious—lay precisely in their nakedness. It was the physicality or corporeality of Greek sculptures that expressed strength and harmony, order and dynamism—in other words, the ideal qualities of both burgher and nation. This ideal of beauty must once again be seen in contrast to the figure of the outsider who was weak, exhausted, unmuscular, and nervous. The youthfulness of the male stereotype symbolized the dynamic of bourgeois society and of the nation as well; outsider figures, by contrast, were generally old. Thus, for example, we do not find many young Jews on the nineteenth-century German stage: they were, almost without exception, old and lonely.

Society expressed its morality in terms of generally accepted ideals of beauty, while projecting its fears and ideas of ugliness onto Jews, homosexuals, criminals, and the mentally disturbed—the very groups the National Socialists eventually determined to exterminate. And, once again, this was no accident, since as mentioned earlier, National Socialism claimed to have saved bourgeois morality from collapse. Or was it only Albert Speer's mother who voted for the Nazis because the youngsters marching through the streets looked so "neat?" Even before the Nazis' electoral victory in 1930 had not Alfred Rosenberg, the Nazi ideologist, written in his characteristically entitled book *The Swamp*, "Democracy has apparently been stabilized. Yet with its pederasty, lesbianism, and procuration, it has been defeated all along the line." And yet it was precisely during the period of National Socialism that the problematical nature of "nakedness without sensuality" found its clearest expression. The open homosexuality of Ernst Röhm, the powerful chief of the S.A.—the storm troopers—and other Nazi leaders, indicates the ambivalent attitude toward bourgeois respectability on the part of members of the early National Socialist movement. This is also true of Hitler, who defended Röhm against attacks by pointing out that the latter's private life was his own affair as long as he used some discretion. The 1934 murder of Röhm and other leaders of the S.A. who were known homosexuals had, in turn, little to do with their sexual inclinations. The S.A. was now threatening Hitler's own power and destroying his relations with the regular army. Be that as it may, the opportunity was seized to underline the role of the party and of the regime as the defender of respectability. Show trials were held in which Catholic priests were accused of homosexuality, and the family was given a central role to play in National Socialist propagands.

The foundations for such a development had already been laid immediately after Hitler's seizure of power on January 30, 1933. As early as February 23, all so-called pornographic literature had been banned and prostitution drastically curbed. It is no wonder that organizations such as the German Evangelical Morality League welcomed Hitler's seizure of power since it apparently brought an end to the moral chaos of the postwar period—and this was by no means the only organization of its kind that saw the Nazis as the saviours of bourgeois morality. But the threat to respectability remained as before. The Nazi Party sought to build upon wartime experiences and first presented itself as a continuation of the male cameraderie which had existed in the trenches. Even when it broadened its base and appeal it never lost its characteristic as a *Männerbund*, a cameraderie of males, a concept which, in any case, had a long tradition in Germany. Important sub-groups of the party like the S.A. or the SS were proud of being male organizations which excluded so-called unmenly men. But such conscious male bonding raised the danger of homoeroticism or even homosexuality, a possibility which frightened some of the leadership.

The driving force behind the purge of all that might pose a threat to respectability was Heinrich Himmler, the leader of the SS. More clearly than anyone else, he articulated the sexual policies of the Third Reich and its underlying fears. These fears went into the making of the Exhibition of Degenerate Art, which would demonstrate to anyone who could see, the consequences of the rejection of social and sexual norms. For Himmler, deviants from the sexual norm were not only outsiders, they were also racial enemies. His concern was directed in the first place at the *Männerbund*—after all, his own SS often represented itself through the image of an idealized, semi-nude male—and if he emphasized the contrast between homosexuality and manliness, it was because of his fear that the one could easily turn into the other. Himmler's obsessional regard for respectability and his fear of all sensuality encouraged him to magnify the homoerotic or even homosexual components of the *Männerbund*. At the same time he affirmed that the Third Reich was a *Männerstaat*, a state based upon the comradeship of men: "For centuries, yea, millennia, the Germans have been ruled as a *Männerstaat*."

But that state was now threatened with self-destruction as a result of homosexuality, as Himmler made clear in November 1937 in a speech delivered to his SS leadership in Bad Tölz. In it even prostitution—otherwise strictly prohibited—was suggested as a remedy. Himmler regarded homosexuality as a sickness which poisoned both body and mind, but he now went a stage further than the metaphorical language of sickness and health and drew on the imagery of "naturalness" and "unnaturalness." In the good old days of the Teutonic tribes, Himmler told his Bad Tölz audience, homosexuals were drowned in the swamps: "This was no punishment, but simply the extinction of abnormal life." Nature simply rectifies her own mistake, and Himmler laments that this kind of extinction is no longer possible today. The death of the outsider, presented here as the goal of the struggle for purity and respectability, points the way to the Holocaust.

It must be stressed that doctors such as Jean-Martin Charcot, who described Jews as subject to nervous diseases, had never for a moment thought of killing them: for Charcot, anyone who was ill could be cured. It was racism which determined Himmler's offensive against outsiders, but also the wish to protect respectability, no matter what the price.

The nakedness of the male stereotype displayed on so many Nazi buildings and monuments played a role that never lost its unsettling and latently threatening effect. In this context it is not without significance that nudism was banned immediately after the Nazis came to power. It was said to deaden women's natural shame. On much the same level is a warning, issued by the Ministry of the Interior in 1935, to the effect that nude bathing by people of the same sex could be seen as the first step toward the violation of paragraph 175, which was directed against homosexual acts.

In its attempt to strip nakedness of its sensuality, the Third Reich not only banned nudism (a ban which, given the powerful influence of the ideal stereotype, was scarcely relevant) but, more especially, drew a sharp distinction between the private and the representational. Arno Breker's nude male sculptures continued to be in official demand, and semi-nude men and women decorated public spaces. But it was an abstract, smooth, almost transparent nakedness and a frozen posture which dominated the representational sphere, a dominance achieved by recourse to Winckelmann's purified concept of beauty.

The Nazis encouraged physical training and here the problem of nudity arose once more. Hans Surèn in his *German Gymnastics, Physical Beauty and Training*, a book which went through several editions during the Third Reich summed up the effort to strip the nude body of its sensuousness in this particular setting. He advocates nearly complete nudity in the pursuit of sport or while roaming through the countryside. But the male body had to be prepared carefully before it could be offered to public scrutiny: the skin must be hairless, smooth, and bronzed. The body had become the abstract symbol of Aryan beauty, as it was, also, in Leni Riefenstahl's film of the 1936 Olympic Games. Sensuality is transcended by being aligned with Greek forms—figures that could be worshipped but neither desired nor loved.

And women? Goebbels insisted that girls should be strong, healthy, and good to look at, which meant that as he put it, in contrast to the male, the muscles of their arms and legs should not be visible. The importance of iconography can be judged from the extent to which the Nazis described physical detail. But how can this ideal of womankind be reconciled with the naked sportswoman, for the latter did indeed exist? The simple answer is that the female athlete's body was often approximated to that of the male. Without obvious feminine contours, it was thus, in principle, identical with that of the male youth: nakedness without sensuality. While, on the one hand, Goebbels launched his attacks on "sports girls," the League of German Girls (BDM) was liberating the mass of young girls for the first time in their history from some home and family commitments, an act of emancipation achieved through sport and country walks. The National Socialist view of women was clearly not free of contradictions, even if those contradictions existed within only a limited framework. Perhaps the reason for this is that National Socialism was based on a consciously male society that often behaved in a contradictory way toward women. Male homosexuality, for example, was strenuously persecuted, as we have seen, but the same was not true of lesbianism which was largely ignored.

In this area, too, the main concern was to separate the private from the representational. In the private sphere, women could be completely naked and sensual—for how else can we interpret the paintings by Hitler's favorite artist, Leopold Ziegler, paintings which hung not only in the Führer's private apartments but also in exhibitions of German Art? Ziegler's fleshy and full-bosomed nudes which left nothing to the imagination hung side by side with Gretchen-like figures, chaste, with blonde plaits—the so-called typical German maiden. The representational world, by contrast, was the political world, and here the aim was to integrate the masses into the Third Reich with the aid of stereotypes that would treat the beautiful as a reflection of the eternal and immutable, revealing it as something pure and removed from all materialism and sensuality.

How deeply respectability and its concept of beauty were embedded in society can be inferred from the different ways in which the term was justified long before National Socialism. At the beginning of the nineteenth century it was religion—and especially Protestantism—that had taken upon itself the task of justifying respectability, whereas by the end of the century that role had been taken over by the people themselves. The stricter attitude towards sodomy, which was made a criminal offense in many countries in *fin-de-siècle* Europe, appealed no longer to religion but to popular sentiment. The clear and unambiguous distinction between the socially normal and the deviant, a distinction that was now medically and iconographically supported—as well as by religion and education—had been internalized. Goebbels knew exactly what he was doing when, in 1936, he banned art criticism on the grounds that the general public should make up its own mind—he was risking very little. That same year the paintings on offer at the Exhibition of German Art sold better than those at almost all earlier art exhibitions.

All this is the indispensable background to the Exhibition of Degenerate Art. It was an exhibition designed to be out of the ordinary, a survey of all that was indecent and ugly and that represented an assault on bourgeois morality through the latter's concept of beauty. Works by modern artists were treated not as evidence of individual creativity but as representative of something else: they were accorded no individual value but only a symbolic status. This, of course, was a mockery of those artists who vaunted their individualism above all else, yet it was the reaction of a society which felt under constant threat, a society, moreover, bonded together by respectability with its eternal values and by the security which it radiated.

And yet foreign newspapers like the Manchester Guardian or the New York Times reported in 1937 that far more people had visited the Exhibition of Degenerate Art than the parallel exhibit devoted to German art. According to the Manchester Guardian there were five times as many visitors each day, while the New York Times reported that there had been 396,000 visitors, as against 120,000, within the space of a week. What is the explanation? Curiosity? It is a question that is difficult to answer, but it is unlikely that an interest in modern art played a part here. Moreover, the Nazis themselves encouraged people to visit the exhibition. Or had the contradiction between bourgeois respectability and the ever latent temptation to act unconventionally become acute once more, a temptation contained in the regime's anti-bourgeois rhetoric?

Notwithstanding the latent contradictions that it involved, respectability—and all that it implied—remained an essential part of the regime, and in the exhibition catalogue all those outsiders were blamed for the degeneration of art which had threatened society's conformist principles since the beginning of the last century. The paintings on display were the work of madmen disfigured by sexual excesses: they represented Marxist and Jewish attacks on all that was German. The text of the catalogue sums up a tradition that sought to draw an increasingly sharp distinction between respectability as something normal, and abnormality; between the healthy and the sick, and between the natural and the unnatural. Thus people could resist the chaos of the age and accept a "slice of eternity" into their lives.

What was sacrificed in the process was sensuality, passion and, to a great extent, individuality itself. The analysis of "beauty without sensuality" undertaken here can be seen as a critique of bourgeois morality with its division of labor according to sex, and as a critique, finally, of the never-ending attempt to draw a distinction between this morality, viewed as the norm, and what was seen as "abnormal." But we must never forget that for most people respectability is much more than merely a form of behavior or an ideal of beauty for their spare time; for many—perhaps even for the vast majority—it offers cogent proof of the cohesiveness of society, a cohesiveness necessary for all systems of government, not just for National Socialism. Hence the favorable response which the Exhibition of Degenerate Art encountered, even in places where we might not expect it. The New Statesman, for example, an English left-wing journal, wrote that the exhibition was the best thing Mr. Hitler had done so far.

The smooth running of a generally accepted morality was just as important for the cohesion of society as the oft-quoted economic and social factors, while, at the same time, it was something that people understood, something that impinged on their daily lives in a wholly concrete and comprehensive way. The ideal of beauty as exemplifying such norms was influenced not only by sentimentalism or Romanticism, it had a social function as well. The aesthetics of politics, of daily life, involved a degree of social control which it had assumed ever since bourgeois morality first came into being. The sculpture that I have mentioned, together with much of the popular literature, is filled with a passion and love that are supposedly devoid of sensuality. For example, Agnes Günther's novel *Die Heilige und ihr Narr* (*The Saint and Her Fool*, 1913), a run-away bestseller during the Weimar Republic, was a sentimental love story in which sensuality is equated with sickness. Seen from such a standpoint, the sculpture and the popular literature that was read at this time readily fall into a tradition which the National Socialists merely took to its extreme.

And today? If my analysis is correct, I can only say that the same needs still exist; that, notwithstanding our modern tolerance toward the individual and sensuality, what seems involved here is more an extension of what is permissible than an actual breach in the principle of respectability. There may be additional proof of this in the fact that, after periods of greater sexual tolerance, the limits are always imposed once again. We are seeing this rhythm repeated once more today, in episodes like that of the Maplethorp exhibit mentioned earlier, and in the continued effort in the United States to control the erotic content of publicly funded art. Marcel Proust gave perhaps the finest expression to that reciprocal relationship between conformism and tolerance that we can see around us today: Swann, the Jewish hero of *A la recherche du temps perdu*, is welcomed among the aristocratic and snobbish Guermantes as an exotic plant until such time as he becomes a Dreyfusard—defending the captain against his reactionary accusers—when they see him as a threat to their political and social position. This seems to me to symbolize the reality of a situation in which we continue to find ourselves today; bourgeois morality, once a newcomer in our midst, now appears so much a part of the way we see ourselves, so essential to our society, that we can scarcely imagine a different kind of morality. We forget that, like everything else in this world of ours, it is the result of historical evolution.

Notes

Introduction

1. See Stanley Payne, *A History of Fascism 1914–1945* (Madison, Wisc., 1995); Robert Eatwell, *Fascism: A History* (London, 1966); and R. Griffin, *The Nature of Fascism* (London, 1991). These are the important works of synthesis to appear in the last decades.

2. i.e. Karl Dietrich Bracher, *Zeitgeschichtliche Kontroversen um Faschismus, Totalitarismus, Demokratie* (Munich, 1976).

3. For this context, see S. Payne, *op. cit.*, 459–461.

4. Victor Klemperer, *LTI* (Frankfurt-am-Main, 1985), 118–119.

5. Manfred Hettling / Paul Nolte, "Bürgerliche Feste als Symbolische Politik im 19. Jahrhundert," in Manfred Hettling / Paul Nolte, eds., *Bürgerliche Feste* (Göttingen, 1993), 8.

6. Anthony D. Smith, "Memory and modernity; reflections on Ernst Gellner's theory of nationalism," *Nations and Nationalism*, Vol. 2, part 3 (November, 1996), 384.

7. See Emilio Gentile, *The Sacralization of Politics in Fascist Italy* (Cambridge, Mass., 1996); George L. Mosse, *The Nationalization of the Masses* (New York, 1975, 1999).

8. Michele Sarfatti, *Mussolini contro gli ebrei* (Turin, 1994), 47, 48.

9. i.e. George L. Mosse, *Toward the Final Solution: A History of European Racism* (New York, 1978, 1997), Chapter 2.

10. Barbara Spackman, *Fascist Virilities: Rhetoric, Ideology and Social Fantasy in Italy* (Minneapolis, 1996), 136.

11. George L. Mosse, *The Image of Man: The Creation of Modern Masculinity* (New York, 1996), Chapter 8.

1. *Toward a General Theory of Fascism*

1. The best recent discussion of fascism and totalitarian doctrine is Karl Dietrich Bracher, *Zeitgeschichtliche Kontroversen um Faschismus, Totalitarismus, Demokratie* (Munich, 1976).

2. Aryeh L. Unger, *The Totalitarian Party: Party and People in Nazi Germany and Soviet Russia* (Cambridge, 1974), 189, 202.

3. Piero Melograni, "The Cult of the Duce in Mussolini's Italy," *Journal of Contemporary History*, Vol. 77 (1976), 223–225.

4. Aryeh L. Unger, *op. cit.*, 1, 264.

5. Cf. George L. Mosse, ed., *Police Forces in History* (London and Beverly Hills, 1975).

6. I am grateful to Eric Johnson for letting me see part of his soon to be published crucial new research on the Gestapo.

7. See J. L. Talmon, *The Rise of Totalitarian Democracy* (Boston, 1952); and the criticism in George L. Mosse, "Political Style and Political Theory," *Confronting the Nation* (Hanover and London, 1993), Chapter 4.

8. Mona Ozouf, *La Fête révolutionnaire 1789–1799* (Paris, 1976), 22.

9. For a more thorough discussion of the point, see George L. Mosse, *The Nationalization of the Masses* (New York, 1975, 1999), and the unjustly forgotten Harold J. Laski, *Reflections on the Revolution of Our Time* (New York, 1943), not for his analysis of fascism but for the weakness of parliamentary government.

10. The term "good revolution" is Karl Dietrich Bracher, *op. cit.*, 68.

11. Stanley Payne, *A History of Fascism 1914–1945*, passim.

12. Renzo De Felice, *Fascism* (New Brunswick, N.J., 1976), 24.

13. Zeev Sternhell, *La Droite révolutionnaire 1885–1914* (Paris, 1978), passim; George L. Mosse, *Toward the Final Solution*, Chapter 10.

14. i.e. Emilio Gentile, *Le origini dell' ideologia Fascista* (Rome/Bari, 1975), 76ff.

15. Renzo De Felice, *Mussolini il rivoluzionario* (Turin, 1965), 591; Paolo Nello, *L'Avanguardismo Giovannile alle origini del fascismo* (Rome, 1978), 26–27.

16. George L. Mosse, *Germans and Jews: The Right, the Left, and the Search for a "Third Force" in Pre-Nazi Germany* (New York, 1970), Chapter 1.

17. See Chapter 6.

18. Otto-Ernst Schüddekopf, *Linke Leute von Rechts* (Stuttgart, 1960), 84.

19. Joseph Goebbels, *Tagebücher 1945* (Hamburg, 1976), 55, 69–70.

20. Ernst Bloch, *Thomas Münzer als Theologe der Revolution* (Munich, 1921), 295.

21. Victor Klemperer, *LTI; Notizbuch eines Philologen* (Berlin, 1947), 116–118.

22. i.e. Clarke Garrett, *Respectable Folly: Millenarians and the French Revolution in France and England* (Baltimore, 1975), 8.

23. Paolo Nello, review of Daniele Marchesini, "La scuola dei gerarchi," *Storia contemporanea* (September, 1977), 586.

24. Quoted in George L. Mosse, ed., *Nazi Culture* (New York, 1966), 116.

25. Giuseppe Bottai, *Il Fascismo e l'Italia Nuova* (Rome, 1923), 19.

26. Horia Sima, *Destinée du Nationalisme* (Paris, n.d.), 19.

27. These qualities are taken from *Voor Volk en Vaderland, De Strijd der Nationaalsocialistische Bewegung 14. December 1931–Mei 1941*, ed. C. Van Geelkerken (n.p., 1941), 315.

28. The remarks on the First World War are taken from George L. Mosse, *Fallen Soldiers: Shaping the Memory of the World Wars* (New York, 1990), Chapters 4, 5; see also his *The Image of Man*, Chapter 6.

29. Antoine Prost, *Les Anciens Combattants et la Société Française*, 3 vols. (Paris, 1978).

30. See George L. Mosse, "La sinistra europea e l'esperienza della guerra," *Rivoluzione e Reazione in Europa* (1917–1924), Convegno storico internazionale—Perugia, 1978 (Florence, 1978), Vol. II, 151–167.

31. Mussolini quoted in Umberto Silva, *Kunst und Ideologie des Faschismus* (Frankfurt-am-Main, 1975), 108. For Hitler, see *Die Fahne Hoch!* (1932), 14; also George L. Mosse, *Fallen Soldiers*, passim.

32. Alfred Steinitzer and Wilhelm Michel, *Der Krieg in Bildern* (Munich, 1922), 97; *Der Weltkrieg im Bild* (Berlin–Oldenburg, 1926), Preface.

33. Goebbels, *op. cit.*, 28.

34. Teresa Maria Mazzatosta, "Educazione e scuola nella Repubblica Sociale Italiana," *Storia contemporanea* (February 1978), 67.

35. Peter Hasubeck, *Das Deutsche Lesebuch in der Zeit des Nationalsozialismus* (Hanover, 1972), 77, 79.

36. Ernst Jünger, ed., *Das Antlitz des Weltkrieges* (Berlin, 1930), Preface.

37. Oldo Marinelli, quoted in Emilio Gentile, *Le Origini del' Ideologia Fascista* (Rome, 1974), 92.

38. Ruggero Zangrandi, *Il lungo viaggio* (Milan, 1948); for a discussion of this revolt of youth, see Michael Ledeen, *Universal Fascism* (New York, 1972), passim.

39. Drieu La Rochelle, *Socialisme Fasciste* (Paris, 1943), 72.

40. For Hans Naumann's speech, see Hildegard Brenner, *Die Kunstpolitik des Nationalsozialismus* (Hamburg, 1963), 188; Bottai, *op. cit.*, 18 ff; and Jean Denis, *Principes Rexistes* (Brussels, 1936), 17.

41. Hugh Seton-Watson, *Nations and States* (Boulder, Colo., 1977), 420, 421.

42. i. e. George L. Mosse, *The Image of Man*, Chapter 8.

43. Charles S. Maier, "Some Recent Studies of Fascism," *Journal of Modern History* (September 1976), 509; and Thomas Childers, "The Social Bases of the National Socialist Vote," in *International Fascism*, ed. George L. Mosse (London, 1979), 161–189.

44. Renzo De Felice, *Fascism* (New Brunswick, N.J., 1976), 46.

45. Gilbert D. Allardyce, "The Political Transition of Jacques Doriot," in *International Fascism*, ed. George L. Mosse, 287.

46. Henry A. Turner, Jr., "Big Business and the Rise of Hitler," in *Nazism and the Third Reich*, ed. Henry A. Turner, Jr. (New York, 1972), 93.

47. i. e. George L. Mosse, *Nazi Culture*, Chapter 1.

48. i.e. George L. Mosse, *Masses and Man* (New York, 1980), Chapter 3.

49. A list of popular novels under fascism will be found in Carlo Bordoni, *Cultura e propaganda nell'Italia fascista* (Messina–Florence, 1974), 85, but without any analysis of their individual content. However, see Pasquale Falco, *Letteratura Populare Fascista* (Cosenza, 1984), which is disappointing.

50. *Storia d'Italia*, ed. Ruggiero Romano and Corrado Vivanti (Turin, 1973), 1526; George L. Mosse, *The Nationalization of the Masses*, 194.

51. Francesco Sapori, *L'Arte e il Duce* (Milan, 1932), 141.

52. *Ibid.*, 123 ff.

53. Adrian Lyttleton, *The Seizure of Power: Fascism in Italy 1919–1929* (London, 1973), 389; Emilio Gentile, *The Sacralization of Politics in Fascist Italy*, passim.

54. George L. Mosse, *The Nationalization of the Masses*, Chapter 7; for the liturgy of Italian fascism, see Emilio Gentile, *The Sacralization of Politics*, passim.

55. Anson G. Rabinbach, "The Aesthetics of Production in the Third Reich," *International Fascism*, ed. George L. Mosse (London, 1979), 189–223.

56. Adrian Lyttleton, *op. cit.*, 19.

57. Oral communication, Albert Speer to George L. Mosse, June, 1974.

58. Schkem Gremigni, *Duce d'Italia* (Milan, 1927), 116.

59. E.g., *Ausstellung der Faschistischen Revolution, erste Zehnjahrfeier des Marsches auf Rom* (1933). Typically enough, the official poster for the exhibition featured soldiers from the First World War.

60. Donino Roncará, *Saggi sull' Educazione Fascista* (Bologna, 1938), 61; George L. Mosse, *The Image of Man*, Chapter 8.

61. Ernst Jünger, *Der Kampf als inneres Erlebnis* (Berlin, 1933), 32 ff.

62. i. e. Hitler at the Reichsparteitag, 1935, *Adolf Hitler an seine Jugend* (Munich, 1940), n.p.

63. See George L. Mosse, *Toward the Final Solution*, Chapter 2.

64. Renzo de Felice, *Fascism*, 56.

65. Domino Roncará, *op. cit.*, 55, 58.

66. *Esposizione Universale di Roma*, MCMXLII, XX E.F. (1942), 83, 88.

67. Giuseppe Bottia wrote that fascism was an intellectual revolution concerned with the problem of its origins—*Pagine di Critica Fascista (1915–1926)* (Florence, n.d.), 322.

68. *Führer Blätter der Hitler-Jugend* (1935), 10.

69. *Lehrplan für Sechsmonatige Schulung* (SS, Hauptamt IV, n.d., n.p.), 25, 79.

70. Typically enough, the newsletter of a Nazi elite school repeated this phrase in Italian, commenting that these ideals were shared by German and Italian youth—*Reichsschule der NSDAP Feldafing* (1940–41), 73.

71. *Ibid.* (1939–40), 17.

72. i.e. Robert Brasillach, *Le Marchand d'Oiseaux* (Paris, 1936), passim.

73. Charles Beuchat, "Le Quartier Latin aux temps du jeune Brasillach," *Hommages à Robert Brasillach* (Lausanne, 1965), 78.

74. Stanley G. Payne, "Fascism in Western Europe," in *Fascism: A Reader's Guide*, ed. Walter Laqueur (London, 1976), 303.

75. Sapori, *op. cit.*, 15ff; George L. Mosse, *Toward the Final Solution*, 42–43.

76. *Rex*, 23 (September 1938); *De Daad*, 2 (September 1933).

77. *Je Suis Partout*, April 18, 1938.

78. Michele Sarfatti, *Mussolini contro gli ebrei* (Turin, 1994), especially 6 ff, 29.

79. Sebastian Haffner, *Anmerkungen zu Hitler* (Munich, 1978), 43.

80. George L. Mosse, *Nationalization of the Masses*, 12, 202.

81. Renzo de Felice, *Fascism*, 65.

82. Sebastian Haffner, *op. cit.*, 154 ff.

83. See Chapter 6; also George L. Mosse, *Toward the Final Solution*, Chapters 7, 18.

84. See also Percy Ernst Schramm, *Hitler als militärischer Führer* (Frankfurt-am-Main, 1965), passim.

85. i. e. Stuart Ewen, *P.R.! A Social History of Spin* (New York, 1996), passim.

3. Racism and Nationalism

1. For the origins of racism, see George L. Mosse, *Toward the Final Solution: A History of European Racism* (New York, 1978, 1997).

2. Roger Chickering, *We Men Who Feel Most German: A Cultural Study of the Pan-German League 1886–1914* (Boston, 1984), passim.

3. George L. Mosse, *op. cit.*, Chapter 2.

4. J. J. Winckelmann, *Gedanken über die Nachahmung der Griechischen Werke etc.* (Stuttgart, 1885), 57.

5. George L. Mosse, *Nationalism and Sexuality*, (New York, 1985, 1997), Chapter 5.

6. Camper, *Dissertation Physique de M. Pierre Camper, etc.*, ed. Adrien Gilles Camper (Utrecht, 1791), esp. 97, 98; Robert Knox, *The Races of Men* (London, 1862), 404.

7. George L. Mosse, *The Image of Man*, Chapters 1, 2, and 3.

8. Thomas Nipperdey, "Auf der Suche nach Identität: Romantischer Nationalismus," *Nachdenken über die deutsche Geschichte* (Munich, 1990), 140.

9. H. de Genst, *Histoire de L'Éducation Physique*, Vol. II (Brussels, 1949), 192, 294.

10. J.C.F. Guts Muths, *Gymnastik für die Jugend* (Schnepfenthal, 1804, first published in 1793), 6.

11. See Chapter 2, page 49.

12. Sander Gilman, *The Jew's Body* (New York and London, 1991); and his *Difference and Pathology: Stereotypes of Sexuality, Race and Madness* (Ithaca, 1985).

13. H. W. Kranz, "Gemeinschaftsunfähigkeit und Ehrwürdigkeit," *Rasse*, Vol. 9, Heft 2 (1942), 235.

14. Sander Gilman, *The Jew's Body*, 134.

15. Adolf Hitler, *Mein Kampf* (Munich, 1931), 762–763.

16. Louis Durieu, *Les Juifs Algérienne (1870–1901)* (Paris, 1902), 87.

4. Fascism and the French Revolution

1. *Oeuvres complètes de J. J. Rousseau*, vol. 5 (Paris, 1907), 43.

2. Mona Ozouf, *La fête révolutionnaire 1789–1799* (Paris, 1976), 55ff; G. L. Mosse, *The Nationalization of the Masses*, Chapter 4.

3. Albert Mathiez, *La Theophilantropie et le Culte Décadaire* (Paris, 1904), 36.

4. Michel Vovelle, *Die Französische Revolution* (Frankfurt-am-Main, 1985), 115.

5. Friedrich Heer, *Der Glaube des Adolf Hitler* (Munich, 1968), 56.

6. Ernst Moritz Arndt, *Entwurf einer Teutschen Gesellschaft* (Frankfurt, 1814), 36.

7. Victor Klemperer, *LTI* (Frankfurt-am-Main, 1985), 118–19.

8. A. Aulard, *Christianity and the French Revolution* (New York, 1966), 106.

9. Mosse, *Nationalization*, 200.

10. Christoph Prignitz, *Vaterlandsliebe und Freiheit* (Wiesbaden, 1981), 138.

11. i.e., Hitler's Proclamation at the Nuremberg Party Day, 1934.

12. G. L. Mosse, *Nationalism and Sexuality*, Chapter 4.

13. Ozouf, *La fête*, Chapter 9.

14. Mona Ozouf, "Le Panthéon: L'École des Morts," in Pierre Nora, ed., *Les Lieux de Memoire* (Paris, 1984), vol. I, *La République*, 155ff.

15. Adolf Hitler, *Mein Kampf*, 286; Ranier Zitelmann has given the best account of Hitler's attitude to the French Revolution, even if it seems too positive. See his *Hitler: Selbstverständnis eines Revolutionärs* (Hamburg, 1987), 44–49.

16. Hitler, *Mein Kampf*, 269.

17. Alfred Rosenberg, *Der Mythos des 20. Jahrhunderts* (Munich, 1935), 500–501.

18. i.e., Hermann Wendel, *Danton* (Königstein/Ts., 1978), 362.

19. Ibid., 344.

20. Hitler, *Mein Kampf*, 371.

21. Jean-Jacques Rousseau, *The Government of Poland* (Indianapolis, 1972), 11, 14.

22. Jean Starobinski, *1789: The Emblems of Reason* (Charlottesville, 1982), 118.

23. Vovelle, *Die Französische Revolution*, 124.

24. See also Alfred Stein, "Adolf Hitler and Gustav le Bon," *Geschichte in Wissenschaft und Unterricht* (1955), 367; Renzo de Felice, *Mussolini il rivoluzionario* (Turin, 1965), 467, n. I.

25. Robert A. Nye, *The Origins of Crowd Psychology* (London and Beverly Hills, 1975), 73.

26. Gustav Le Bon, *The Crowd* (New York, 1960), 68.

27. Ibid., 118–19.

28. Emilio Gentile, *The Sacralization of Politics in Fascist Italy*, 86, 87.

29. Piero Melograni, "The Cult of the Duce in Mussolini's Italy, *Journal of Contemporary History* II (October 1976), 228.

30. Ibid., 223.

31. Mosse, *Nationalization*, 200.

32. Emilio Gentile, *Le Origini dell'Ideologia Fascista* (Rome–Bari, 1975), 184.

33. G. L. Mosse, *Masses and Man*, 97.

34. Gentile, *Le origini*, 184.

35. Ozouf, *La fête*, 97.

36. G. L. Mosse, *Fallen Soldiers*, Chapter 3.

37. Sergio Panunzio, *Italo Balbo* (Milan, 1923), 36–37.

38. Hans-Peter Gorgen, *Düsseldorf und der Nationalsozialismus* (Düsseldorf, 1969), 98. See also Jay W. Baird, *To Die for Germany: Heroes in the Nazi Pantheon* (Bloomington and Indianapolis, 1990).

39. Emil Ludwig and Peter O. Chotjewitz, *Der Mord in Davos* (Herbstein, 1986), 139.

40. Avner Ben-Amos, "Les Funerailles de Victor Hugo," in Pierre Nora, ed., *Les Lieux de Mémoire* (Paris, 1984), vol. I, *La République*, 474, 487ff.

41. As, for example, in the "L'Apoteosi del Caduto" in the "Sala dedicata alle Medaglie d'Oro," *Redipuglia*, ed. Ministero della Difesa, Commissariato Generale Onoranze Caduti in Guerra (Rome, 1972), 18.

42. Ozouf, "Le Panthéon," 145ff.

43. G. L. Mosse, "National Cemeteries and National Revival: The Cult of the Fallen Soldiers in Germany," *Journal of Contemporary History* 14 (January 1979), 1–20.

44. John McManners, *Death and the Enlightenment* (New York, 1981), 359–60.

45. Mosse, *Masses and Man*, Chapter 4.

46. Vovelle, *Die Französische Revolution*, 117.

47. Renzo de Felice, *Intervista sul fascismo*, ed. Michael A. Ledeen (Rome-Bari, 1975), 53–54.

48. Gentile, *Le Origini*, 328; Felice, *Intervista*, 53.

49. Emilio Gentile, *Il Mito dello State Nuovo dall'Antigiolittismo al*

Fascismo (Rome-Bari, 1982). I should like to thank Professor Gentile for his valuable suggestions.

50. Alberto Maria Ghisalbert, "Giacobini," *Enciclopedia Italiana* (1932), 16:934.

51. Ibid., 934.

52. Zeev Sternhell, *Neither Right nor Left: Fascist Ideology in France* (Berkeley, 1986), 106.

53. *Je Suis Partout*, Numéro Speciale sur la Révolution, no. 449 (30 June 1939), I.

54. Ibid., I.

55. Robert Brasillach, "Jacobins et Thermidoriens," *Oeuvres complètes de Robert Brasillach* (Paris, 1964), 12:604.

56. Roger Joseph, "Alcibiade et Socrate," *Cahiers des Amis de Robert Brasillach*, no. 13 (6 February 1968), 63–64.

57. Brasillach, "Jacobins," 605.

58. Joseph, "Alcibiade," 64.

59. Robert Soucy, *Fascist Intellectual: Drieu La Rochelle*, 214.

60. Brasillach, "Jacobins," 605.

61. *Je Suis Partout*, I.

62. Philippe Burrin, *La Dérive Fasciste* (Paris, 1986), 404.

63. Hitler, *Mein Kampf*, 536.

5. Fascism and the Intellectuals

1. Hayden White, "Benedetto Croce and the Renewal of Italian Culture: Croce as a Historian," (MS read at the annual meeting of the American Historical Association, December 29, 1966), 9.

2. Aldo Garosci, *La Vita di Carlo Roselli*, Vol II (Rome, n.d.), 70.

3. *Ibid.*, Vol. I, 143.

4. John R. Harrison, *The Reactionaries* (London, 1966), 127; Robert Brasillach, *Léon Degrelle* (Paris, 1936), 78.

5. Stanley Payne, *Falange* (Stanford, 1961), 49; Joris van Seeveren, *La Constitution des Pays-Bas* (St. Nicolas-Waes, 1938), 24.

6. Robert Brasillach, "La Poésie du national-socialisme," *Notre Combat*, No. 42 (April 1943), 6–7.

7. Julie Braun-Vogelstein, *Was Niemals Stirbt* (Stuttgart, 1966), 282. See also the accusations of Carlo Roselli against Italian socialism: Garosci, *op. cit.*, Vol. I, 143–144.

8. Christopher Caudwell, *Illusion and Reality* (New York, 1955), 288.

9. S. H. Harris, *The Social Philosophy of Giovanni Gentile* (Urbana, 1966), 172–173.

10. Louis Ferdinand Céline, *Journey to the End of the Night* (New York, 1960), 10.

11. Céline, *Bagatelles pour un Massacre* (Paris, 1937), 70.

12. Quoted in Harrison, *op. cit.*, 132.

13. Céline, *Bagatelles pour un Massacre*, 70; Pound quoted in Harrison, *op. cit.*, 137.

14. Céline's manifesto in *Au Pillori* reprinted in *L'Affaire Céline* (documents), *Les Cahiers de la Résistance*, No. 4 (n.d.), 33; his appointment by Otto Abetz, *ibid.*, 32. For Céline's career under the occupation, see Léon Poliakov, "Le cas Louis Ferdinand Céline et le cas Xavier Vallat," *Le Monde Juif*, 5 Year, No. 28 (February 1950), 5–7.

15. André Gide, "Les Juifs, Céline et Maritaine," *Nouvelle Revue Française*, Vol. L (January–June 1938), 631.

16. Gottfried Benn, "Das moderne Ich," *Der neue Staat und die Intellektuellen* (Stuttgart, 1933), 129–151. Hans Richter, *DADA, Art and Anti-Art* (New York, 1966), 112. For Benn's nihilism see Edgar Lohner, quoted in Reinhold Grimm, *Strukturen* (Göttingen, 1963), 309.

17. Benn, *op. cit.*, 20, 25.

18. Quoted in Peter de Mendelssohn, *Der Geist in der Despotie* (Berlin, 1953), 251.

19. Benn, "Antwort an die literarischen Emigranten," *op. cit.*, 31.

20. Ladislao Mittner, "Die Geburt des Tyrannen aus dem Ungeist des Expressionismus," *Festschrift zum achzigsten Geburtstag von Georg Lukacs* (Neuwied, 1965), 402–420.

21. Camillo Pelizzi, *Una Rivoluzione Mancata* (Florence, 1951?), esp. 30–35; Benn, *op. cit.*, 25.

22. Drieu La Rochelle, *Gilles* (Paris, 1939), 74.

23. Walter Benjamin, "Theorien des deutschen Faschismus," *Das Argument*, 6 Jahrg., Heft 3 (1964), 136.

24. La Rochelle, *op. cit.*, 393.

25. Harrison, *op. cit.*, 32.

26. Gottfried Benn, *Kunst und Macht* (Stuttgart, 1934), 106–107. Harrison, *op. cit.*, 137.

27. La Rochelle, *op. cit.*, p. 385.

28. Lucien Rébatet, *Les Décombres* (Paris, 1942), 20.

29. Harrison, *op. cit.*, 83.

30. See George L. Mosse, *The Crisis of German Ideology* (New York, 1964; Reprinted 1998).

31. Alfred Bäumler, "Die verwirklichte Idee," in Léon Poliakov and Josef Wulf, *Das dritte Reich und seine Denker* (Berlin, 1959), 268.

32. Harris, *op. cit.*, 172.

33. Quoted in Adrian Lyttelton, "Fascism in Italy: The Second Wave," *Journal of Contemporary History*, Vol. I, No. I (1966), 77.

34. La Rochelle, *op. cit.*, 484.

35. Harris, *op. cit.*, 92.

36. Julien Benda, *The Betrayal of the Intellectuals* (New York, 1955). First published in Paris in 1928.

37. Ernst Jünger, *Der Arbeiter* (Hamburg, 1932), 66, 129.

38. Quoted in Robert Soucy, "The Nature of Fascism in France," *Journal of Contemporary History*, Vol. I, No. I (1966), 52; Walter Muschag, *Die Zerstörung der deutschen Literatur* (Munich, n.d.), 143, 145.

39. Robert Brasillach in *Je Suis Partout*, Vol. XII, No. 593 (December 2, 1942), 6.

40. Quoted in Franz Schönauer, *Deutsche Literatur im dritten Reich* (Olten and Freiburg, 1961), 44.

41. Gastone Silvano Spinetti, *Vent'anni dopo Ricominciare da Zero* (Rome, 1964), 109. I owe this reference, as well as others on Italian fascism, to Michael Ledeen, *Universal Fascism: The Theory and Practice of the Fascist International* (New York, 1972), 39 ff.

42. *Arnolt Bronnen gibt zu Protokoll* (Hamburg, 1954), 302 and *passim*.

43. *L'Universale* (1931–41) and *La Sapienza* (1933 ff.).

44. As reported in *L'Oeuvre* (August 24, 1937).

45. Marc Augier, *Götter-Dämmerung, Wende und Ende einer Zeit* (Buenos Aires, 1950), 116.

46. H. Naumann and E. Luethgen, *Kampf wider den undeutschen Geist* (Bonn, 1933).

47. Cesare Rossi, *Mussolini Com'era* (Rome, 1947), 227.

48. Quoted in Lionel Trilling, *Matthew Arnold* (New York, 1955), 211.

49. George L. Mosse, *Nazi Culture*, 162.

50. Dante L. Germino, *The Italian Fascist Party in Power* (Minneapolis, 1959), *passim*.

51. La Rochelle, *op. cit.*, 419.

6. The Occult Origins of National Socialism

1. See also Ellie Howe, *Urania's Children: The Strange World of the Astrologers* (London, 1967); Dusty Sklar, *Gods and Beasts: The Nazis and the Occult* (New York, 1977); Nicholas Goodrick-Clarke, *The Occult Roots of National Socialism* (Wellingborough, Northamptonshire, 1985). This book contains an extensive bibliography of some of the men discussed in this chapter.

2. It is significant that one common tie among all those men was their frustration in being denied academic recognition. Schuler and List were kept at arm's length by the academic world whose company

they sought, while Paul de Lagarde had to teach in a Gymnasium for twelve years before he finally obtained a chair at the University of Göttingen. Julius Langbehn failed to obtain an academic post despite repeated efforts. These experiences undoubtedly deepened their aversion to intellectualism and to what they called academic pedantry. Langbehn's *Rembrandt as Educator* is full of diatribes against the professors whose world outlook he opposed. Such men were part of what has been called the "academic proletariat." Langbehn eventually converted to Catholicism (1900). This is not mentioned in C. T. Carr, "Julius Langbehn—A Forerunner of National Socialism," *German Life and Letters*, III (1938–39), 45–54. For Paul de Lagarde, see Robert W. Lougee, *Paul de Lagarde* (Cambridge, 1962).

3. Julius Langbehn, *Rembrandt als Erzieher* (Leipzig, 1900), 8.

4. *Ibid.*, 82.

5. *Eugen Diederichs Leben und Werke*, ed. Lulu von Strauss and Torney-Diederichs (Jena, 1936), 180.

6. *Ibid.*, 82.

7. *Freideutsche Jugend: Zur Jahrhundertfeier auf dem Hohen Meissner* (Jena, 1913), 98 ff.

8. Langbehn, *Rembrandt*, 131.

9. *The Life and Letters of Jacob Burckhardt*, trans. Alexander Dru (London, 1955), 225.

10. Langbehn, *Rembrandt*, 65.

11. R. Burger-Villingen, *Geheimnis der Menschenform* (Leipzig, 1912), 23, 27.

12. Langbehn, *Rembrandt*, 315.

13. *Eugen Diederichs*, 74, 452.

14. Quoted in the National Socialist article, Karl Friedrich Weiss, "Individualismus und Sozialismus," I, *Der Weltkampf*, IV (1927), 66–70.

15. *Paul de Lagarde, Lebensbild und Auswahl*, ed. K. Boesch (Augsburg, 1924), 52.

16. Johannes Baltzli, *Guido von List* (Vienna, 1917), 18, 23.

17. *Ibid.*, 26, 27.

18. Alfred Schuler, *Fragmente und Vorträge aus dem Nachlass*, ed. Ludwig Klages (Leipzig, 1940), 33, 159.

19. *Ibid.*, 51.

20. Claude David, *Stefan George* (Paris, 1952), 200.

21. Baltzli, *Guido von List*, 45; Alvin Boyd Kuhn, *Theosophy* (New York, 1930), 116–117.

22. Baltzli, *Guido von List*, 55n.; Kuhn, *Theosophy*, 144.

23. *Ibid.*, 135, 133.

24. Besser, "Die Vorgeschichte . . . ," 773.

25. Franz Hartmann, *The Life and Doctrines of Jacob Boehme* (Boston, 1891), 166 n. 1.

26. *Erste Gesamtausstellung der Werke von Fidus zu seinem 60. Geburtstage* (Woltersdorf bei Erkner, 1928), 9, 11.

27. *Eugen Diederichs*, 171, 207, 220.

28. *Ibid.*, 267.

29. Langbehn, *Rembrandt*, 93. "With a dose of mysticism one can gild the life of a nation" (203).

30. *Prana, Organ für angewandte Geisteswissenschaften*, VI, 1–2 (1915), 4.

31. *Ibid.*, 348–349. Nourishment and the development of the soul go hand in hand. Anti-alcoholism plays an important role here as well. At the Hohen Meissner gathering, the Temperance League said that it too wanted to serve the race—*Freideutsche Jugend*, 16; see also Langbehn, *Rembrandt*, 296–297.

32. Kuhn, *Theosophy*, 297; *Prana*, 46–47.

33. Arthur Dinter, *Die Sünde wider den Geist* (Leipzig, 1921), 236.

34. Besser, "Die Vorgeschichte . . . ," 773.

35. Baltzli, *Guido von List*, 185. His name was Friedrich Wannieck, and he contributed more to the List Society than all other members put together (79). Wannieck and Franz Hartmann had at least one séance together (185).

36. Langbehn, *Rembrandt*, 94–95. Blavatsky and G. R. S. Meade

believed that "of all mystics, Swedenborg has certainly influenced Theosophy most . . . ," though his powers did not go beyond the plane of matter. H. P. Blavatski, *The Theosophical Glossary* (Hollywood, 1918), 293.

37. *Eugen Diederichs*, 15.

38. Baltzli, *Guido von List*, 155, 199.

39. Langbehn, *Rembrandt*, 130–131.

40. *Ibid.*, 158, 159.

41. H. F. K. Günther, *Ritter, Tod und Teufel* (1920). Quoted in R. Walther Darré, *Das Bauernthum als Lebensquell der Nordischen Rasse* (Munich, 1937), 97. Darré was the National Socialist Minister of Agriculture.

42. Langbehn, *Rembrandt*, 5.

43. *Paul de Lagarde*, 96; *Reichsschule der NSDAP Feldafing* (1939–40), 17.

44. *Eugen Diederichs*, 351–352.

45. Langbehn, *Rembrandt*, 158, 160.

46. *Eugen Diederichs*, 72. On *Die Tat*, see Klemens von Klemperer, *Germany's New Conservatism* (Princeton, 1957), 97–100.

47. *Paul de Lagarde*, 64.

48. Langbehn, *Rembrandt*, 218–219.

49. Gerhard Heine, *Ferdinand Avenarius als Dichter* (Leipzig, 1904), 45.

50. Langbehn, *Rembrandt*, 113. Tudel Weller, *Rabauken! Peter Moenkemann haut sich durch* (Munich, 1938), 114; cf. George L. Mosse, *Germans and Jews*, Chapter 2.

51. *Weltkampf*, IV (1927), 189.

52. Baltzli, *Guido von List*, 29; Klages in Schuler, *Fragmente*, 43.

53. *Paul de Lagarde*, 104.

54. Schuler, *Fragmente*, 163 ff.; Review of Guido von List, *Die Ursprache der Ario-Germanen und ihre Mysterien-Sprache in Prana*, VI, 11–12 (February–March 1916), 560.

55. Langbehn, *Rembrandt*, 353, *Eugen Diederichs*, 84–85.

56. Melanie Lehmann, *Verleger J. F. Lehmann: Ein Leben im Kampf für Deutschland* (Munich, 1935), 23 ff. Lehmann was intimately involved with the growth of the National Socialist Party in Munich.

57. Langbehn, *Rembrandt,* 326–327.

58. *Eugen Diederichs,* 73.

59. Langbehn, *Rembrandt,* 95.

60. Guido von List, *Die Namen der Völkerstaemme Germaniens und deren Deutung* (Leipzig, 1909), 4.

61. *Weltkampf,* IV (1927), 92.

62. Alfred Rosenberg, "Rebellion der Jungend," *Nationalsozialistiche Monatshefte,* Heft 2 (May 1930), 50 ff.

63. Hans Blüher, *Wandervögel, Geschichte einer Jugendbewegung* (Berlin, 1916), II, 83 ff. Blüher blamed Christianity for the degeneration of the romanticism of the *Wandervögel* (172).

64. Alfred Andreesen, *Hermann Lietz* (Munich, 1934), 101.

65. Hermann Lietz, *Deutsche Nationalerziehung* (Weimar, 1938), 123–124.

66. *Ibid.,* 114, 120; H. Lietz, *Lebenserinnerungen* (Weimar, 1935), 41, 47. Christ symbolized struggle (189).

67. For his developing attitude toward Jews, see Lietz, *Lebenserinnerungen,* 115. From 1909 on, only students of Aryan descent were admitted (161). On the Jewish spirit, see Lietz, *Deutsche Nationalerziehung,* 14.

68. *Lebenserinnerungen,* 194; Andreesen, *Hermann Lietz,* iii; for Lietz's own hymn on patriarchal society, see *Lebenserinnerungen,* 194.

69. Hermann Lietz, *Des Vaterlandes Not und Hoffnung* (Haubinda, 1934), 86.

70. *Ibid.,* 76. *Eugen Diederichs,* 64; Lehmann, *Verleger,* 38, 277. The close collaborator was Alfred Andreesen, from 1909 his deputy director at Bieberstein. Lietz, in his social-political confession of faith during the war, tells of his allegiance to the world view of German idealism—*Lebenserinnerungen,* 196. The schools were also represented on the Hohen Meissner in 1913 (*Freideutsche Jugend,* 18).

71. David, *Stefan George,* 208.

72. For the relationship of Strindberg and Lanz von Liebenfels, see Wilfried Daim, *Der Mann der Hitler Die Ideen Gab* (Munich, 1958), 92–99.

7. Fascism and the Avant Garde

1. Robert O. Paxton, *La France de Vichy* (Paris, 1973), 251.
2. Henry de Montherlant, *Le Songe* (Paris, 1922), 374.
3. Antoine de Saint-Exupéry, "Terre des Hommes," *Oeuvres* (Paris, 1959), 169–170.
4. Quoted in Rolf Italiander, *Italo Balbo* (Munich, 1942), 137. H. G. Wells saw the "Coming of Blériot" (1909) as the end of natural democracy—*The Works of H. G. Wells*, XX (New York, 1926), 422; Guido Mattioli, *Mussolini Aviatore* (Rome, 1936?), 3.
5. Mattioli, *op. cit.*, 3.
6. Bertold Brecht, "Der Ozeanflug," Brecht, *Versuche 1–12* (Berlin, 1959), 14. I owe this reference to Reinhold Grimm.
7. *Ibid.*, 24.
8. Rolf Italiander, *Marschall Balbo*, 11.
9. Giuseppe Fanciulli, *Marschall Balbo* (Essen, 1942), 116.
10. Anson Rabinbach, "The Aesthetics of Production in the Third Reich," *International Fascism*, ed. George L. Mosse (London, 1979), 189–223.
11. Hans Poelzig, quoted in Anna Teut, *Architektur im Dritten Reich* (Frankfurt-am-Main, 1967), 32.
12. See, for example, Jost Hermand and Frank Trommler, *Die Kultur der Weimarer Republik* (Munich, 1978), 382 ff. "Omagio a Terrgani," *L'Architettura: Chronache e Storia*, XIV, No. 3 (July 1968).
13. Hildegard Brenner, *Die Kunstpolitik des Nationalsozialismus* (Hamburg, 1963), 64 ff.
14. *Ibid.*, 73; Barbara Miller Lane, *Architecture and Politics in Germany, 1918–1945* (Cambridge, Mass., 1963), 152, 172 ff. Mies van der Rohe was a member of the Reichskammer für Bildende Kunste, 264, n. 73. He designed an exhibit for the exhibition "German People, German Work" in 1934—Philip C. Johnson, *Mies van der Rohe* (New

York, 1947), 53. Mies, so one book claims, did not leave Germany until 1937, while Barbara Miller Lane gives the impression that he left shortly after 1933. Cf. Arthur Drexler, *Mies van der Rohe* (New York, 1960).

15. Albert Speer, *Erinnerungen* (Frankfurt-am-Main, 1969), 94.

16. George L. Mosse, *The Nationalization of the Masses*, 186. For the relationship of *Neo Klassizismus* and *Neue Sachlichkeit*, see Georg Friedrich Koch, "Speer, Schinkel und der Preussische Stil," in *Albert Speer; Architektur* (Frankfurt-am-Main, 1967), 136 ff.

17. E. Crispolti, B. Hinz, and Z. Birolli, *Arte e Fascismo in Italia e in Germania* (Milan, 1974), 129.

18. "Omaggio a Terragni," 180.

19. Ute Diehl, "Der lange Weg in die Abstraktion. Die italienische Kunst und der Faschismus," *Frankfurter Allgemeine Zeitung*, No. 89 (May 2, 1978).

20. Emilio Gentile, *Le Origini dell' Ideologica Fascista* (Rome, 1975), 6.

21. Alexander J. de Grand, *Bottai e la Cultura Fascista* (Rome, 1978), 251.

22. Calro Bordoni, *Cultura e propaganda nell'Italia fascista* (Messina-Florence, 1974), 167.

23. Cited in *ibid.*, 44, 46.

24. Emilio Gentile, "Bottai e il fascismo. Osservatione per una biografia," *Storia Contemporanea*, X, No. 3 (June 1979), 559.

25. "Novocento," *Enciclopedia Italiana* (1934), XXIV, 995.

26. Mosse, *op. cit.*, 224

27. "Novocento," *Enciclopedia Italiana*, 994.

28. Adrian Lyttleton, *The Seizure of Power*, 391–393.

29. Francesco Sapori, *L'Arte e il Duce* (Milan, 1932), 37, 49, 66.

30. *Ibid.*, 124, 125, 129; Bordoni, *op. cit.*, 71.

31. Marcello Piacentini, *Architettura d'Oggi* (Rome, 1930), 56–57.

32. i.e. George L. Mosse, *Die Völkische Revolution* (Frankfurt-am-Main, 1991).

33. "Omaggio a Terragni," 161.

34. Cited in Nicolas Slonimsky, *Music Since 1900* (New York, 1946), 355.

35. Mussolini ignored Pound, who bombarded him not with poetry but with bizarre political and economic tracts—Niccolo Zapponi, "Ezra Pound e il fascismo," *Storia Contemporanea*, IV, No. 3 (September, 1973), 423–474.

36. See Chapter 5.

37. Gottfried Benn, "Rede auf Stefan George" (1934), *Essays, Reden. Vorträge* (Wiesbaden, 1959), 473.

38. *Ibid.*, 627.

39. Crispolti, *et al.*, *op. cit.*, 59.

40. Renzo De Felice, *Fascism*, 56.

41. "Fascismo," *Enciclopedia Italiana*, XIV (1932), 847.

42. See Robert Soucy, *Fascist Intellectual: Drieu La Rochelle* (Berkeley and Los Angeles, 1979).

43. Drieu La Rochelle, *Gilles* (Paris, 1939), 405–406.

44. i.e. George L. Mosse, "The Poet and the Exercise of Political Power: Gabriele D'Annunzio," *Masses and Man*, Chapter 5.

45. Quoted in Soucy, *op. cit.*, 2.

46. David L. Shalk, *The Spectrum of Political Engagement* (Princeton, 1979), 99.

47. J.-L. Loubet del Bayle, *Les non-conformistes des années 30* (Paris, 1969), 101.

48. Walter Laqueur, *Young Germany* (London, 1962), 102.

49. i.e. Ulrich Linse, *Anarchistische Jugendbewegung 1918–1933* (Frankfurt-am-Main, 1976).

50. Giovanni Sabbatucci, *I Combattenti nel Primo Dopoguerra* (Rome, 1974), 358.

51. Ferdinando Cordova, *Arditi e Legionari Dannunziani* (Padua, 1969), 22.

52. Donino Roncará, *Saggi sull'Educazione Fascista* (Bologna, 1938), 65.

8. Nazi Polemical Theater: The Kampfbühne

1. Gunther Rühle, *Zeit und Theater,* III, *Diktatur und Exil* (Berlin, n.d.), 27, 28.

2. i.e. Klau Vondung, *Magie und Manipulation* (Göttingen, 1971).

3. George L. Mosse, *The Nationalization of the Masses,* 192.

4. Johann von Leers, quoted in Eugen Hadamovsky, *Propaganda and National Power* (New York, 1972), 175, 176; see also "Politisches Streitgesprach ist der Ausdruck Unseres Theaters," *Der Aufmarsch* (März, 1931), 8.

5. Ulrich Mayer, *Das Eindringen des Nationalsozialismus in die Stadt Wetzlar* (Wetzlar, 1970), 46.

6. See, e.g., *Der Junge Nationalsozialist* (September 1932), 12, 13; *Der Junge Sturmtrupp* (März, 1932), n.p.

7. This play is included in the *Eine Materialsammlung Vorgelegt vom Centralverein Deutscher Staatsburger Jüdischen Glaubens* (Berlin, 1932). This collection of documents was to be submitted to President von Hindenburg.

8. Adolf Gentsch, *Die Politische Struktur der Theaterführung* (Dresden, 1942), 303.

9. *Ibid.,* 307; *Illustrierter Beobachter* (1931), 21.

10. Gentsch, *op. cit.,* 305.

11. *Ibid.,* 308.

12. A. E. Frauenfeld, *Der Weg Zur Bühne* (Berlin, 1940), 33.

13. *Illustrierter Beobachter* (1927), 132.

14. *Ibid.,* 312.

15. *Ibid.,* (1930), 14.

16. *Ibid.,* 773.

17. *Ibid.,* 72.

18. *Ibid.,* 14.

19. *Ibid.,* (1931), 119.

20. *Ibid.,* (1930), 13, 14.

21. *Ibid.,* (1931), 321.

22. *Ibid.,* (1930), 211.

23. *Volkischer Beobachter,* 2 Beilage (October 6, 1932), n.p.

24. Richard Biedrzynski, *Schauspieler, Regisseure, Intendanten* (Heidelberg, 1944), 53.

25. Rühle, *op. cit.,* 778.

26. Eberhard Wolfgang Möller, *Rothschild siegt bei Waterloo* (Berlin, 1944), preface to the 4th edn., 11, 41, 124.

27. *Nationalsozialistische Monatshefte* (März, 1934), 109.

28. Erwin Piscator, *Das Proletarische Theater* (Berlin, 1929), 41, 243.

29. *Gott, Freiheit, Vaterland, Sprech-Chöre der Hitler-Jugend* (Stuttgart, n.d.), 7.

30. Mosse, *op. cit.,* 110.

31. Ernst Lenke, "Richard Elsner zu seinem 50. Geburtstage am 10, Juni, 1933," *Das Deutsche Drama* (1933), 9, 13.

32. Hans Brandenburg, *Das Theater und das Neue Deutschland; Ein Aufruf* (Jena, 1919), 36, 20, 11, 33; Mary Wigman, *Die Sprache des Tanzes* (Stuttgart, 1964), 17.

33. Ernst Brandenburg, *Das Neue Theater* (Leipzig, 1926), 490.

34. *Ibid.,* 449.

35. Hans Brandenburg, "Der Weg zum Nationaltheater. Ein Zweigesprach," *Die Neue Literatur* (July 1936), 402.

36. Christian Jensen, "Hans Brandenburg, Volkhafter Deutscher Dichter," *Die Neue Literatur* (January 1936), 10–15.

37. Rudolf Mirbt, *Laienspiel und Laientheater* (Cassel, 1960), 15, 16.

38. Gerhard Rossbach, *Mein Weg Durch Die Zeit* (Weilburg-Lahn, 1950), 90–93.

39. These are listed and described in *Wille und Werk; Bühnenvolksbund Handbuch* (Berlin, 1928), 96–99.

40. There is unfortunately no investigation so far as I know of the similarity and differences between plays staged by such organizations.

41. *Das Laienspiel, Erfahrungen, Grundsätze, Aufgaben* (Berlin, Arbeitsfront publication, n.d.), 11.

42. See Eugen Kurt Fischer, *Die Neue Vereinsbühne* (Munich, 1926?), 208.

43. *Das Volksspiel im NS Gemeinschaftsleben* (Munich, 1938), 19.

44. Christian Hermann Vosen, *Kolpings Gesellenverein in Seiner Sozialen Bedeutung* (Frankfurt-am-Main, 1866), 12.

45. *Ibid.*, 17, 18.

46. These and the following plays will be found bound together in the British Museum, London, catalogue number 11747 d. 5. (Familein und Vereinstheater in Paderborn). They were published as *Kleines Theater.* I owe this reference to Sister Dr. Charlotte Klein.

47. See Adolf Kolping, "Gebet, und es wird euch gegeben," *Ausgewahlte Volkserzahlungen von Adolf Kolping* (Regensburg, 1932), VI, 33–85.

48. Gentsch, *op. cit.*, 53, 203; *Die Volksbühne* (July 1930), 119.

49. Gentsch, *op. cit.*, 206.

50. *Die Volkstümliche Bühne* (1918), 191; *ibid.*, 2 ff, 51.

51. George L. Mosse, *Germans and Jews*, 50 ff.

52. *Die Volktümliche Buhne* (1918–19), 97 ff.

53. Demetrius Schrutz, *Handlexicon des Theaterspiels* (Munich, 1925), 40.

54. Gentsch, *op. cit.*, 204.

55. *Die Volksbühne* (February 1931), 482.

56. Gentsch, *op. cit.*, 55.

57. Gerschom Scholem, *Walter Benjamin—die Geschichte einer Freundschaft* (Frankfurt-am-Main, 1975), 220.

58. *Dramatiker der HJ, Sonderheft Zur Theaterwoche der Hitler-Jugend verbunden mit einer Reichstheatertagung der Hitler-Jugend*, Vol. II, April 18, 1937 (Bochum, n.d.), 26.

59. Rühle, *op. cit.*, 787.

60. *Wille und Macht* (1937), V, 21.

61. Paul Alverdes, *Das Winterlager* (Munich, 1935), *passim;* Herbert Georg Gopfert, "Paul Alverdes," *Die Neue Literatur* (September 1936), 503–509.

62. Speech by Baldur von Schirach at the Weimarer Tagung of the Hitler Youth, in 1937, *Die Neue Literatur* (May 1938), 223, 224.

63. *Die Spielschaar* (January 1943), 12.

64. *Volktums Arbeit im Betrieb* (Berlin, Kraft Durch Freude publication, 1938?), 23.

65. Hermann Kretzschmann, *Unterricht und Erziehung im Deutschen Arbeitsdienst* (Leipzig, 1933), 8.

66. *Die Neue Literatur* (June 1936), 328. The typical phrase stems from Martin Luserke.

67. Hans Hinkel, *Einer unter Hunderttausend* (Munich, 1937), 261. I am indebted to Barry Fulkes, who supplied the knowledge about Nazi films.

9. On Homosexuality and French Fascism

1. Giovanni Dall'Orto, "Omosessuale e stato," *Quaderni di Critica Omossuale*, supplemento no. 11 (Rome, 1977), 44, 46, 47.

2. Pieter Koenders, *Homosexualiteit inBezet Nederland* (S-Gravenhage, 1983), 95ff, 109.

3. Lucien Steinberg, *Les Autorités Allemandes en France Occupée* (Paris, 1966), 280.

4. Jean Quéval, *Premiere Page, Cinquième Colonne* (Paris, 1945), 280, 281.

5. Jean-Paul Sartre, *Situations*, III (1949), 58; Jean Guehenno, *Journal des Années Noires* (Paris, 1947), 123, 118.

6. Andre Halimi, *Chantons sous L'Occupation* (Paris, 1976), 225.

7. J. L. Loubet del Bayle, *Les non-conformistes des annees 30* (Paris, 1969), *passim*.

8. Robert Brasillach, *Notre Avant Guerre* (Paris, 1941), 283.

9. George L. Mosse, *The Crisis of German Ideology*, 217.

10. Robert Soucy, *Fascist Intellectual: Drieu La Rochelle*, 203, 326.

11. quoted in Dominique Desanti, *Drieu La Rochelle* (Paris, 1975), 315.

12. Drieu La Rochelle, *Gilles* (Paris, 1939), 455; Solange Leibovici, *Le sang et l'encre: Pierre Drieu La Rochelle. Une psychobiographie* (Amsterdam, 1994), 289.

13. Robert Brasillach, *Anthologie de la poésie grecque* (Paris, 1950, written 1943/44), 10.

14. Ginette Guitard-Auviste, "Le Precaire bonheur de vivre," Supplement, *Le Monde* (7. Fevrier, 1970), 4.

15. Robert Brasillach, *Comme le temps passe* (Paris, 1937 and 1938), 74ff.

16. d'Étiemble, "A propos de Brasillach," *Le Monde* (February 14, 1970), 11.

17. Robert Soucy, *op. cit.*, 326; see also Robert Brasillach, *Comme le temps passe*, 72, for men preferring the company of men to that of women.

18. i.e. George L. Mosse, *Nationalism and Sexuality*, 175.

19. Robert Brasillach, *Notre Avant Guerre*, 214.

20. Arthur Mitzman, *Michelet, Historian* (New Haven, 1990), 71, 107.

21. Jules Michelet, *The People* (Urbana, 1973), 158, 159–160.

22. quoted in Maud de Belleroche, *Le ballet des crabes* (Paris, 1975), 12.

23. i.e. Drieu La Rochelle, *Gilles*, 406; Robert Brasillach in *Je Suis Partout* (December 11, 1942), 6.

24. Louis Ferdinand Céline, *Bagatelles pour un Massacre* (Paris, 1937), 70.

25. See Chapter 5.

26. Jacques Isorny, *Le Procès de Robert Brasillach* (Paris, 1946), 138–140.

27. i.e. George L. Mosse, *Nationalism and Sexuality, passim.*

28. Christian Bourqueret, "Die Invertierten von Paris," 100 Jahre Schwulenbewegung, Eine Ausstellung des Schwulen Museums and der Akademie der Kunste (Berlin, 1997), 151.

29. George L. Mosse, *The Image of Man*, Chapter 8.

Index

Naumann, Hans, 113
Nazi aesthetics, 183–97
Nazi art, 145, 183–84
Nazi symbols, 20, 42–43
Nazi theater. *See Kampfbühne*
Nietzscheanism, 110, 112
nudity
  banning of, 192
  male, 188–89, 192. *See also* male
  body

obedience, 110
occult origins of National Socialism,
  117, 120–35. *See also* mysticism
occult symbolism, 123–25
"organic state," 133

parliamentary government, 5
patriotism, 62, 68
poetry, 97–99
police, secret, 4
populism, 28–29, 48, 137, 163
positivism, 118, 122, 135
Pound, Ezra, 102, 148, 180
Prana, 135, 136
precedent, xvii, 9
propaganda, 3
puritanism, 21

race, superior, 59–60
"race mysticism," 131
race war, xv–xvi
racial purity, 77
racial revolution, 66–67
racial stereotype, 62, 63, 67
racial utopia, 66–67
racism, xiii–xvi, 31, 35–36, 56–58, 67.
  See also fascist movements, nonracist
  aesthetic adopted by, 58
  as aggressively masculine, 59
  depends upon having enemies, 63
  foundations, 57
  functions, 36
  gender division, 59
  substitute for religion, 20
  transcendent beauty and, 58
racist symbol(s), 57, 59, 62
  human body as, 58

Rassemblement National Populaire
  (RNP), 91
religious overtones in fascism, xvi, 10,
  18, 27, 81–82
Republic of Virtue, 89
respectability, 185, 190, 191–92,
  194–95
revolution, xi–xii, 6, 7, 42, 77. *See also*
  French Revolution
  based on the already familiar, xvii
  from the Right, 67
revolutionaries, social, 17, 21
  fascist leaders' attitudes toward, 8
revolutionary nationalism, 73
Rexist movement in Belgium, xiii–xiv,
  20, 36
Robespierre, Maximilien, 76, 78, 79,
  90
Röhm, Ernst, 190
romanticism, 23–25, 108, 114, 119,
  120, 134–35, 145, 148
Roselli, Carlo, 96–97
Rosenberg, Alfred, 77–78, 132, 189

Saint-Exupéry, Antoine de, 139
Sartre, Jean-Paul, 177, 178
Schiller, Friedrich, 161, 165, 187–
  88
Schuler, Alfred, 121, 122
science, attitudes toward, 28, 125. *See
  also* technology
socialist and Bolshevik revolutions,
  fascists' view of, 77
socialist rhetoric, borrowed by fascism,
  27
Soviet Union, 2–3
Spain. *See* Franco
Spanish Falange, xiv
stereotypes, 48, 49, 62, 63, 67
  as symbols, 67
symbolism, 49, 59, 83
  occult, 123–25
  in speeches, 48
symbol(s), 46, 49. *See also* national
  symbols and myths
  Nazi, 20, 42–43
  racial, 57, 59, 62, 67, 123–24
  sun as symbol, 123–24

Talmon, Jacob, 4. *See also* Jacobins
technology, 137–39
   attitudes toward, 28
theosophy, 123–25, 128
Thing theater, 157
"Third Force," 7–9, 11, 18, 116
"Third Way," 9, 40, 42
"totalitarian democracy," 4–5
totalitarianism, 4–6
traditionalism, xvii, 10, 19–20, 114, 143

urbanism, 122, 129
utopianism, xv, 10, 30, 66–67, 72, 88.
   See also apocalypticism

Valois, George, 89

war, acceptance of, 16
war experience, 15–17
   deification of fallen soldiers, 16, 84

wartime camaraderie, xvi, 18, 30
Weimar Republic, 184
will of the people, general, 70–72,
   74–75, 78, 79, 83, 148
Winckelmann, J. J., 188
women, 50–51
   aesthetics of, 51
   artistic portrayals of, 188–89
   contradictory attitudes toward, 193
   devaluation of, 178–79
   ideal of beauty in, 188–89, 193
   stereotyped passive role of, xvi,
      188
world view, importance of, 22

youth, fascism as movement of, 13–14,
   83, 87, 150, 153, 170–72. *See also*
   Hitler Youth

Ziegler, Leopold, 193